WILHELM MÜLLER

The Poet of the Schubert Song Cycles

THE PENN STATE SERIES IN GERMAN LITERATURE

General Editor
   Joseph P. Strelka, State University of New York at Albany

Editorial Board
   Stuart Atkins, University of California at Santa Barbara
   Peter Demetz, Yale University
   Reinhold Grimm, University of Wisconsin
   Karl Guthke, Harvard University
   Erich Heller, Northwestern University
   Victor Lange, Princeton University
   Henry Remak, Indiana University
   Oskar Seidlin, Indiana University
   Walter Sokel, University of Virginia
   Blake Lee Spahr, University of California at Berkeley

German Baroque Poetry, 1618–1723, by Robert M. Browning

German Poetry in the Age of the Enlightenment, by Robert M. Browning

Kafka's Narrative Theater, by James Rolleston

War, Weimar, and Literature: The Story of the Neue Merkur, 1914–1925, by Guy Stern

The Leitword in Minnesang: A New Approach to Stylistic Analysis and Textual Criticism, by
   Vickie L. Ziegler

WILHELM MÜLLER

The Poet of the Schubert Song Cycles:
His Life and Works

Cecilia C. Baumann

The Pennsylvania State University Press
University Park and London

Library of Congress Cataloging in Publication Data

Baumann, Cecilia C 1943–
  Wilhelm Müller, the poet of the Schubert song cycles.

  (The Penn State series in German literature)
  Includes bibliography and index.
  1. Müller, Wilhelm, 1794–1827. 2. Authors, German
—19th century—Biography. 3. Schubert, Franz Peter, 1797–
1828. I. Title. II. Series: Penn State series
in German literature.
PT2436.M7Z58   831'.6 [B]   80-12806
ISBN 0-271-00266-2

PT
2436
m7
258

This book is dedicated to my husband, Ronald, and my mother, Mary Louise Cloughly, without whose assistance in many ways it would never have become a reality.

Contents

List of Illustrations

Preface

Johann Ludwig Wilhelm Müller (1794–1827) is usually remembered today as the German Romantic poet whose lyrics Franz Schubert set to music in *Die schöne Müllerin* and *Die Winterreise*. Students of German literature of the early nineteenth century may recognize the nickname Griechen-Müller and recall the impassioned lyrics that philhellene Müller wrote in support of the Greeks in their struggle for independence from the Turks. Few who have sung "Das Wandern ist des Müllers Lust" or "Im Krug zum grünen Kranze" or "Am Brunnen vor dem Tore" will, however, know these "folk songs" as the work of lyric poet Müller. Fewer still will be aware that Goethe very likely became acquainted with Christopher Marlowe's *The Tragical History of Doctor Faustus* through Müller's 1818 translation. The influence of editor Müller's collections of Italian and modern Greek folk songs upon later research is seldom noted. If one also takes into account Müller's literary criticism and scholarship, his close association with the prestigious firm of F. A. Brockhaus in Leipzig, and his Italian memoirs of 1820 (republished in 1956 in Bremen, and in 1978 in East Berlin), what emerges is the profile of a man whose features, when viewed separately, are the enduring portrait of an age, reflecting the landscape of literary concern and endeavor from the Romantic movement to that of Junges Deutschland.

Although previous studies of Müller have dealt with specific aspects of his life and works—especially the poetry—no monograph on Wilhelm Müller has ever appeared in print. At the beginning of this century a monograph on Müller was to have been published by the Palaestra Publishing Company, but the author, Bruno Hake, who had written his doctoral dissertation on Müller, was killed in World War I. A single chapter dealing with *Die schöne Müllerin* was all that appeared in print. Other efforts have dealt with one or another of the individual "features" of Müller: his relationship to the folk song; his views on art; his philhellenism; the numerous musical settings of his poems; his critical writings; his translation of the Marlowe *Faustus;* and his song cycles. This book brings together all that has gone before and presents a portrait of Wilhelm Müller, poet, prose writer, translator, critic, editor, philhellene, traveler, and man.

Since the book represents a compendium of all available materials

about Wilhelm Müller, its organization was considered of great impor-
tance. The chosen structure—a detailed biography, chapters on Mül-
ler's various literary efforts, and an exhaustive chronology—is meant to
facilitate practical use of the book by readers from different fields and
with divergent interests, who (it is expected) will elect to read only
selected chapters or sections. That this design has necessitated some
reiteration of facts and interpretations is acknowledged, and the author
here begs the reader's indulgence for the occasional sacrifice of ele-
gance for the sake of clarity and greater usefulness.

The biographical information about Wilhelm Müller available to the
modern scholar is based on scanty and sometimes inaccurate sources.
The first such source was the biography of Müller written in 1830,
shortly after the poet's death, by a longtime but not very intimate
friend, the poet Gustav Schwab, for a five-volume edition of Müller's
collected works. Schwab drew upon written accounts of the poet's
widow, Adelheid, and his friends Baron Alexander Heinrich von Simo-
lin and Count Friedrich von Kalckreuth. Some of the facts apparently
were edited for publication, especially those concerning the social
standing of Müller's father and the sudden death of the poet. Drawing
upon childhood memories, the poet's son F. Max Müller (1823–1900)
wrote an introduction to the 1868 edition of his father's poetry. This
introduction as well as the biography that F. Max wrote in 1885 for the
Allgemeine deutsche Biographie were both based on the questionable
Schwab biography.
    Where then are the private papers of the poet, which might shed
light on the basic facts of Müller's life (such as the number of brothers
and sisters in his family, and his father's occupation)? The American
editors of *Diary and Letters of Wilhelm Müller,* Philip Schuyler Allen and
James Taft Hatfield, were told by the poet's elderly son that a "fire
which consumed the poet's library in Dessau destroyed almost all of the
materials upon which studies of his intimate life could be based." In
1914, however, the official historian of Anhalt, Hermann Wäschke,
published a documented account of Müller's youth based on research
among the records of the city of Dessau. In this study Wäschke ques-
tions the alleged fate of Müller's private papers. He calls attention to
the son's apparent lack of interest in providing an accurate account of
his father's life; observes that the otherwise reliable chronicler of the
city of Dessau, L. Würdig, made no mention of any such fire in the "list
of fires in Dessau from 1820 to 1874" in his *Chronik der Stadt Dessau;*
and cautiously hints at a possible suppression of some facts about the
family circumstances: "Zu allem kommt nun noch eine gewisse,—ich
will nicht sagen absichtliche,—aber tatsächliche Verschleierung der
Familienverhältnisse."[1]
    It is also curious that several items from the poet's library (which had

supposedly burned) appeared at different times during the following century. In the introduction to Müller's unfinished collection of Italian poetry that O. L. B. Wolff completed in 1829, Wolff makes passing reference to manuscripts lent to him by the family of the deceased. Letters to Müller from Heine, Fouqué, and the Dessau poet Matthisson came to light in 1845, when they were published by F. Max Müller in *Blätter für literarische Unterhaltung*. Shortly before his death in 1900, F. Max released for publication his father's Berlin diary, along with several of the poet's letters, "lately discovered" among his mother's papers.[2] (His mother, Adelheid von Basedow Müller, it may be noted, had died seventeen years earlier in 1883—surely a more likely occasion for the discovery of such papers.) Then, in 1927, the family produced a diary from the couple's 1827 journey along the Rhine and an album containing family documents, letters of condolence to the widow Adelheid, drawings, and miscellany for the exhibit at the Anhaltische Landesbücherei in Dessau on the occasion of the centennial of the poet's death. In this same year Heinrich Lohre published a collection of Müller's letters, finally released from the Brockhaus archives. A detailed biography by Lohre precedes the letters, which were addressed to Friedrich Arnold and Heinrich Brockhaus. The unpublished diary of Müller's last trip, several poems, and some letters were published four years later in 1931 by Paul Wahl in Dessau. Finally, in a 1934 article for the *Anhaltische Geschichtsblätter,* Wahl reports the unusual circumstances surrounding Müller's death. All of these subsequent discoveries and publications tend to discredit F. Max Müller's evaluation of the severity of the supposed fire: "Seine Collegienhefte [wurden] . . . leider in späteren Jahren *sammt [sic] seiner ganzen von ihm hinterlassenen Bibliothek* [italics added] ein Raub des Feuers. . . ."[3]

Müller's heirs probably had good reasons for not wanting to expose the poet's papers and other family documents to the scrutiny of the curious. In addition to a natural desire for privacy, the widow's family, which was of the lower nobility and which held a powerful political position in the duchy, may have wished to conceal the lower-class background of the poet. The early biographer Schwab (whose manuscript the widow herself edited and approved) describes Müller's father as quite respectable: "Sein Vater war ein wohlhabender, für seinen Stand gebildeter und in seiner Vaterstadt allgemein geachteter Handwerker."[4] This statement, which was repeated verbatim by the poet's son thirty-eight years later in the 1868 biography, contrasts sharply with that which Wäschke presents when he reports that the ducal archives contain two requests by Müller's father for alms.

It is interesting to note that—despite the absence of documentation —unofficial and unwritten speculation has continued over the years (even into the 1970s) that Müller might have been an illegitimate child of the ducal house. (The ruler of Anhalt-Dessau at the time was Leopold Friedrich Franz [1740–1817], who was nicknamed "Vater Franz" by the people, partially because of the unusually large number of children he sired. His successor was Leopold Friedrich [1794–1871], nicknamed "der Burschbolte" ["Boy Leopold"], who was born the same year as Wilhelm Müller.)

This speculation is supported by several puzzling aspects of Müller's life, such as the financial support the Duke gave his father on at least two occasions. Furthermore, as a boy—both in school and at home—Wilhelm was given an unusual amount of freedom and encouragement. Upon completing his schooling in Dessau, Müller, the supposed son of a tailor, was admitted to the newly founded university in Berlin and given entrée to the best homes and salons in the city. Later, Müller was given a dual job as ducal librarian and teacher in Dessau, even though he had failed to complete his university studies in Berlin. In his violent disagreements with the school principal in Dessau, the independent and nonconformist young man eventually won complete freedom from all school duties he considered onerous, an unusual situation in a school bureaucracy.

In general, it is clear that Müller was favored in his career and marriage by the Dessau court and that he was given great independence and recognition, including the title Hofrat. Finally, these unsubstantiated rumors about Müller's background were certainly fed by the mysterious and still unexplained circumstances surrounding his sudden death at the age of thirty-two. Without any proof, Müller's possible hereditary connection to the ducal house of Anhalt, which is discounted today by some Dessau residents, must remain speculation. Nonetheless, this tenacious rumor about Müller's life is another piece in the puzzle which literary historians must attempt to put together.

Although F. Max Müller wrote next to nothing about his father's family, he wrote much in his several autobiographical works about his maternal ancestors. This one-sided view of his family background may be explained in part by his having lived much of his childhood in the Basedow household, to which Adelheid returned immediately after her husband's death. Indeed, it would seem that F. Max was very much impressed by the titled side of his family—so much so, in fact, that, according to Wäschke, he once referred to his grandfather Basedow as having been "Premierminister des Herzogs" at a time when such a position did not even exist.

Another reason for the family's secrecy may have been that some of Müller's published works contained controversial political opinions, at a time when political repression and censorship were the rule. Publication of Müller's letters and other unpublished writings might well have embarrassed the widow's family, perhaps even have compromised its enviable political position.

Whatever the reasons, then, it remains a fact that our knowledge of

Wilhelm Müller's life is less than complete. With few exceptions, there remains only the Müller side of an active correspondence with several important men and women of the time. There are indications, for example, that Heinrich Heine wrote letters to Müller which are no longer extant.[5] It is a loss to the study of the Romantic movement in Germany that the majority of the letters written to Müller have not survived.

It was considered necessary to detail here some of the problems of biographical research on Müller because, through repetition by later scholars, some of the errors in the early reports have become firmly entrenched. To avoid further perpetuation of inaccuracies, the first chapter of this study is based on documented biographical material about Wilhelm Müller and is supplemented with such autobiographical information as can be gleaned from the poet's own letters and other writings. A detailed chronology of the poet's life and publications—the first ever compiled—is included here as an appendix. Also published for the first time is a sketch of the house in which Müller was born, drawn by Rudolf Hugk, the son of the last owner. Hugk's wife Margarete was for many years the librarian in Dessau most familiar with the Müller papers. Margarete Hugk and her successor at the Stadtbibliothek, Irmgard Lange, have over the past decade kindly provided every piece of information available in Dessau about Müller, in order that this study on Dessau's native son might be as complete as possible. I am grateful to them for their help.

I would also like to acknowledge the assistance of several other persons who have contributed to the development of this book: Erich Heller, Northwestern University; Joseph P. Strelka, State University of New York at Albany; Reinhold Grimm, University of Wisconsin; Johannes Irmscher in the German Democratic Republic; Ulrich Urban in the Federal Republic of Germany; librarians in several countries; and many colleagues and friends who have encouraged and advised me during the past twelve years.

Appreciation is also due to Pomona College and the University of Kiel, whose generous grants have enabled me to complete this work.

Wilhelm Müller (1794–1827), as sketched by his friend Wilhelm Hensel (husband of Fanny Mendelssohn) on December 8, 1822.

CHAPTER ONE

Biographical Sketch

Das Wandern ist des Müllers Lust,
Das Wandern![1]

The title of Wilhelm Müller's best-known poem is a fitting motto for the life of the young poet who so loved to travel. Although Müller lived most of his life in the provincial town of Dessau on the Mulde River north of Leipzig, he was unusually well traveled for a man of his station in life. It is believed that as a boy he accompanied a family friend to Frankfurt, Dresden, and Weimar. It is known that he studied in Berlin, the capital of Prussia, and that his studies were interrupted by his participation in the War of Liberation against Napoleon, during which he traversed much of the European continent from Prague to Brussels with the Prussian army. After the war he returned to his studies at the University of Berlin. Later he spent about fifteen months traveling in Italy, finally settling down as schoolteacher and librarian in his hometown.

Young Müller continued to feel the urge to travel, to escape occasionally from the small-town atmosphere of Dessau: "Obschon meine Lage nicht eben unbehaglich ist und mein Geschäft als Bibliothekar meinen Studien nicht widerstrebt, so will mir doch die Ruhe nicht zusagen, und ich sitze immer noch wie auf Kohlen und kann nicht heimisch werden."[2] Until his death a week before his thirty-third birthday, Müller made visits of varying duration at least once a year to Dresden, Leipzig, Berlin, or some more distant place. During these trips he conferred with his publishers and maintained friendships with many of the prominent literati of his time.

In a letter to his wife he describes the love of travel that he so often expressed in his simple lyrics: "Ich habe eine so glückliche Reisenatur, dass, sobald ich im Wagen sitze u[nd] die Unterstadt hinter mir habe, dass ich dann gleich frank u[nd] frei bin, wie ein junger Bursch."[3]

Childhood in Dessau

Born in Dessau on October 7, 1794, the future poet was baptized Johann Ludwig Wilhelm. His birthplace was a small one-story house, part of a three-house complex at Steinstrasse 53. The house was separated from the Mulde River only by a small garden, from which steps led directly down to the water.

Wilhelm Müller's birthplace in Dessau as viewed from the side facing the Mulde River. This original aquarelle or water color was painted for publication in this monograph by artist Rudolf Hugk, who was also born in the house and who lived there many years. Hugk was awarded the "Wilhelm Müller Art Prize of the City of Dessau" in 1975.

Müller's father, Christian Leopold Müller (1752–1820), was one of sixty-eight tailors in the local guild. His mother, Marie Leopoldine Cellarius Müller (1751–1808), bore seven children (not six, as reported by Gustav Schwab and F. Max Müller).[4] Wilhelm alone survived early childhood. Because of the many illnesses in the family, the hard-working father was forced more than once to call upon the Duke for monetary assistance, which was granted to him. However, the financial situation of the family appears to have improved later. Wilhelm apparently had a very happy childhood. His parents, thankful that fate had spared at least one of their children, allowed the boy much freedom.

According to Otto Francke's 1887 study of Müller's school records and the unpublished Gymnasium records from the papers of Pastor Schmidt (now in the Dessau city archives), he was an excellent pupil, especially in languages, but was criticized for being too independent, too arrogant, and too unsettled. Although he displayed an interest in several subjects, Wilhelm showed a strong resentment of authority. Apparently, he had become attached to a fellow pupil, a certain Hesekiel, who was considered a bad influence by the teachers.

Wilhelm's mother Marie died in her son's fourteenth year (not in his eleventh year, as Schwab reported and F. Max repeated).[5] This year also marked his church confirmation and saw his first attempts at literary composition. The young would-be writer prepared elegies, odes, small poems, and a tragedy as if they were to be published. He sold nothing for several years, however, and it was only Christian Müller's marriage to the relatively wealthy widow Marie Gödel Seelmann (1769–1853) that made it financially possible for young Müller to continue his formal education. This second marriage produced a daughter, Wilhelm's half sister Wilhelmine, about whom it is known only that she married a minister named Franke, who served in Raguhn, a little village on the outskirts of Dessau, and that she died in 1889.

After successfully completing the Abitur examination in the spring of 1812, Müller matriculated at the newly founded University of Berlin. (The small duchy of Anhalt-Dessau did not have a university.) Although the University of Berlin, founded by Wilhelm von Humboldt (1767–1835), had arranged its first lectures only two years before in 1810, and had only 600 students during the academic year 1812–1813, its prestigious faculty included such professors as Friedrich Schleiermacher, Johann Gottlieb Fichte, Karl von Savigny, and F. A. Wolf. Wilhelm Müller fell immediately into the rhythm of student life in Berlin, enjoying the freedom and stimulating pace of life in the large, bustling city.

War of Liberation
Events in the world at large interrupted Müller's first year of study in Berlin. Upon learning of Napoleon's retreat from Russia, the Prussian king called for volunteers for the army on February 10, 1813. By February 16 Müller had petitioned for and been granted permission to join the Prussian army; by February 24 he had withdrawn from the university along with 258 of his fellow students, forty-three of whom never returned.

Unfortunately, there is no record of Müller's feelings and experiences during this troubled time. It is known only that he became a lieutenant, as did many of his fellow student volunteers, and that he was not wounded during four battles with the French. On May 2, 1813, Müller fought in the Battle of Lützen (near Leipzig), which was a

Street view of Wilhelm Müller's birthplace, ca. 1880. The house was completely destroyed on March 7, 1945, by American bombs during an air raid. Since 1960 the Mulde River Project has encompassed the area where the house once stood.

French "victory" despite heavy losses. He was at Bautzen (east of Dresden) when Napoleon attacked on May 20–21, forcing the allied forces to retreat east of the Spree River. Five days later, on May 26, the troops again engaged at Haynau (Chojnow today) to the east of Bautzen. (Schwab—and later writers—have mistaken Haynau for Hanau near Frankfurt am Main, where a battle occurred during Napoleon's retreat across the continent on October 30–31, 1813.)[6] Müller fought again at Kulm on August 30, when the French general, Vandamme, who had attempted to join the main French force, was defeated. During the Battle of the Nations at Leipzig on October 16–19, 1813, Müller was stationed at Prague. He finished out the War of Liberation in a minor post at the headquarters in Brussels.

Müller's military tour of duty in the garrison of the Belgian capital was marked by serious personal problems, one of which was a painful love experience with a certain Thérèse. In his "Studien," Alfred Wirth draws the conclusion that the passionate affair affected Müller so deeply that he actually deserted his regiment, an act which caused the regimental commander to contact Müller's father through the University of Berlin. Although the details surrounding the episode will doubtless remain unknown, the first entry in Müller's Berlin diary written on his twenty-first birthday shows the importance of the experience: "Vor einem Jahre habe ich meinen Geburtstag in Brüssel verlebt, ich weiss selbst nicht recht, wie. Aber einen Brief schrieb ich an diesem Tage, der hat mir und meinem Vater manche Thräne gekostet. Gottlob, dass alles überstanden ist! Das vergangene Jahr liegt so weit hinter mir oder vor mir, als wär ich seitdem von einem Kinde zum Greise oder von einem Greise zum Kinde geworden."[7] The literary product of this unhappy time of transition was a collection of nine pessimistic sonnets, which were first published in 1902 by the American scholar Philip Schuyler Allen.

Leaving Brussels on November 18, 1814, Müller returned to Berlin via Dessau. Happy to resume his studies and renew friendships in Berlin, he looked back on the time in Brussels as an interlude of sensuality and freethinking (". . . eine Zeit der Sinnlichkeit und Freigeisterei, die mich nur zu lange in ihren Fesseln hielten").[8]

In his biography of Müller, Otto Hachtmann speculates that military discipline did not appeal to the independent and undisciplined youth who occasionally broke regulations and who did not seek out a hero's role for himself.

Study in Berlin

Much of Müller's second period of study in Berlin (January 1815 to August 1817) is recorded in detail in a diary begun on his twenty-first birthday, October 7, 1815. Entries appear with great regularity through January 1816, but there are only sixteen short ones from February until the end of the year, when they cease altogether. This diary, published in 1903 by the American Germanists James Taft Hatfield and Philip Schuyler Allen, is a valuable source of information about Müller, the religious poetess Luise Hensel, and the Berlin Romantic period. The diarist's entries are intimate conversations with himself, obviously never intended for publication: "Denn ich habe es fest in mir beschlossen, dass ich mir in dir (denn nur für mich will ich dich schreiben) keinen bösen Gedanken, kein böses Wort, keine böse That verschweigen will, wenn sie anders mir selbst bemerkbar werden."[9] More than one scholar has rightly observed the "Werther-like" nature of this and similar passages in this diary.

The unifying experience described in the diary is Müller's romantic attraction to Luise Hensel (1798–1876), the younger sister of his good friend Wilhelm. Wilhelm Hensel (1794–1861) later married Fanny Mendelssohn (1805–1847), the granddaughter of the Dessau philosopher of the Enlightenment Moses Mendelssohn and the older sister of Felix. Hensel was a poet by avocation and a painter by occupation. His drawings of members of the Berlin Romantic movement (e.g., those of Rahel Varnhagen von Ense and Baron de la Motte Fouqué) are still used today as illustrations in books dealing with the period.

The two Wilhelms had met briefly during their military service, but their lasting friendship dated from their return to Berlin, when Müller became a regular guest in the Hensel home, a Lutheran parsonage. It was here that the young poet fell in love with the talented, attractive, and deeply religious sister of his friend. Müller was not Luise Hensel's only suitor; she also attracted, among others, the attentions of Ludwig Berger, teacher of Felix and Fanny Mendelssohn, and the dashing Clemens Brentano. Luise, however, who wrote poems of a religious nature and who converted to Catholicism in 1818, remained unmarried to the end of her days, devoting her life to religious service and her poetry, published in *Gedichte* (1858) and *Lieder* (1869).

Luise obviously enjoyed Müller's company. However, her biographer, Frank Spiecker, published an English translation of a section of his *Luise Hensel als Dichterin* under the title "Luise Hensel and Wilhelm Müller," in which he expresses the view that "as a suitor Wilhelm Müller made no impression on Luise."[10] This may well have been the case, but it should be mentioned that Luise did little to discourage the attentions of the enamored youth. In fact, Luise, an attractive girl of seventeen, exhibited what seem to have been signs of genuine affection toward Müller, which he ecstatically recorded in his diary. The pair spent a good deal of time together; at least twenty-three meetings between the two are noted in the diary during a period of ten weeks. For example, Müller accompanied her arm in arm on a long walk through the festively lighted streets of Berlin on the occasion of the arrival of the Russian Czar. Most often, however, they met at the Hensel home. Once when Müller had not visited for a week, he was greeted with questions about his health and was urged by Luise not to stay away for so long. Luise asked him to write poems for her: "Wenn Sie ein Lied im Herzen haben, so unterdrücken Sie es nicht und schreiben Sie es nieder. Denken Sie, dass es mir grosse Freude macht!"[11] Once she coquettishly asked if her name might be found in his diary—and blushed when he replied in the affirmative. On another occasion she gave Müller her hand to kiss, and once in a game he kissed her cheek. Luise told the hopeful suitor that she had played a card game in which one learned the name of one's future spouse. Blushing, she then coyly hinted that Müller's card had been the one that she had drawn.

According to Allen and Hatfield in their notes to Müller's diary, there is only one poem by Luise Hensel which reflects her relationship with Müller, "Die Siebenzehnjährige [*sic*] auf dem Balle":[12]

> Du liebst mich, weil durch braunes Haar
> Sich schlingt der grüne Lebenskranz,
> Weil frisch und voll der Wangen Paar
> Und leicht der Fuss sich hebt im Tanz.

O, armer Jüngling! wisse, bald
Ist all das hin, was du geliebt,
Geknickt die blühende Gestalt,
Die jetzt den Zauber auf dich übt.[13]

Even if Luise was simply enjoying his company and his attentions, the impact of the relationship on Müller was profound. The two exchanged poems and discussed their readings of *Der arme Heinrich*, E. T. A. Hoffmann's *Phantasiestücke, Des Knaben Wunderhorn*, Novalis, Jakob Böhme, and others. Before going to sleep, Müller addresses Luise in his diary: "Was ich Gutes u[nd] Schönes gethan, gedacht, gefühlt, gesprochen u[nd] gedichtet habe, dichtete, sprach, fühlte ich aus dir."[14]

During his military service Müller had matured to a degree that the boisterous society of his Berlin student comrades no longer held the appeal for him that it once had. In his diary he describes sitting as if alone in the midst of a swirling throng of students in a drinking tent: "Nun sass ich so gleichgültig da, als wäre ich allein: das bunte Gewühl schien mir einem Automaten ähnlich." After departing early from his fellow students of Anhalt, he questions his motives: "Ich bin darüber weg—vielleicht zu früh—! Denn die schönen Studentenjahre kehren nicht wieder."[15] A couple of weeks later, however, he feels the need to record merely that he found the company in a favorite student gathering place "large, but boring."

Müller now became a more serious student at the university. His literary productivity began to accelerate and broaden in scope, keeping pace with an ever-widening compass of friends and acquaintances in the intellectual circles of Berlin. During his military service he had struck up friendships with several young noblemen, among them Count Friedrich von Kalckreuth. Thanks to these contacts and to his personal charm and ready wit, the impecunious tailor's son from Dessau quickly gained entrance into the best houses in Berlin. He was invited to the salons of Elisa von der Recke, Friedrich August Stägemann, Rahel Varnhagen von Ense, and Helmina von Chézy. He made the acquaintance of many talented and educated people, including Friedrich de la Motte Fouqué, Adolf Müllner, Karl August Varnhagen von Ense, Gustav Schwab, Christoph August Tiedge, August Zeune, Christian Rühs, and Ludwig Berger. In the home of the privy councillor, Stägemann, the small drama that later formed the basis for *Die schöne Müllerin* was written and produced.

Although the small-town boy often felt ill at ease in the higher circles of society and was embarrassed about his inability to dance, he was a welcome guest, whose company people enjoyed: "Ich kann überhaupt von dem Glücke sagen, dass die meisten Menschen, bekannte und unbekannte, mir mehr Zutrauen zu schenken pflegen, als ich verdiene."[16] Since he also worried about the financial strain that his studies placed upon his father, Müller moved into less expensive quarters and repeatedly applied for university scholarships. His diary at this time shows that he was at once unsure of himself and yet confident of his abilities. "Ich weiss es wohl, wenn ich ein Drittel meines Herzens vertauschen könnte mit einem Drittel Lebensverstand, so würde ich im Umgange, wie auch in meinen Liedern zwei Drittel mal mehr Menschen gefallen als jetzt. Und doch, wenn mir Einer den Tausch anbieten könnte, ich nähme ihn nicht an."[17]

Müller's major area of study at the university was classical philology, but he also attended lectures on medieval history, Dante, Roman history, early German literature, the English language, and Milton. Among his professors were Philipp Buttmann, Friedrich August Wolf, Christian Rühs, August Boeckh, and Benjamin Beresford. The highly respected but controversial professor F. A. Wolf invited Müller to join him for meals several times. In the home of the English teacher Benjamin Beresford, who was the official English lecturer to the Prussian court, Müller spoke French and English with the teacher, his family, and other guests. He also knew Professors Boeckh and Buttmann personally. Independently, Müller read many contemporary works, such as Goethe's *Dichtung und Wahrheit*. He immersed himself in Middle High German masterpieces, which had recently aroused the interest of his contemporaries, and he studied languages. He was interested in Old French poetry and worked on a German version of the story of the troubadour Geoffrey Rudel. For Müller language study was an intellectual exercise to limber the mind: "Je mehr Sprachen man wisse, desto kräftiger u[nd] gelenkiger werde der Geist."[18] But he was also interested in the literature of the languages he studied. From the Berlin diary there emerges a picture of an intelligent, highly talented student, who studied a number of different fields because he was genuinely interested in them.

At this time Berlin was a center of German Romanticism, and the young Müller acquired many of the tastes and interests of the literary personalities with whom he associated in the capital. The Romanticists were enthusiastic in their admiration for everything German—especially the German past. Müller adopted the fashion of wearing old German attire. He studied early German literature and translated parts of the *Nibelungenlied* and many Middle High German poems. A collection of these poems appeared in March 1816, under the title *Blumenlese aus den Minnesingern*. Further testimony to his absorption in the mood of the time was his voracious reading of the works of other Romanticists. He was especially impressed by Novalis: "Ich habe in diesen Tagen viel im Novalis gelesen, der mich oft gar wunderlich ergriff, es schien die Stimme desselben nicht von aussen zu mir hereinzuklingen, sondern aus mir hervor. Es schien mir, als hätte ich das Alles schon lange sagen wollen, wäre aber stumm gewesen."[19]

On January 4, 1815, a group of Berlin intellectuals founded a society for the study and ennoblement of the German language, the Berlinische Gesellschaft für deutsche Sprache, which was created with some of the same goals as the Sprachgesellschaften of the seventeenth century. Members, who were interested in "purifying" the German language from foreign influences, included teachers, clerics, lawyers, young noblemen, and poets. Many of the younger men had just returned from the war against the French. Among those attending the weekly Thursday evening meetings were Friedrich Ludwig Jahn, a patriot and political reformer; Theodor Heinsius, a grammarian and lexicographer; August Zeune, a professor; and the Romantic poets Baron de la Motte Fouqué and Clemens Brentano.

After joining the society on July 26, 1815, Müller attended meetings regularly and was eventually elected to office. On October 11 of the same year, he read the introduction to his *Blumenlese* to the membership. During the following summer (June 12 and 19) he lectured on his theories regarding the origin of the *Nibelungenlied*.

The young Müller greatly admired the popular Romantic poets Ludwig Tieck, Ludwig Uhland, and especially Baron de la Motte Fouqué. Schwab gives the following account of Müller's introduction to Fouqué in a coffeehouse on August 4, 1815:

> Er stand erröthend vor dem Meister, dessen Poesie auf ihn wie auf die meisten jüngern [*sic*] Dichter jener Zeit einen so grossen Einfluss geübt hatte; sein Gesicht blühte in der ersten Jugend, eine fast jungfräuliche Scham färbte mit einem schnell wachsenden und vergehenden Roth die durchsichtige Haut seiner Wangen; im Auge glänzte der Stolz des werdenden Dichters; ein voller Kranz von blonden, halbgelockten Haaren umgab seine hohe Stirne. In dieser Gestalt ist er mir später immer erschienen, wenn ich die begeisterungsvollsten seiner Gesänge, namentlich seine "Griechenlieder" las.[20]

On the next day the youth sent Fouqué a manuscript of his soon-to-be-published collection of translations of Middle High German poems, *Blumenlese*. In the letter accompanying his manuscript, Müller humbly declared that Fouqué's *Undine* had "seduced" him away from his studies of classical philology and had given him a "new soul" as well as a new understanding of the *Nibelungenlied*. Fouqué soon asked Müller to contribute to his Romantic journal, *Frauentaschenbuch*.

In addition to studying and making friends, Müller spent much time writing poetry. In this he was encouraged by Luise Hensel and several of his other literary friends. Poetry seemed to come to him naturally: "Es ist ein gar liebes Dichten, das Dichten im Innern, das auch wieder zum Innern dringt. Ich trage so manchmal ein Lied lange Zeit mit mir herum, es vollendet sich in mir, es feilt sich sogar—dann aufgeschrieben schnell und ohne Veränderung. Das sind dann meine besten Sachen."[21] In January 1816 a collection of poetry, *Die Bundesblüthen*, was published by five companions back from the War of Liberation: Wilhelm Müller, Wilhelm Hensel, Count Friedrich von Kalckreuth, Count Georg von Blankensee, and Wilhelm von Studnitz. Müller's contributions, which were not included in the 1906 critical edition of his poetry, were published by Hatfield in 1898 under the title "Earliest Poems."

Müller also contributed to *Die Sängerfahrt*, a volume of poems and stories edited by Friedrich Förster. Although dated 1818, it appeared in 1817 and included contributions from both well-known and amateur Romantic writers. In addition to the first printing of Brentano's *Aus der Chronika eines fahrenden Schülers*, *Die Sängerfahrt* contained works by Achim von Arnim, Adelbert Chamisso, Count Otto Heinrich von Loeben, the brothers Grimm, Max von Schenkendorf, Helmina von Chézy, Karl Förster, Hedwig von Stägemann, and Wilhelm and Luise Hensel. Müller contributed four poems to this volume: "Die Sage vom Frankenberger See bei Aachen," "Der blaue Mondschein," "Freie Glosse," and "Wechselreigen."

The year 1817 marked the beginning of Müller's journalistic work. In addition to having poems published in the *Frauentaschenbuch für das Jahr 1817*, *Zeitung für die elegante Welt, 1817*, and *Wiener Zeitschrift für Kunst, Literatur und Mode, 1817*, Müller began writing for Friedrich Wilhelm Gubitz's *Der Gesellschafter, oder Blätter für Geist und Herz*. As a result of his articles about Berlin opera and drama in this journal, Müller became involved in an extended literary debate with the disputatious Adolf Müllner, literary critic and author of the popular fate tragedy *Die Schuld* (1813).

In addition to his critical writings, Müller's contributions to the *Gesellschafter* were short poems; the ballad "Der Glockenguss zu Breslau"; translations from Scottish, Spanish, and English; and a series of short prose tales explaining the names of various flowers. These Blumendeutungen and Märchen, slavishly imitative of the style of Tieck and Novalis, were later republished in 1845 in *Moderne Reliquien*, edited by Arthur Müller (no relation to Wilhelm Müller). During 1816 and 1817 Müller apparently had also been working on his translation of Christopher Marlowe's *The Tragical History of Doctor Faustus*, for which Achim von Arnim wrote the introduction.

Travel in Italy

A fortuitous turn of events led Müller to decide to cut short his studies at the University of Berlin. In the summer of 1817, a wealthy Prussian courtier and dilettante, Baron von Sack (who later became Vize-Oberjägermeister Graf Sack), had been planning to make an extended journey through Greece, Asia Minor, and Egypt. Hoping to gain recognition at court for his trip, he asked the Akademie der Wissenschaften in Berlin to recommend a suitable traveling companion—someone who might cast an aura of scientific or literary worth upon his travels. It happened that Professor August Boeckh had been working for some time on a thesaurus of classical inscriptions and, as early as 1815, had suggested the need for the Academy to send scholars to search out and transcribe previously unrecorded inscriptions. The Academy, however, had no funds for such a project, and Baron von Sack's proposal was welcomed by the scholars. They selected the promising classical philology student Wilhelm Müller, who had been active in the philology seminar and who was a favorite student of F. A. Wolf. Müller accepted the offer eagerly. It was a great honor and opportunity for a youth of his background and financial situation. The professors, doubtless aware of the splintering of Müller's interests and his lack of real concentration in one field of study, may have hoped that the change of environment and the opportunity to apply his knowledge of philology in the field would give direction to the talented but unsettled youth. Philipp Buttmann, president of the Royal Prussian Academy of Sciences, and Friedrich Schleiermacher, secretary of the Academy, signed Müller's credentials as collector of inscriptions in Greece and Asia.

On August 20, 1817, the Baron and his young companion left Berlin for Vienna, where they stayed for two months. It was here in the Austrian capital that the future Griechen-Müller acquired his keen interest in modern Greece. Vienna, the site of the Congress of 1814 and 1815, had important mercantile interests in Greece and the Orient. It was also the European center of the Philikí Etairía (Hetaireia), a group whose avowed purpose was to promote the cause of Greek independence from Turkey. Through Professor Wolf's personal letters of recommendation, Müller came into contact with the crusading editors of the Greek literary-patriotic newspaper *Hermes Logios*. During his two-month stay in Vienna, Müller devoted himself conscientiously to the mastering of modern Greek under the tutelage of native Greeks—a skill he later put to use in making his translations of modern Greek folk songs. Müller's involvement with modern Greece and its language, his interest in the Viennese folk theater, and his friends in the Viennese artist colony often separated him from Baron von Sack, whose interests centered mainly around the society of the Viennese court.

After an outbreak of plague in Constantinople was reported, the travelers altered their itinerary. On November 6, 1817, they departed for Italy in the company of the artist Julius Schnorr von Carolsfeld (1794–1872). The journey led from Trieste to Venice, where Müller became acquainted with examples of the Italian commedia dell'arte. They visited Ferrara, Bologna, and Florence, where Schnorr remained while Müller and the Baron proceeded to Rome, arriving on January 4, 1818. In letters to his father and brother, Schnorr describes the relationship between the Baron and the much younger Müller: "Der Baron hat sich in den Kopf gesetzt, nichts zu übersehen, besonders seines

Begleiters wegen, den er (einen jungen talentvollen, auch anerkannten Gelehrten) mehr aus Eitelkeit mitgenommen hat, weil dieser über die Reise dann etwas schreiben wird, was dem König dediciert werden soll. Sonst ist er ein ganz guter Mann und legt uns nichts in den Weg, wenn wir nach unserer Art sehen wollen." Partly because of the Baron, Schnorr parted company with the two in Florence: "Als sie gingen, hatte ich noch keine Lust, Florenz zu verlassen, und auch keine Lust mit dem alten Sack weiter zu reisen, der ein alter unerträglicher Sack ist, obwohl sonst ein guter Mann. Bisher musste sein lieber Begleiter, Herr Müller, mir des Alten Unerträglichkeit ausgleichen; . . . am Ende hatte ich doch keine Lust mehr."[22]

Müller and the Baron remained together until Easter, finally parting company in Rome. The precise nature of the discord that resulted in their going their separate ways is not known. Müller's independent and headstrong personality may have been a contributing factor. It is known that the wealthy aristocrat enlisted the aid of Müller's friend Count Kalckreuth in an attempt to convince the young scholar to remain with him—but to no avail. The Baron finally continued on from Rome in the company of an architect. In January 1819 Müller gave his version of the reasons for the separation in a letter of application for a teaching post in Dessau: "Dafür mag meine schnelle Trennung von dem H. Baron von Sack sprechen, die keinen andern Grund hatte, als die feste Überzeugung, dass seine Methode zu reisen mit der Erreichung meiner Absichten nicht vereinbar wäre. Ich zog es also vor, wenigstens Italien in Hinsicht auf Alterthum, Kunst und Sprache genauer kennen zu lernen, als viele ferne Länder, wie Bilderbücher, zu durchfliegen."[23]

Müller's decision to leave the Baron must have been a difficult one to make, for it left him without a source of funds and certainly disappointed his Berlin professors. Schnorr wrote to his father that he had lent money to Müller, whom he described as being "unquestionably honorable."[24] The artist Schnorr also introduced Müller to the German artists in Rome, especially the Nazarenes.

After the Baron's departure, Müller visited Naples and the ruins in Pompeii and Paestum, returning to Rome on May 29. Preferring the cooler air of nearby Albano, he left behind the oppressive Roman summer. During July and August, Müller shared lodgings in Albano with the young Swedish poet Per Daniel Amadeus Atterbom (1790–1855). Müller and Atterbom, who had similar misgivings about the political situation in Europe, corresponded intermittently during Müller's later years in Dessau. In his letters to Atterbom, Müller is especially candid in expressing his opinions about contemporary affairs, both literary and political:

Über Politik ist nichts Erfreuliches zu melden. *S'isch doch a Lumpenescht das Deutschland,* sagt der alte Tyroler Koch [painter Josef Anton Koch] in Rom. . . . . Aber *Presszwang* und *die politische Inquisition in der deutschen Bundesfestung* (und in der Stadt, in der die Druckerkunst erfunden ward) bleiben: Das sind die Trophäen der deutschen Völkerschlacht bei Leipzig.—Und die Patrioten verfluchen dennoch die Leipziger, die die Ehrensäule auf dem Schlachtfelde umgestürzt haben, und die Berliner sagen dennoch, Ihr König sei ein Franzose. Gott segne seine französische Herrschaft und bewahre ihn vor deutschem Patriotismus.[25]

It was during this stay in the Roman countryside that Müller saved the life of the orientalist and poet Friedrich Rückert (1788–1866), an incident first recorded in 1845 by Müller's son in the *Allgemeine deutsche Biographie* and later retold by him in English in *Auld Lang Syne:*

Rückert and my father were travelling on foot, and they had often to sleep in the poorest *osterias.* In these wretched hovels they got more than they had bargained for, and one fine morning, after getting out into the fresh air, they saw a lake, and my father jumped in to have a bath. Rückert could not resist, and followed. But he could not swim, the lake was deeper than he had thought, and he was on the point of drowning when my father swam towards him and rescued him. "I wrote my first epic poem then, in the style of Camoens," said Rückert, with a loud chuckle, "and I called it the 'Lousiade,' but it has never been published."[26]

The months in Italy were a happy time for Müller, who, unlike many visitors to Rome, passed over the remnants of the past in preference to the present. He observed the ordinary people at work and at play. Although he frequented the caffès of the foreigners (including the famous Caffè Greco, still a popular rendezvous spot), he devoted most of his time to studying the everyday life, customs, language, and folk songs of Italy. The collection of Italian folk songs which Müller began during his stay in Italy was later expanded. Its publication in 1829 under the title *Egeria* made it the first significant collection of such songs ever printed, preceding by twelve years the first important collection made by an Italian.[27]

On August 30, 1818, Müller began his four-month return journey to Dessau, passing through Orvieto, Perugia, Florence, Verona, the Tyrol, Munich, and Dresden. He arrived in Dessau in December. From the memoirs of the Dresden professor Karl Förster comes a description of the impression the handsome, twenty-four-year-old Müller made:

Wilhelm Müller aus Dessau erfreut mich durch seinen Besuch und persönliche Bekanntschaft. . . . Müller ist ein junger Mann, ausser dem lebendigen Auge, wenig ausgezeichnet durch sein Äusseres. Einfach, fast wortkarg, bis das Gespräch ihn interessirt, dann wird er immer lebendiger, liebenswürdiger. Wir verstanden uns bald; der erste Handschlag nach dem kurzen Besuche gab uns Beide Gewähr, dass unsere Bekanntschaft nicht vorübergehend sein werde.[28]

Their friendship was indeed a lasting one. Förster assumed the editor-ship of the *Bibliothek deutscher Dichter des siebzehnten Jahrhunderts* after Müller's death.

Adulthood in Dessau

The twenty-four-year-old Müller now found himself in his hometown without a formal degree from the University of Berlin and without a position to support himself. The uncompleted research assignment from the Berlin Academy of Sciences made it unlikely that he would be able to find a position in that city, although he apparently had been forgiven his decision to remain in Italy, especially by Professor Wolf, whose close friend he remained. Professors Boeckh, Wolf, and Rühs wrote letters of recommendation for him at this time.

Plans for the restructuring of the school system in Dessau made a teaching position available, and Müller applied for it on December 28, 1818. He was hired soon thereafter. In addition to his light teaching duties, the organization of several private libraries—among them the Duke's—into one large public library became Müller's responsibility on April 1, 1820, making him the second ducal librarian, after Christian Friedrich Stadelmann's brief tenure of less than one year.

Although he would have preferred to find a position in Berlin, Dresden, or Leipzig, Müller was relatively satisfied with his position in Dessau, which allowed him much variety and freedom to come and go without strict supervision. Early in his Dessau days he writes Helmina von Chézy, the librettist of Weber's opera *Euryanthe,* that he is not unhappy with his lot: "Ich bin in Dessau nicht unzufrieden: der Ort ist, wie Sie wissen werden, nicht unfreundlich, wenigstens giebt es vor den Thoren grüne Baüme u[nd] in den Thoren rothe Backen: das über-rascht schon angenehm, wenn man aus Berlins Sandwüsten u[nd] Bleichsuchtlazarethen kömmt. Mein Italien trage ich aber in mir."[29] Müller enjoyed the beauty of his surroundings in Dessau but missed the intellectual stimulation and companionship that he had found in the cities. In 1820 he writes his Swedish friend Atterbom: "Von mei-nem Leben in Dessau habe ich Ihnen wohl schon etwas geschrieben: Die Natur ist gut und grün, die Menschen von gutem Schlag, hübsche Gesichter—aber wenig dahinter. Mein geselliger Umgang beschränkt sich auf Wenige: mehr Frauen als Männer."[30]

F. Max Müller writes in the *Allgemeine deutsche Biographie* that his father never had any desire to move to a larger city or to assume a more influential post. Wilhelm Müller's friend Karl Förster paints a different picture: "Er ist gesund und heiter und mit seiner Stellung in Dessau sehr zufrieden; dennoch ist's sein grosser Wunsch in Dresden heimisch zu werden."[31] Actually, Müller kept his eyes open for possible positions elsewhere and maintained numerous contacts in several cities in Germany.

At a time when his name was being mentioned in connection with the librarianship at Wolfenbüttel (once held by Lessing), Müller refers to this possible opportunity in letters in October 1825 and August 1826. In the August communication, written from Weimar to his wife Adelheid, he writes about Dessau with some ambivalence: "Denn das Weimar ist ein wunderlicher Ort u[nd] von seinen bösen Seiten *böser* als Dessau. Namentlich ist das Kliquenwesen und das Klatschen hier toller als in Dessau u[nd] es muss sehr schwer sein, sich als Neueintretender durchzuschlagen. . . . Lass uns daher in Geduld unser Dessau tragen u[nd] ertragen."[32]

In 1819 Müller began his adult career in Dessau in three fields at once: teaching, librarianship, and creative and critical writing. Although he obviously considered teaching secondary in importance to his other activities, he was a popular and versatile teacher. During the next eight years, his obligations as a teacher varied with respect to the number of hours he taught, grade level, and subject. In 1820 he taught Greek, Latin, and classical geography. In his language courses he discussed, among other subjects, Cicero, Sallust, and Homer's *Odyssey*. Müller happily reports to his former professor Wolf that he has been successful with his pupils: "Meine Schüler zeigen Eifer und Liebe zu meinem Unterricht u[nd] meiner Person und das macht mir die Arbeit leicht."[33]

Müller also enjoyed his work as the director of the first public library in Dessau—the ducal library. He was ultimately credited with the successful organization and cataloguing of a library of over 18,000 volumes, a job which took up much of his time, particularly during the summer of 1819. (This ducal library existed independently until 1924, when it was combined into the state library, the Landesbibliothek. The Dessau historian Dr. Franz Brückner described in 1978 the early history of this library in his *Häuserbuch der Stadt Dessau*.) Müller especially enjoyed the freedom he had with respect to the acquisition of materials and their organization: "Da gibt es denn vollauf zu thun; jedoch scheint das Geschäft mir leicht, weil es mir zusagt und weil ich darin ganz unbeschränkt bin."[34] This freedom granted to library director Müller in the selection of materials for the library proved especially useful to Müller the book reviewer and critic. He ordered numerous books, journals, and newspapers; after perusing them, he determined which should be added to the ducal library and which to his own private collection. (Letters to Brockhaus reveal that he was scrupulous in the recording of the costs to the two accounts.) Thanks to this virtually unlimited access to newspapers and journals (he read the Duke's newspaper before it was sent to the palace), Müller was extremely well informed about contemporary literary activity in Europe. He made good use of this knowledge in his many critical writings for various journals.

After becoming settled in his new life in Dessau, Müller began to write his firsthand observations and impressions of Italy, which became a 564-page travel book entitled *Rom, Römer und Römerinnen*. The book was published in Berlin early in 1820 and was well received by the public. (The book's lively style and detailed descriptions of the Rome of 1818 has inspired two twentieth-century editions, one in 1956 in Bremen, and another in 1978 in East Berlin.)

During the winter of 1819 Müller conceived the idea of publishing a literary journal that would compete with the well-established *Gesellschafter* in Berlin for the readership of educated, literarily inclined persons. Müller announced the forthcoming publication of the *Askania* (*Anhaltische Blätter für Leben, Literatur und Kunst*) by sending out many letters to friends and acquaintances, soliciting contributions to the journal. Increased teaching duties, however, left him little time to write for his own publication; even the pleasant task of writing the introduction to the new journal had to be assigned to another, Wilhelm von Schütz. Although the *Askania* received contributions from several well-known writers, such as Achim von Arnim, Jakob Grimm, Count Otto Loeben, Baron de la Motte Fouqué, Helmina von Chézy, Karl Förster, J. M. Schottky, and Otto von der Malsburg, it suffered the fate of many such idealistic ventures: it failed after six months (January–June 1820). The reason for ceasing publication was simple: fewer than 150 copies of each issue were sold. The articles were too serious and too sophisticated to win a wide readership, and Dessau was too small to support such a literary venture.

In December 1819 Müller received a letter from the prominent liberal publisher Friedrich Arnold Brockhaus, suggesting that Müller write a series of reviews of all the travel books about Italy for the *Hermes oder Kritisches Jahrbuch der Literatur*. This was a turning point in Müller's life, for it marked the beginning of his close relationship with the firm of F. A. Brockhaus, an association that continued after Heinrich Brockhaus assumed control of the firm upon the death of the founder in 1823.

During the following year, 1820, Müller continued his many enterprises, doing more work for Brockhaus, organizing the Dessau library, teaching, and completing his first volume of poetry, *Siebenundsiebzig Gedichte aus den hinterlassenen Papieren eines reisenden Waldhornisten*. On June 23 Müller's father died. In July and August Müller spent four weeks in Dresden and the surrounding area, where he met Ludwig Tieck and Karl von Holtei. Upon his return to Dessau, he writes to his Swedish friend Atterbom:

> Ich war vier Wochen in Dresden und der Umgegend. . . . Ich habe kostbare Jelängerjelieber-Tage mit dem *herrlichen* Manne [Tieck] gelebt, und bilde mir etwas darauf ein, dass er mir und meinen poetischen Kleinigkeiten so viel Theilnahme gezeigt hat. Wir sind ganze Tage zusammen gewe-

sen—Morgens auf der Gallerie, Mittags in irgend einem Wirtshause und Abends bei ihm. Haben Sie ihn lesen hören?—Ich habe unter andern den *Ulyss von Ithaka* von Holberg von ihm vortragen hören, und dieser Genuss ist unbeschreiblich.[35]

Müller left Dessau again in October, this time traveling to Berlin, where he visited friends.

On May 21, 1821,[36] Müller married the lovely Adelheid von Basedow (1800–1883), to whom he had become engaged in November of the preceding year. His bride was the granddaughter of the reformer of public education in Germany, Johann Bernhard Basedow (1723–1790), a forerunner of Pestalozzi and Froebel as well as the founder of the experimental school in Dessau, the Philanthropinum, in 1774. Adelheid's father and brother were high officials in the duchy. In this marriage into one of the leading families of Dessau, the tailor's son led home a pretty twenty-one-year-old bride, who was said to be small, lively, and personable. She was not only an energetic housewife who was in the market by seven, but was also an accomplished musician who sang contralto solos beautifully and played the piano. As was not uncommon for a daughter of well-to-do parents, Adelheid was also well educated; she knew English, French, and Italian.[37]

Wilhelm and Adelheid's marriage was by all accounts a happy one, based on mutual affection and respect. Some of Müller's frequent letters to her when he was away on trips and she was at home in Dessau with the two children have been preserved. They contain many terms of endearment and show the casual ease of a secure, satisfying relationship. He teases her about an apparent overweight problem: "Iss keine Kartoffeln!" The granddaughter of the educational reformer is also cautioned not to be too strict with their young children: "Küsse die lieben Kinder von mir u[nd] verziehe sie nicht mit den vielen Prügeln, sonst muss ich mich nachher zu sehr mit der Liebe u[nd] Güte anstrengen, u[nd] das entgeht dann dir."[38]

In letters to others Müller testifies to the happiness of his marriage: "Gott segne auch Sie, mein lieber Atterbom, mit einem guten Weibe. Es giebt doch auf Erden nichts, was über häusliches Glück ginge! Könnten Sie doch einmal ein Zeuge des meinigen sein!" After four years of marriage, Müller writes Atterbom again on the occasion of his friend's marriage: "Glück und Segen Ihrem Bunde, so ruft Ihnen ein Ehemann zu, der nach 4 Jahren der Verheirathung sich noch so glücklich fühlt, wie als Bräutigam."[39]

On New Year's Day 1826, Müller writes Adelheid a striking testament to the happiness of their marriage: "Glück auf zum Neujahr, meine liebe Adelheid! Wir haben uns nichts zu wünschen, als dass Alles uns so bleibe, wie es ist, und gewiss giebt es heute nicht viele Menschen auf der grossen Erde, die sich so glücklich u[nd] so zufrieden fühlen."[40]

Their first child, Auguste, was born April 20, 1822. She later married Dr. A. Krug of Chemnitz, who compiled *The Dictionary of Philosophy.* Auguste died in 1868, having outlived her children.

Friedrich Max Müller was born December 6, 1823. His name had been chosen in an unusual manner. The Müllers were staying with the Carl Maria von Weber family in Dresden. It was decided that the next baby in each family would be named after either Max or Agathe, the leading figures in Weber's Romantic opera *Der Freischütz.* Both babies were boys; hence the names Max Maria von Weber and Friedrich Max Müller.[41]

F. Max (as he called himself in England) inherited from his father the ability to work quickly and made a remarkable career for himself in the specialized field of Sanskrit and comparative philology. After earning a doctorate in philosophy at the University of Leipzig (1843), he went to England, where he became a respected professor at Oxford, holding the chair of comparative philology from 1868 until 1873. F. Max, who died in Oxford on October 28, 1900, became a naturalized Englishman and a member of the Privy Council, a rare honor for a foreigner. He was particularly known for his voluminous publication of the *Sacred Books of the East* and the *Rig-Veda,* which were republished in the 1960s. F. Max's scholarly work is honored still today in India, where cultural institutes bear his name.

During F. Max's brilliant career, marked by contact with many important people in both Germany and England (including Queen Victoria and Prince Albert), the friends and admirers of Wilhelm Müller showed an interest in his son. Musicians especially were pleased to welcome the son of the poet of Schubert's song cycles. Felix Mendelssohn, Robert and Clara Schumann, Ferdinand Hiller, and Franz Liszt were among F. Max's acquaintances. In *Auld Lang Syne* Müller's son records the greeting he received from soprano Jenny Lind: "What? the son of the poet of the *Müllerlieder!* Now sit down, . . . and let me sing you *Schöne Müllerin.*"[42]

Friedrich Max was not yet four when his father died; he made his brilliant career despite this early tragedy.

Family obligations did not keep Wilhelm Müller from his literary work. During the first year of his marriage (1821) he began writing poems about the Greek War of Independence, which had begun officially on March 25. As his family grew, he increased the amount of his journalistic writing to help out financially. His work for Ersch and Gruber's *Allgemeine Enzyklopädie der Wissenschaften und Künste* began slowly during 1821 with a few articles. His poetry and prose appeared in *Literarisches Konversationsblatt, Hermes, Urania, Zeitung für die elegante Welt, Gesellschafter,* and *Frauentaschenbuch.* Travels during 1821 included one trip to an unknown destination in April, a journey with

Adelheid to Leipzig in August, and a stay in Leipzig at the end of the year.

Besides *Die Winterreise,* which was sent to Brockhaus on January 16, Müller's writings during 1822 included the second volume of the *Lieder der Griechen,* a long article on Byron for *Urania,* reviews for *Hermes* and *Literarisches Konversationsblatt,* and poems for three different journals. He also continued working on Ersch and Gruber's *Enzyklopädie* and began work on the *Bibliothek deutscher Dichter des siebzehnten Jahrhunderts* by writing the first three volumes.

The trips of 1822 were to Magdeburg in October and to Dresden for a two-week stay at the home of Count Kalckreuth in July and August, followed by a stopover in Leipzig on the return trip. Wilhelm writes Adelheid of the warm reception that he enjoyed in Dresden, with so many invitations that he could accept only half of them:

> ... da ich hier sehr bekannt u[nd]—ich darf es ohne Schmeichelei gegen mich selbst sagen—geschätzt bin. Überall kömmt man mir entgegen—was ich leider nicht gern thue—und macht mir so zu sagen die Cour—was ich auch nicht kann. Den vielen Einladungen von alten und neuen Bekannten kann ich kaum zur Hälfte Genüge leisten. Vorgestern war ich zu Tische bei der Gräfin von der Recke, wo—die guten Sorten gar nicht zu erwähnen— eine Prinzessin (von Augustenburg) meine *Moitié* u[nd] ein Minister (Schuckmann) mein *Vis à Vis* war.[43]

These days in Dresden were filled with cultural activities, which Müller describes in letters to his wife. After seeing the Viennese court actress Antoinette Schroeder in Schiller's *Die Braut von Messina,* Müller joined a group of friends at Ludwig Tieck's home. On the following evening, the singer Eduard Devrient performed for the group gathered at Tieck's. In honor of Müller, Devrient sang Ludwig Berger's settings of *Die schöne Müllerin.* During this stay in Dresden Müller also heard a stirring performance of the popular *Der Freischütz,* directed by Weber himself. On the day after the performance he was a guest in Weber's home. Earlier, he had joined Count Kalckreuth and the Tieck family on an excursion into the country southeast of Dresden.

During the following year, 1823, Müller continued the literary activities he had begun earlier: *Neue Lieder der Griechen, Zweites Heft;* poems ("Tafellieder," "Devisen zu Bonbons," and the end of *Die Winterreise*); two volumes of the *Bibliothek deutscher Dichter;* and increased work for the *Enzyklopädie.* He produced critical writings for *Hermes, Literarisches Konversationsblatt,* and *Morgenblatt für gebildete Stände.* This was also the year of Müller's brief attempts at writing drama. "Herr Peter Squenz: Oder die Komödie zu Rumpelskirch, Posse in zwei Abtheilungen, nach Gryphius und Shakespeare frei bearbeitet" appeared in *Jahrbuch deutscher Nachspiele, Zweiter Jahrgang für 1823,* edited by Karl von Holtei. This version of the Andreas Gryphius comedy was the result of Müller's interest in the baroque poet, whose works he had published for Brockhaus in the second volume of the *Bibliothek deutscher Dichter*. The changes Müller made in his version of "Peter Squenz" were mainly in the arrangement of the speeches. He also attempted to make some of the lines more intelligible to the nineteenth-century audience. However, although the action in the Müller version may move more quickly than in the Gryphius play, it cannot be said that Müller really improved the comedy.

In May 1823 the first act of Wilhelm Müller's only original drama appeared in Breslau in *Deutsche Blätter für Poesie, Litteratur [sic], Kunst und Theater*. "Leo, Admiral von Cypern," written partly in prose and partly in blank verse, shows the influence of Shakespeare, Lessing's *Nathan der Weise*, Goethe's *Götz von Berlichingen*, and Schiller's *Wallenstein*. A letter to F. A. Brockhaus dated June 15, 1823, indicates that Müller had sent him the second act, which apparently was not published. Nor was the drama ever completed. Rudolf Koepke, the biographer of Ludwig Tieck, relates an incident which may explain why Müller never pursued a career as a dramatist: "Als er [Müller] einst Tieck einen dramatischen Versuch mitteilte, und dieser ihm auseinandersetzte, dass das Drama nicht sein Beruf sei, verwarf er ohne Empfindlichkeit und mit voller Anerkennung der dagelegten Gründe seine Dichtung, und hielt sich seitdem von dieser Gattung fern."[44] Since it is known from other sources that Müller often read his poetry (e.g., *Die schöne Müllerin*) aloud to Tieck for approval and criticism, and that Tieck also encouraged Müller in his later attempts in the Novelle (novelette) form, this statement of Koepke sounds quite plausible. Müller valued Tieck's opinion greatly.

During the first months of 1823 there developed a lengthy and extremely bitter fight between the young schoolteacher Müller and Christian Friedrich Stadelmann, a stiff, pedantic, conservative pedagogue who was Müller's immediate superior in the Dessau school system.[45] Throughout the struggle, which concerned Müller's independence in all school matters, Müller's coolly calculated maneuvers showed his determination to retain his special privileges. Insofar as the conflict was largely one of personalities, both parties were probably equally at fault. It is known, however, that Müller, although an unorthodox teacher, had much to offer his pupils, and that he was much admired by them: "Man nimmt ihn wie er ist. Es war, trotz Stadelmanns kühlen Berichten, kein Geheimnis geblieben, dass sein freier Unterricht den Schülern etwas bot, dass sie ihn liebten und dass er 'die unschätzbare Gabe besass, Autorität allein auf geistiges Übergewicht zu gründen.' "[46] Müller won a decisive victory, receiving from higher authorities all that he had requested. Besides retaining his privileged position as librarian, he was named ausserordentlicher Lehrer and as such was freed from the obligation to attend faculty meetings. In addition, he was permitted to lecture exclusively to advanced classes. From this time on, Müller welcomed his teaching duties as a pleasant and challenging diversion from his writing obligations.

Müller's greater freedom at the school also made it easier for him to arrange his travels. In January 1823 he went on an excursion to Leipzig with the Dessau Choral Society (Liedertafel). He made a trip to Dresden in June and paid a two-week visit to the Hensel home in Berlin during July. He writes Adelheid that his social activities in Berlin will delay his return to Dessau: "Statt meiner kömmt [*sic*] ein Briefchen von mir. Sei darum nicht böse. . . . Diese Woche warte nicht auf mich. Meine Abend [*sic*] sind von alten und neuen Bekannten schon bis Sonnetag [*sic*] besetzt, ohne einmal das Theater in Anschlag zu bringen, das doch auch wohl noch einen oder den andern in Beschlag nehmen wird."[47] It was during this visit to Berlin that he first met Felix Mendelssohn.

During 1824 Müller more than doubled his previous year's production of critical writings. This remarkable increase may have been due in part to new financial burdens, since his second child Friedrich Max had been born in December. Heinrich Brockhaus also kept requesting more and more work from him. In addition to his work on the *Enzyklopädie* and the *Bibliothek deutscher Dichter,* Müller wrote numerous book reviews, especially for the *Literarisches Konversationsblatt.* At the request of Brockhaus, he also agreed to write at least eighteen articles for the latest edition of the *Konversationslexikon.*

Müller's poetic productions for the year 1824 were the second volume of *Gedichte aus den hinterlassenen Papieren eines reisenden Waldhornisten* (dedicated to Carl Maria von Weber) and yet another group of patriotic poems on the Greeks, *Neueste Lieder der Griechen.* His single contribution to classical scholarship, *Homerische Vorschule,* also appeared in this year. With this work (dedicated to Duke Leopold Friedrich in gratitude for the freedom allowed him in the Duke's service), Müller sought to popularize the theories of F. A. Wolf, who had inspired him and many other students in Berlin.

In 1824 Duke Leopold Friedrich gave Müller the title Hofrat, an honor which at the same time made him eligible to join the society of the ducal court. Recognizing the value of social and political acceptance for the further progress of his career as well as the security of his family, Müller modified to a degree his independent manner and outspokenness so as not to jeopardize his newly acquired status. Nevertheless, he had little respect for the nobility in general, and not even the bestowal of the title changed his critical attitude, which his poetry frequently reflects.

From May 29 until June 13, 1824, Müller vacationed outside Dresden, at his friend Count Kalckreuth's Villa Grassi. These two weeks were filled with walks in the countryside, poetry writing ("Frühlingskranz aus dem Plauenschen Grunde"), and hours of friendly discourse with Tieck and Weber. Several evenings were spent at Tieck's home, where it was the custom of the host to read aloud to his guests. Müller escorted Tieck's daughter Agnes to a performance of Haydn's *The Seasons* at the Zwinger. He also accompanied Tieck and Agnes on a visit to Weber's home in the country. Müller describes the reception of his drinking songs at Tieck's: "Nachher wurde gelesen u[nd] meine neuen Trinklieder besonders mit grossem Applaus aufgenommen. Tieck hat sich den Bauch dabei gehalten, so sehr ergötzten ihn die Romanzen von dem Sechsmonatkinde [*sic*] ['Der Trinker von Gottes und Rechtes wegen'] und dem Est Est."[48]

Müller and his wife participated in the celebration in Quedlinburg of the hundredth anniversary of the poet Friedrich Klopstock's birth on July 2, 1824. This celebration in Klopstock's birthplace was essentially an elaborate music festival under the direction of Carl Maria von Weber. Musicians from all over Germany, including the Dessau composer Friedrich Schneider (1786–1853), gathered in the little town to perform the works of Händel, Beethoven, Mozart, Weber, Rossini, and Schneider. Adelheid Müller was one of the soloists at the festival; Müller attended in the role of reporter by recording the events in uninspired newspaper fashion in two issues of the *Literarisches Konversationsblatt*. Schwab reprinted the description in his fourth volume of Müller's *Vermischte Schriften*.

On June 20, 1824, Müller received word of Lord Byron's death at Missolunghi. Almost immediately, Müller began collecting everything he could find written about the English poet. He then proceeded to write a poem on Byron's death, a review of eight works about him, and the first German biography of the poet. At this time Müller also translated Claude Fauriel's collection of neo-Greek folk songs, but this work was not finished until 1825.

In addition to these labors, Müller's literary work in 1825 consisted of the Novelle *Der Dreizehnte;* much critical writing for five different journals; one volume of the *Bibliothek deutscher Dichter*; poems (mostly drinking songs); and encyclopedia work. In December he assumed joint editorship with Georg Hassel of the second section of the Ersch and Gruber *Allgemeine Enzyklopädie*.

Somehow Müller still found time to travel in 1825. In March and April he and Adelheid spent about three weeks in Berlin. At the end of July Müller left by himself for a month's vacation on the island of Rügen, where he was the guest of the poet Adolf Friedrich Furchau (1787–1868). Müller observed the customs of the inhabitants of the island with great interest. From this holiday came the cycle of lyrics "Muscheln von der Insel Rügen," which includes his "Vineta." Returning from this trip, Müller passed through Putbus, Stralsund, Rostock, and Berlin, where he dined at the Mendelssohns' and enjoyed the opera. A week after his return to Dessau he made a short trip to Magdeburg. After Christmas, Müller left his family again for a trip to Dresden via Leipzig, returning home on January 9, 1826. During his Dresden visit he spent several evenings, including New Year's Eve, with Ludwig Tieck. To Adelheid he writes:

> Die Glocke der letzten Stunde des alten Jahres hat mir bei Tiecks geschlagen in ganz kleinem Kreise, bei Austern u[nd] Champagner. Auch deine Gesundheit ist da getrunken worden, u[nd] wie gern hätten wir dich bei uns gehabt—nicht allein der Austern wegen. . . .
> Die Novelle [*Der Dreizehnte*] kann ich erst Dienstag bei Tieck lesen, weil ich sie zuerst ihm allein mittheilen will. . . . Gestern habe ich Trinklieder gelesen u[nd] Tieck hat recht herzlich darüber gelacht, auch über die schlanke, blanke ["Die schlanke Kellnerin und die schlanken Flaschen"].
> Auch heute gehe ich wieder zu Tiecks, wie überhaupt wohl alle Tage, sei es Morgens oder Abends.[49]

During 1826 the second edition of *Siebenundsiebzig Gedichte aus den hinterlassenen Papieren eines reisenden Waldhornisten, Band I*, appeared with the following dedication to Ludwig Tieck: "Seinem hochverehrten und inniggeliebten Freunde Ludwig Tieck zum Danke für mannichfache Belehrung und Ermunterung." In addition to his usual work for the various journals, Müller wrote poems and epigrams, having adopted the epigrammatic form from the baroque poet Friedrich von Logau, whose works appeared in Volume 6 of the *Bibliothek deutscher Dichter*.

In March 1826 Müller caught whooping cough from his children. Recovery was slow. To speed Müller's recuperation, Duke Leopold Friedrich allowed him to occupy the little teahouse (nicknamed the Schlangenhaus because of its fanciful, snakelike water spouts) in the park area Luisium outside of Dessau. (Previous biographers have written that Müller lived in Luisium, which gave the false impression that the poet was actually living in the elegant ducal residence, which is also called Luisium.) Müller was pleased with the secluded teahouse in the peaceful park surroundings and relished the opportunity to rest in solitude away from the hectic bustle of his family life and journalistic writing.

Although his relaxing stay in the beautiful surroundings of the park outside Dessau improved his health, Müller's physician Dr. Franz Olberg prescribed a stay at a spa during the months of July and August. Accompanied by his adventurous friend Alexander Baron von Simolin, Müller underwent a month-long health cure at Franzensbad, which is now part of Czechoslovakia and lies near the West German border to the east of Bayreuth.

Müller's letters to Adelheid during this stay at the spa are detailed descriptions of the ordered and restricted life of the spa visitors, whose main amusements were nature walks, gossip, and flirtations with fellow guests. Müller assures Adelheid of his improved health: "Die Reise ist mir sehr gut bekommen, der Husten hat aufgehört und schon die Bergluft hat angefangen, mich zu stärken. So hoffe ich denn, dass der Brunnen u[nd] die Bäder gut anschlagen werden. . . . Grüsse doch Olberg von mir u[nd] danke ihm dafür, dass er mich hierher geschickt hat. Wenn die zweite Hälfte der Kur so anschlägt, wie die erste, so komme ich um 10 Jahre verjüngt nach Dessau."[50]

The happily married Müller was concerned about the difficulties experienced by Adelheid, who was alone at home with the children, the household duties, and, during this particular journey, preparing a move into rooms adjacent to the ducal library, which was to be Müller's last residence:

> Es ist das Schicksal des Zurückbleibenden, die Trennung schwerer zu tragen, u[nd] dein Temperament verschlimmert deinen Stand. Hoffentlich werden die lieben Kinder das Mögliche thun, dich zu zerstreuen u[nd] zu beschäftigen. Der Auszug u[nd] Einzug ist nun wohl überstanden, u[nd] ich muss mich in Gedanken wieder nach unsrer Stadtwohnung versetzen, wenn ich bei dir sein will. Das geschieht oft, aber nie traurig u[nd] immer denke ich nur an die Freude des Wiedersehns, nicht an die Leiden des Getrenntseins. Das schöne Pärchen aus Dresden auf dem Balkon gegenüber thut indessen sein Mögliches, meine Sehnsucht nicht einschlafen zu lassen.[51]

About this time he dedicated to Adelheid a poem, "Auf der Höhe von Schönberg," which he wrote while enjoying the panoramic view of the Egerland, Fichtelgebirge, and Erzgebirge.

Müller's last letters from Franzensbad refer to the "Dangerous Neighbor," a beautiful Jewish woman from Prague who happens to rent near Müller and Simolin during the last week of the cure. Müller assures Adelheid that he has been a faithful husband and has merely written poems to the beautiful neighbor. The payments he received from both the woman and the newspaper *Zeitung für die elegante Welt* for his poems depicting the artificial, regimented life of the spa, "Lieder aus Franzensbad bei Eger," helped to finance his own expenses at the spa. In fact, the husband assures his practical wife that his writings have practically paid for both the trip and the health cure.

> Bei uns im goldnen Engel wird jetzt angeführt: Die gefährliche Nachbarschaft. Muss uns das noch in der letzten Kurwoche begegnen! Eine schöne Jüdin aus Prag, deren Ruf schon über die Berge von Karlsbad u[nd] Marienbad lange vor ihrer Ankunft zu uns gedrungen war, hat sich neben uns einlogiert. Du kannst denken, welche Noth ich habe, Simolin's Tugend zu bewachen. . . . Ich phantasiere mich aus, wie gewöhnlich, u[nd] halte mich im Reiche der Poesie schadlos für das verbotene Reelle, u[nd] so habe ich gestern in einem Morgen 7 Badegedichte an die Schöne gemacht, von denen ein Paar bereits in ihren Händen sind. Eine so aufrichtige

Beichte wird dich hoffentlich über die Treue deines Eheherrn beruhigen. Die schöne Frau muss ihre Beisteuer zu meinem Reisegeld geben, das ist Alles. . . . Zu deinem Troste kann ich dir auch sagen [*sic*]. Die ganze Reise wird mir [*sic*] sehr wenig kosten. Die Reise hierher u[nd] den Aufenthalt im Bade bestreite ich ganz mit dem Geschenk, so dass ich nur eine Kleinigkeit von dem Meinigen zur Heimreise zuzulegen brauche. Wenn ich das ausrechne, was ich hier—auch für die Enzyklopädie—gearbeitet, so bin ich *gratis* hin u[nd] her.[52]

In a letter to Adelheid two days later, Müller continues to describe the youthful "adventures" of Simolin and himself. Apparently Simolin had placed Müller's green slippers before the door of the beautiful neighbor, who suddenly departed. The gossip surrounding her departure mentioned boyish pranks involving Müller's green slippers, a tall figure in white skulking around her door, a peephole in her door, and an order for her departure from her older and absent husband. Simolin supposedly was overcome by pangs of unrequited love and wanted to drown himself in the spring. Müller concludes that these innocent carryings-on were proof of his good spirits and waxing health: "Diese Tollheiten mögen dir mehr als alle Versicherungen, dass ich wohl u[nd] munter sei, beweisen, dass ich es wirklich bin."[53] (For the modern reader, this amusing anecdote reveals the human side of Müller, who was—unlike so many poets—relatively happy both in his marriage and his career. Unfortunately, the fun-loving and faithful husband was to die just a little more than a year after this Franzensbad escapade with Baron Simolin.)

The return trip from Franzensbad brought Müller and Simolin to Wunsiedel, Bayreuth, Nuremberg, Bamberg, Coburg, Rudolstadt, Jena, and Weimar. In the *Zeitung für die elegante Welt* appeared the article "Reise von Wunsiedel nach Bayreuth" (reprinted in Schwab's *Vermischte Schriften*), in which Müller painted a sensitive portrait of the writer Jean Paul Friedrich Richter, who had died the previous year.

The main stopover on the return trip was Weimar, where the two friends arrived on August 23. Müller saw Goethe the next day. On the twenty-sixth, he was among a large crowd attending a tea party at Goethe's, and he also joined the many admirers who greeted the older poet on his birthday, August 28. Müller writes Adelheid: "Dein Mann wird hier bei guter Laune erhalten und mit Komplimenten, Ehrenbezeugungen u[nd] Einladungen nach Möglichkeit heimgesucht. . . . Was soll ich dir von Göthe sagen? Er war freundlich, aber, wie immer bei der ersten Zusammenkunft mit Fremden, etwas befangen, ja fast verlegen, so dass er mich mehr sprechen liess, als selbst sprach." Later he writes Tieck: "Der alte Herr war wohl auf, gut gelaunt, mit mir sehr höflich und freundlich, aber das ist auch Alles, und was ich aus seinem Munde gehört, das kann mir jeder gebildete Minister sagen."[54]

The following winter in Dessau, imitating the practice of Tieck,

Müller read plays aloud for his friends. He had recovered from his illness so well that he was able to read an entire Shakespeare play almost without stopping. A bust of Ludwig Tieck—a gift from Adelheid on Wilhelm's thirty-second (and last) birthday—graced the room in which the readings were held.

Another activity was added to Müller's already full schedule in 1826: the directorship of the court theater, which opened on January 1, 1827. Just as Schiller had written a prologue for the reopening of the Weimar court theater in 1787, Müller was asked to write the prologue for the opening in Dessau. Müller writes to an acquaintance in Berlin:

> Ich hatte den Plan, diesen Winter nach Berlin zu kommen, aber nun ist mir eine Theaterregie dazwischen gekommen, die ich habe übernehmen müssen. Ich sehe Sie lachen. Schule, Bibliothek, Enzyklopädie, Kritik, Poesie und Theaterregie—wie reimt sich das zusammen?—Aber sehen Sie, da ich nun einmal Hofrath heisse, und der Hof hier in Dessau keinen Rath wusste, sich diesen Winter zu amüsieren, so habe ich als wirklicher Hofrath Rath schaffen müssen durch ein Dilettanten-Hof- und Schlosstheater.[55]

Müller apparently was involved not only in writing the prologue, but in directing and acting as well. "Unser Herzog, des herumziehenden Theaterwesens müde, lässt nämlich im Schlosse ein kleines hübsches Bühnchen für Dilettanten einrichten, u[nd] da habe ich mich *nolens volens* nicht bloss als Spieler, sondern auch als *quasi* Regisseur engagiren müssen. Der Hof wusste keinen andern Rath, da musste ich denn einmal mehr sein, als Titular-Hofrath."[56] Hofrat Müller resented the time he was required to devote to the small ducal court. As court librarian and school official, however, and as husband of Adelheid von Basedow, he had to fulfill certain social obligations. Adelheid also took part in the amateur theatrical productions.

Müller's last collection of poetry was published in the year of his death, 1827. *Lyrische Reisen und epigrammatische Spaziergänge* gathered together eight groups of poems and 200 epigrams, which had been published previously in various journals. In this year Müller also wrote prose articles on miscellaneous subjects for seven different journals and newspapers. To Brockhaus he delivered some sixty-five articles for the seventh edition of the *Konversationslexikon*. The editorial work on the *Enzyklopädie* and the *Bibliothek deutscher Dichter* also occupied much of his time. His second Novelle *Debora*, begun in the autumn of the previous year, was in progress. However, it was not published (in *Urania*) until 1828, after his death.

In June 1827 Müller made another excursion with the Dessau singing group, this time to nearby Zerbst. On July 1 he reported being confined to bed: "Schon seit 14 Tagen theils bett- theils sofa-lägerig, jetzt in Besserung und schon wieder der Stube und dem Hause entlassen, bin ich doch mit meinen Arbeiten noch auf ein strenges Regime gesetzt."[57]

On July 31 Wilhelm and Adelheid departed from Dessau on Müller's last trip, one which satisfied a desire he had had as a young man interested in the German past: to make a "pilgrimage to the hoard of the Nibelungen."[58] Müller and his wife both wrote brief entries about this trip in a notebook, which was not published until 1931 (edited by the Dessau librarian and historian Paul Wahl).

The Rhine journey lasted from July 31 until September 25 and was filled with sightseeing, theater evenings, and visits with many friends. In Frankfurt they saw the journalist Georg Döring and their friend Baron Simolin and visited the house in which Goethe was born. They enjoyed the beauty and wine of the Rhine: "Ein schöner heller Tag. Den Morgen war der Rhein bewegt. Adelheid schwärmte die Nacht hindurch von Wein und Natur, von 1825 [er] und 1827 [er], und guckte aus ihrem Bett in den Rhein."[59] Rüdesheim, Bingen, Rochuskapelle, the Lorelei, and Siebengebirge were all on the itinerary.

In Bonn the Müllers visited August Wilhelm von Schlegel. Then, after seeing Wiesbaden, Heidelberg, Karlsruhe, Baden-Baden, and Strasbourg, the travelers arrived in Stuttgart, where they enjoyed the company of old acquaintances and made new ones among the Swabian poets. As guests of Gustav and Sophie Schwab, they met with Ludwig Uhland, Friedrich von Matthisson, Wilhelm Hauff, Wolfgang Menzel, and Friedrich Haug.

After Müller and Schwab had drunk Brüderschaft (a toast of brotherhood) with one another, the travelers proceeded on to Weinsberg and the home of the poet Justinus Kerner (1786–1862), where an eerie coincidence cast a shadow over the brief visit.[60] Kerner, who shared Müller's enthusiasm for the cause of the Greeks, had put up a homemade Greek flag outside in honor of his guest. Arriving at sunset, Müller appeared tired, but he nevertheless became very involved in a discussion of the supernatural—life after death, mediums, and similar subjects. Kerner, who was also a physician, was treating at the time the so-called Seeress from Prevorst (Friederike Hauffe), a somnambulist and clairvoyant. In spite of Adelheid's admonitions, Müller insisted upon seeing the woman, whose trances were sometimes marked by convulsions. As they departed the next morning at dawn, the thirty-two-year-old poet of the *Griechenlieder* and his wife looked back at the house where they had just spent the night. There on the old tower was not the familiar blue-and-white Greek flag, but a wet white cloth with a black cross—an omen of death. Kerner had mistakenly painted a black cross (instead of white one) on a blue- and white-striped field. Rain during the night had completely washed the blue color away, leaving just the black cross. (A mere two weeks after this visit with Kerner, Müller died without forewarning in his sleep.)

On September 20, 1827, the couple arrived in Weimar, where they met with Goethe.[61] According to F. Max Müller, Goethe greeted them coolly. The older poet had been displeased with the arrogance of the young Müller for daring to criticize the translations of modern Greek poems that he had published in *Kunst und Alterthum, 1823*. When Goethe asked Adelheid about her parentage, she answered insolently: "Excellenz sollten das eigentlich riechen! Ich bin die Enkelin 'des Propheten rechts oder links,' Ihres alten Freundes Basedow, dessen Tabak und Stinkschwamm Ihnen im J. 1774 so viel Kummer bereiteten."[62] Adelheid was referring to the journey along the Rhine which Goethe had made in the summer of 1774 with her grandfather Johann Bernhard Basedow (1723–1790) and Johann Kaspar Lavater (1741–1801). The "Child of the World" Goethe had described his older companions as "prophets" in the poem "Diné zu Coblenz" ("Zwischen Lavater und Basedow / Sass ich bei Tisch des Lebens froh"). This is the final stanza of the poem:

> Und, wie nach Emmaus, weiter ging's
> Mit Geist- und Feuerschritten,
> Prophete rechts [Basedow], Prophete links [Lavater],
> Das Weltkind [Goethe] in der Mitten.[63]

Also, in *Dichtung und Wahrheit* Goethe had called the tinder with which Basedow lit his pipe "Stinkschwamm":

> Schon dass er [Basedow] ununterbrochen schlechten Tabak rauchte, fiel äusserst lästig, um so mehr als er einen unreinlich bereiteten, schnell Feuer fangenden, aber hässlich dunstenden Schwamm, nach ausgerauchter Pfeife, sogleich wieder aufschlug, und jedesmal mit den ersten Zügen die Luft unerträglich verpestete. Ich nannte dieses Präparat Basedow'schen Stinkschwamm, und wollte ihn unter diesem Titel in der Naturgeschichte eingeführt wissen; woran er grossen Spass hatte, mir die widerliche Bereitung, recht zum Ekel, umständlich auseinandersetzte, und mit grosser Schadenfreude sich an meinem Abscheu behagte.[64]

Goethe apparently forgave Adelheid her lack of respect, but remained unsympathetic toward Wilhelm; he spoke of the young couple at another time, criticizing Müller for wearing glasses: "Er [Müller] ist mir eine unangenehme Personnage, ... suffisant, überdies Brillen tragend, was mir das Unleidlichste ist. Frau von Varnhagen und die Arnim haben mir Müllers Gattin ganz richtig geschildert, die wirklich recht liebenswürdig ist."[65]

After their departure from Weimar on September 23, Wilhelm and Adelheid passed through Leipzig, where they visited Heinrich Brockhaus. They arrived home in Dessau on September 25, 1827. During the next few days Müller enjoyed the company of his family and discussed his literary plans. On September 27 he went on an outing with friends on the Mulde River. The evening of September 29 was spent at the home of his father-in-law Basedow. The next day he enthusiastically discussed with Baron Simolin plans for a complete edition of the *Grie-*

chenlieder. That evening he wrote more than a dozen letters for the encyclopedia, one to Brockhaus, and one to Karl Förster. These letters disclose no hint of illness or any premonition of death. In fact, the letter to Brockhaus refers to the poet's safe arrival ("glückliche Heimkehr") and requests that Müller's complimentary copy of the *Konversationslexikon* be sent to him as soon as possible; he would need it for his critical writing. The copy was never used for this purpose. Müller died during the night of September 30/October 1, 1827.[66]

Premature Death

The immediate physical cause of Wilhelm Müller's death is unknown. Tradition has it that he suffered a heart attack and passed away quietly in his sleep. Although no evidence of either foul play or suicide has ever come to light, the fact remains that rumors of a less than peaceful death began circulating in Dessau shortly after the event, rumors that have persisted through the years and which are lent at least a small measure of credibility by a letter discovered and published in 1934 in an obscure journal in Dessau.

All biographers of Müller who have written of his sudden but "quiet" and "peaceful" death have based their comments on the following description of the death written by Gustav Schwab in the *Vermischte Schriften* of 1830, as related by the widow Adelheid:

Um halb 10 Uhr gingen wir nach der Schlafstube, und indem ich ihm vorwarf, dass es noch so früh sei, dehnte er sich gemächlich im Bette, indem er sagte: im Bette wäre Einem doch am wohlsten. Er war müde, sagte mir gute Nacht, ohne dass auch nur ein Wort verrathen hätte, dass er sich unwohl fühle, was er, da er sonst sehr ängstlich war, gewiss gethan hätte. Nach 11 Uhr wache ich auf und höre ihn sehr schnarchen, was er öfters that; ich rede ihn an und bitte, er möchte sich anders herum legen, denn ich könnte davor nicht schlafen. Ich spreche immer auf ihn ein, rufe ihn, springe auf, will sein Gesicht anfassen und fühle seinen Mund so kalt, während er immer fortschnarcht. Ich rufe die Magd, um Licht zu haben; doch noch ehe ich dies bekam, lief sie, von meiner furchtbaren Angst getrieben, zum Arzte, welcher nur einige Häuser davon wohnte. Während dieser Zeit dauert mein Bitten und Schreien fort, ich lege mich auf seinen Mund, um ihm warme Luft einzuhauchen, reibe ihm die Brust und glaubte, nur in der Angst den Herzschlag nicht fühlen zu können; doch endlich kommt Licht, und der erste Blick zeigt mir das todtenblasse Gesicht; ich richte ihn auf, setze ein Glas Wasser an seine Lippen: ein tiefer Seufzer drang hervor, und der Kopf sank in meinen Arm zurück. Er war todt—eine plötzliche Ausdehnung des Herzens hatte ihn schlafend durch einen Schlagfluss getödtet. Kein Glied war verzuckt; ruhig beide Arme unter der Decke auf der Brust, die Augen geschlossen, lag er da im ewigen Schlafe; sein Gesicht, wie das eines Schlafenden, gab den ungestörtesten Abdruck zu einer von dem geschickten Bildhauer Hunold verfertigten Büste.[67]

Lohre includes a shortened version of this account in his detailed biography of 1927. In a review of the Lohre book, however, Hatfield (who had himself described no unusual circumstances surrounding the death in his critical edition of the poetry in 1906) alludes to a different story. He mentions that information he has obtained from the Dessau historian Wilhelm Hosäus leads him to believe that the real facts about the death may not agree with the scene described in the Schwab version, which the widow and Schwab had probably "rearranged for personal reasons."[68]

In 1927 Dr. Schulze of Dessau published a short article, "Wilhelm Müllers letzte Lebensjahre und sein Ende," in a special commemorative section of the *Anhaltische Rundschau*. As a native of Dessau, Dr. Schulze had long been acquainted through local oral tradition with the rumors which had circulated about Müller's sudden death—rumors of a mysterious poisoning as part of an intrigue against the ducal court. In his article he states the following about the poet's death:

> Das jähe Hinscheiden des gefeierten Lyrikers und Sängers der Freiheit rief weit über die Grenzen Anhalts das lebhafteste Bedauern und die wärmste Anteilnahme hervor. Aber nicht lange nachher kamen hässliche Gerüchte in Umlauf, die grösstenteils daraus zu erklären sind, dass der im ganzen gesunde und stets lebensfrohe Mann so völlig unerwartet aus seinem Schaffen herausgerissen wurde, ein Fall, der nach dem Urteil sachkundiger Ärzte, wenn nicht schwere Krankheit vorausgegangen ist oder Belastung durch Alkoholismus vorliegt, in diesen Lebensjahren—der Dichter stand vor dem Eintritt in das 34. [33.]—kaum jemals eintritt. Am meisten scheint das Gerede von seiner Vergiftung sich eingewurzelt zu haben, das, wie ich feststellen konnte, auch heute noch älteren Dessauer Bürgern bekannt ist, und meinem längst heimgegangenen Vater zuerst von unserem alten Chronisten L. Würdig mitgeteilt wurde. Die am meisten verbreitete Version desselben ist folgende: Durch einen verhängnisvollen, niemals aufgeklärten Irrtum sei der Dichter das Opfer einer gegen das Herzogliche Haus gerichteten Intrige geworden.[69]

Seven years later in 1934, another Dessau historian, Paul Wahl, who had mentioned nothing unusual about the poet's death in his 1931 publication of the diary from Müller's Rhine journey, published a document which tells an unusual story.[70] While searching among the manuscripts of the poet Friedrich von Matthisson (1761–1831)[71] in the Landesbibliothek in Stuttgart, Wahl found a previously unpublished letter written by Matthisson to the wife of August von Hartmann, a longtime friend. The letter dated November 22, 1827—not quite two months after Müller's sudden death—reports that the experienced and highly respected court physician Dr. Franz Olberg (1767–1840) was unsure of the cause of the poet's death because of the black spots which had appeared all over the body and the unusually rapid decomposition of the body. Olberg, the personal physician of the Duke, was an early proponent of immunization and the founder and director of the Dessau Medical Library. He had also been Müller's physician, as indicated in the poet's letter of August 2, 1826, to Adelheid from Franzensbad, in which he instructs her to thank Olberg for sending him to the spa. The strange circumstances of Müller's death as described in the Matthisson letter are as follows:

> . . . —Die Ursache von Müllers plötzl. Tode ist selbst dem sehr erfahrenen Herzogl. Leibarzte[72] noch räthselhaft. Er behauptet, dass er, um die Sache klar zu sehen, beym Sterben hätte gegenwärtig seyn müssen. Wenige Stunden nach dem Hinscheiden zeigten sich auf dem[73] Leichnam hin und wieder schwarze Flecken und bald darauf erfolgte eine völlige Auflösung. Die Aerzte versichern, nie einen so schnellen Übergang in Verwesung erlebt zu haben. Gleich nach dem Tode des Mannes rannte die unglückliche Frau im Nachtkleide, mit blossen Füssen, vom Wahnsinne der Verzweiflung ergriffen, zum Hause des Arztes und rief auf eine jammervolle Weise um Hülfe. Die Folgen hiervon waren, dass auch sie auf das Krankenlager geworfen wurde. Jetzt soll sie wieder ausser dem Bette seyn können. Sogleich nach ihrem Unglück verliess sie die Wohnung auf der Bibliothek und zog zu ihren Eltern. Anfangs war ihr der Anblick ihrer Kinder zuwider, weil ihr jedes freundliche Gesicht einen unangenehmen Eindruck machte, und diese ahnungslosen Geschöpfe nach wie vor fröhlich und guter Dinge waren. . . . So eben war mein ältester Schwager[74] bey mir und sagte, der Leibarzt habe gestern gegen ihn geäussert, Müllers plötzlicher Tod habe wahrscheinlich eine gesprengte Arterie am Herzen zur Ursache. Von einer Section konnte wegen der furchtbar-schnellen Auflösung gar keine Rede seyn.— . . . [75]

Despite the admittedly unusual circumstances of Müller's death, the fact remains that no proof either of foul play or of death from accident has ever been produced. There seems to have been no reason for this successful and happily married man to have committed suicide. His general health was poor enough—especially after his bout with whooping cough in the spring of 1826—to warrant the conclusion which both Schulze and Wahl drew: the sudden death with the unusual postmortem symptoms of black spots and rapid decomposition cannot be definitely explained by modern medicine due to a lack of information. However, the death of the thirty-two-year-old poet was probably due to natural causes because of his general poor health, which could perhaps have been consumption (Schwindsucht). Wahl writes:

> Bei alledem ist es natürlich schwer, heute ein völlig eindeutiges Bild der Todesursache zu gewinnen, aber soviel steht fest, dass der Tod des Dreiunddreissigjährigen aus ganz natürlich-pathologischen Ursachen herbeigeführt wurde. Man darf auch nicht vergessen, dass Müller, der am Tage vorher noch dem Arzt [Dr. Franz Olberg] gesagt hatte, "dass er sich ganz erstaunlich wohl fühle," keineswegs ein gesunder Mensch war, der besser getan hätte, statt der anstrengenden Rheinreise wiederum die Kur in Franzensbad zu gebrauchen.[76]

The Life and Letters of the Right Honorable F. Max Müller records that
Adelheid made daily visits to the cemetery, where she sobbed as if her
husband had just died. A notice in the family album (which in 1934 was
in the possession of the poet's grandson, Sir William G. Max Müller of
London) was written by the widow after she had visited the grave for
the first time: "Ich hätte hinsinken mögen, als ich vor dem vermauer-
ten Hause stand, wo mein liebstes dieser Erde auf ewig verborgen
war. . . . Die Abendsonne stand gross und hell gerade über dem
Gewölbe; für mich gieng sie aber unter, wo auch die Sonne meines
Lebens untergegangen war. . . ."[77]

This first visit to the grave was on November 8, 1827, five weeks
after Müller's funeral; the grief and consequences of her frantic run to
the physician's house (reported by Matthisson, but not mentioned in
the Schwab version) had confined her to bed for several weeks after
her husband's death.

Duke Leopold Friedrich provided Adelheid with a yearly stipend
until F. Max became twenty-one; then the widow (who never remar-
ried) received half of the amount. This sum allowed her to live mod-
estly until her death in 1883, when she was buried in Dessau next to
her husband.

Wilhelm Müller is still remembered today in his hometown of Des-
sau, which lies between Leipzig and Berlin in the German Demo-
cratic Republic. The Stadtbibliothek conscientiously and enthusiasti-
cally preserves his remaining papers. The cultural life of Dessau is
occasionally enriched with performances of *Die Winterreise* and *Die
schöne Müllerin*, poetry readings, scholarly lectures, and exhibits about
Müller. The large marble monument donated by the Greek Parlia-
ment and erected on the hundredth anniversary of the poet's birth
today graces a newly replanted city park surrounded by modern
apartment buildings, which have replaced the buildings destroyed in
1945. The graves of Wilhelm and Adelheid Müller were also care-
fully restored in 1971, when the historic old cemetery and its sur-
rounding wall were renovated.

The one hundred and fiftieth anniversary of Müller's death in 1977
was marked in Dessau by lectures and concerts and highlighted by the
publication of a booklet completely about Müller in the series *Zwischen
Wörlitz und Mosigkau*. This well prepared publication of thirty-six pages
contains several articles about the poet and—of special value—a listing
of the Müller holdings in the Stadtbibliothek Dessau, prepared by Irm-
gard Lange. In addition, the issue contains several interesting photo-
graphs, including those of details of the monument in the City Park, a
sketch by Wilhelm Hensel of Müller with Adelheid sitting on his lap,
the marble plaque, with inscriptions in Greek and German, donated by
the Greek government in 1891, and several Müller autographs.

Wilhelm Müller monument in Dessau in 1973. The monument was carved from marble sent by the Greek Parliament and erected on September 29, 1891.

Perhaps Dessau's most interesting living memorial to the poet is the Wilhelm Müller Art Prize, which the City Council established in 1971 as an annual award. A generous sum of money, a plaque, and a certificate are awarded each year to one or two individuals or to a collective for the "development of socialist work in art, architecture, music or folk art; for the interpretation of particularly socialist works of art; for exceptional examples of the socialist reception of the cultural heritage; and for the encouragement of the intellectual and cultural life of the working class and the socialist collective."[78] The encouragement of the application of the socialist political philosophy to art is the announced purpose of the prize. (One of the recipients of this award was the painter Rudolf Hugk, whose sketch of Müller's birth house appears in this study.)

The official socialist adoption of Wilhelm Müller as a symbol for the working class and the common people is worth noting. In his own life, Müller, the supposed son of a tailor, appeared to understand not only the mentality of the common people but also that of the nobility and the intelligentsia. He described and praised the life of the common people but still spent his adult life in the intellectual and social circles of the wealthy. Müller's "barbs" aimed at the nobility and the clergy, as well as his calls for the freedom of the Greeks from the Turks, were all tempered by his realization that he had to adapt to the reality of the social system of his times. The court poet Müller would be surprised that today's Socialist party leaders in Dessau have cast him in the role of a socialist cultural model. Nonetheless, he would be pleased that his "songs" and prose writings are still read and studied 150 years after his death by people of all political persuasions, wherever German is read or sung.

CHAPTER TWO

The Poet

Ich kann weder spielen noch singen und wenn ich dichte, so sing' ich doch
und spiele auch. Wenn ich die Weisen von mir geben könnte, so würden
meine Lieder besser gefallen, als jetzt. Aber, getrost, es kann sich ja eine
gleichgestimmte Seele finden, die die Weise aus den Worten heraushorcht
und sie mir zurückgiebt.[1]

Although Müller was active in several fields of literary endeavor, it is as
the poet of simple lyrics in the folk-song style that he is most often
remembered. As early as 1821 a critic in *Literarisches Konversationsblatt*
describes Müller as an unusually talented poet. (". . . der so hold im
Scherz, so süss in der Wehmut, so reich in der Liebe, so leicht und
kühn im Aufschwunge ist, den die kommenden Zeiten lieben werden
wie die jetzige Zeit, weil er echt volkstümlich ist, was so wenige zu sein
verstehen.")[2] The anonymous critic was correct; the popularity of
Müller's poetry in the folk-song style did outlast the poet's lifetime.

Many of his poems seem old-fashioned and naïve today. Adjectives
such as sentimental, trite, light, imitative, popular, shallow, and pa-
thetic have all been applied to his poetry in the various histories of
German literature, and Müller has been called a "poet of the young."[3]

Nevertheless, several of his poems have become part of the German
cultural heritage. "Das Wandern ist des Müllers Lust," for example, is
still sung today to a melody composed by Karl Friedrich Zöllner (1800–
1860). "Im Krug zum grünen Kranze" ("Brüderschaft") is often sung
to the folk melody "Ich stand auf dem hohen Berge." Some of Müller's
seemingly naïve poems conceal a surprising maturity and depth of
thought: "Unter der Fülle leichtfertiger, spielerischer Lieder ist eine
ernstere Veranlagung zu erkennen, die Müller in einer sehr per-
sönlichen Erlebnisweise seine Ansichten von der tieferen Bedeutung
des Lebens aussprechen lässt."[4]

Despite the undeniably uneven quality of Müller's poetry, his better
poems have found many admirers. For example, Willibald Alexis, whom
Heine considered a literary critic in the same league as the Schlegel
brothers, called Müller "the first lyricist of his time." Friedrich Hebbel
writes the following words of praise in a review of the fourth edition of
Müller's poetry published by Brockhaus in 1858: "Die Sänger kommen
und gehen, und nur die auserwähltesten überdauern das grüne Laub

und verbinden das Alter des Adlers mit dem Jugendschmelz der Nachtigall. Wo ist Hölty, wo sein Freund Bürger, wo sind Salis und Matthisson? Der 'Dichter der Griechenlieder' ist noch nicht im Andenken seines Volkes erloschen, wie diese neue geschmackvolle Auflage beweis't, er verdient auch eine liebevolle Erinnerung. . . . "[5]

As early as 1847 the philosopher and literary critic Gustav Theodor Fechner complained that Wilhelm Müller was underrated.[6] The same claim was repeated 125 years later by Alan P. Cottrell in his 1970 book *Wilhelm Müller's Lyrical Song-Cycles: Interpretations and Texts:*

> There is no question but that Müller's works abound with clichés, conventional imagery, and motifs drawn from all manner of sources ranging from Italian popular poetry to the *Wunderhorn*. At the same time, however, many of the poems are of the most lilting musicality and show a naïve and original manner of expression which cannot be accounted for simply in terms of a dilettante's juggling of conventional themes. It is perhaps most of all this curious mixture of the trite and spontaneous, the conventional and the unique which has caused the poems to have been largely passed over by literary research. . . . A careful reading discloses the fact that beneath the cloak of conventionality there is to be found in Müller a lyric poet of depth and sensitivity. We are convinced that his works have been unjustly ignored and that it is time to reëvaluate them.[7]

In addition to Cottrell's book, several articles about Müller's poetry (including one in 1977 by Günter Hartung in the *Weimarer Beiträge*) have appeared during the past decade. In fact, scholarly interest in Müller 150 years after his death seems to be increasing, rather than the reverse.

CHARACTERISTICS OF THE POETRY

Forms and Metrics

James Taft Hatfield published the critical edition of Müller's poetry in 1906. This edition includes 783 poems, all of which were written in the short span of twelve years between 1815 and 1827.

Although Müller composed many of the poems quickly, there is little monotony in his forms and metrics. In a study of his influence upon the early poetry of Heinrich Heine, it has been determined that Müller uses 154 different metrical patterns, whereas Heine employs "only 78 in a larger bulk of poetry covering a much longer period of time."[8] According to this study, Müller shows a slight preference for iambic and anapestic rhythms, with 88 iambic-anapestic as opposed to 65 trochaic meters. In addition to the more usual forms, Müller uses the distich and the so-called political verse line (an iambic line of 15 syllables with a caesura after the eighth). Along with his friend Friedrich Rückert, Müller introduced into German poetry the Italian *ritornello* (a type of tercet) later adopted by Theodor Storm and Paul Heyse.

The Lyric Cycle

It was within the relatively unrestrictive framework of the lyric cycle form that Müller's poetic talents found what was perhaps their best— certainly their most enduring—expression. In Hatfield's opinion: "Hauptsächlich in seinen lyrischen Zyklen zeigt sich unser Dichter als bahnbrechender Schöpfer einer dichterischen Form. Kein anderer Dichter in irgend einer Sprache hat diese rein lyrische Behandlung durch eine Reihe locker zusammenhängender Gesänge, welche zu gleicher Zeit einen klaren anschaulichen Fortschritt in der dramatischen Handlung zu Tage bringen, mit so glänzendem Erfolge durchgeführt."[9] A noted contemporary scholar of the Biedermeier period, Friedrich Sengle, maintains that Müller's song cycles were more influential than Goethe's *West-östlicher Divan* of 1819. He further asserts that Müller's work in this area—without which Heine's cycles would have been un- thinkable—was a perfect reflection of the times, during which lyric cycles were considered in their entirety.

> Für die weltliche Lyrik waren die Zyklen Wilhelm Müllers wahrscheinlich noch ein wirksameres Vorbild als Goethes *Divan*. Mit der Mischung von Ironie und Empfindsamkeit, Spass und volksliedhafter "Gemütlichkeit" wurden hier Kombinationen hervorgebracht, die den Stilwillen der Zeit genau trafen und ohne deren Anregung auch Heines grosse Leistung auf dem Gebiete zyklischer Lyrik nicht zu denken ist. Man betont hier mit Recht, dass man diese Zyklen im Zusammenhang interpretieren muss. Zy- klen werden in der Biedermeierzeit von Anfang bis Ende durchgelesen, *weil eben dem Einzelgedicht keine absolute Autonomie zukommt.* Man ist nicht ständig auf der Jagd nach dem einzigartigen Gedicht, wie der moderne Liebhaber.[10]

Müller arranged his poems for publication in loosely connected groups with descriptive titles, such as "Wanderlieder eines rheinischen Handwerksburschen," "Frühlingskranz aus dem Plauenschen Grunde bei Dresden," and "Die Kellnerin von Bacharach und ihre Gäste." Of his several cycles, *Die schöne Müllerin* and *Die Winterreise* are more tightly structured and are considered excellent examples of the lyric cycle, in which a series of poems forms a dramatic entity. Helen Meredith Mus- tard, the author of a study on the lyric cycle in German literature, writes:

> *Die schöne Müllerin* is more coherent in structure than any narrative cycle of this period. The narrative progresses smoothly and consistently, and the many inner thematic links help to unify the group. The symmetrical ar- rangement of the poems according to the various stages of the story gives the group balance and grace of proportion. Müller's successful treatment of this cycle seems to me to be due to two factors, first, the definite narra- tive outline which served from the beginning as a framework, and second, the fact that the poems were written specifically for this group and not simply collected and arranged as best they might.[11]

Although other early nineteenth-century poets wrote lyric cycles, few were as successful as Müller and Heinrich Heine. Cycles by Gustav Schwab, Justinus Kerner, Anastasius Grün, Emanuel Geibel, and Paul Heyse have all been called "descendants of the lyric cycles of Müller and Heine."[12]

Müller's Use of Roles

One of the most striking features in Müller's poetry is his frequent use of roles. The poet very often assumes a role and speaks through it. His figures are all representatives of the common people; often they are stereotypes, such as shepherds, hunters, wanderers, musicians, and sailors. Among the rustic figures one finds exotic ones, such as a bride from the island of Rügen or a small Hydriot lad from Greece. Although the stereotyped figures remain faceless, their joys and sorrows are so universal that the reader can readily identify with them. No definite picture of the miller lad or the winter wanderer emerges in either cycle; nevertheless, we share their innermost feelings.

Müller's Relationship to the Folk Song

In his collection *Unsere volkstümlichen Lieder,* Hoffmann von Fallersleben lists poems whose universal popularity has transformed them into folk songs. No fewer than nineteen of Müller's poems are included. In 1910 Hermann Hesse and two other editors entitled a collection of German folk songs *Der Lindenbaum,* after Müller's poem of the same title. Müller's "Der Lindenbaum" and "Im Krug zum grünen Kranze" are included in the Hesse collection.

The close affinity between Müller's poetry and the German folk song has often been noted. The poet's son F. Max writes: "He certainly had caught the true tone of the poetry of the German people, and many of his poems have become national property, being sung by thousands who do not even know whose poems they are singing." A critic in 1820 writes that a poem of Müller sounds like "a true folk song" ("klingt frisch aus voller Brust, wie ein echtes Volksliedchen").[13] This relationship between Müller and the folk song has been examined in detail by Philip S. Allen. Additional articles on the subject have been published by Alfred Wirth. Influences of the German folk song are found not only in his subject matter and form, but also in his meters and idioms.

> Der Einfluss der Volksdichtung auf Müller ist ein vielfacher. Die Freude an der Natur, die Beseelung von Baum, Bach, Vogel, Blume, die Symbolisierung fallender Blätter und Äpfel, von Rosmarin und Rosen, die bildhafte, auf sinnlicher Anschauung beruhende Sprache statt des wesenlosen Abstraktums, die Übernahme ganzer Wendungen aus dem Volkslied, die kurze plastische Zeichnung der Landschaft im Liedeingang, die Verwendung des Kehrreims, der Kettentechnik und Wortwiederholung, der rhetorischen Frage, der Verkleinerungsformen und schmückenden Beiwörter,

die Unbestimmtheit der Beschreibung, das alles und noch manches mehr schöpft Müller aus dem unversiegbaren Born des Volksliedes.[14]

Müller did not attempt to imitate the folk song as such. Instead, the collector of Italian folk songs and the translator of modern Greek folk songs sought to capture the essence of the folk-song spirit without resorting to the mere adoption of archaic forms and diction. As a critic Müller was quick to rebuke those of his contemporaries who did resort to such superficial tricks when writing poetry in the folk-song style. In *Hermes, 1827,* Müller published the article "Über die neueste lyrische Poesie der Deutschen—Ludwig Uhland und Justinus Kerner," in which he discusses his concept of the folk song and its imitation by popular contemporary writers:

> Daher ist ein heilloser Irrthum einiger Modedichter der nächsten Vergangenheit, dass sie Volkslieder zu geben meinten, wenn sie alterthümliche Phrasen, unbeholfene Wendungen, auch wohl gemeine Derbheiten aus den alten Vorbildern nachäffend zu neuen Verbindungen zusammenfügten. Keiner Dichtungsart liegt es mehr ob als der lyrischen, zeitgemäss zu sein; denn ihr Genuss und ihre Wirkung, am weitesten von jedem Studium getrennt, gehen lebendig von Mund zu Mund und haben keine Zeit zu Erklärungen. Das gemeine Volk nun vollends, wenn jene Volkslieder etwa für dieses gesungen sein sollen, wird durch dergleichen altväterischen Schmuck keineswegs angezogen.[15]

Müller believed that the folk song is characterized by the immediateness of its influence on life—a quality not to be imitated with dead, archaic forms: "Die eigenthümliche Natur des Volksliedes ist die Unmittelbarkeit seiner Wirkung auf das Leben. Das Leben kann aber nur durch das Leben lebendig angesprochen werden."[16]

Müller's attempts to infuse the spirit of the folk song into his poetry were based on an encyclopedic knowledge of the subject. For example, he was familiar with Friedrich Nicolai's *Eyn feyner kleyner Almanach,* Johann Büsching and Friedrich von der Hagen's *Sammlung deutscher Volkslieder,* Johann Meinert's *Alte deutsche Volkslieder in der Mundart des Kuhländschens* [sic], Franz Ziska and Julius Schottky's *Österreichische Volkslieder,* Johann Gottfried Herder's *Stimmen der Völker,* and, of course, Achim von Arnim and Clemens Brentano's *Des Knaben Wunderhorn.* Like Herder, Müller was also interested in the folk poetry of other nations. He had read Bishop Thomas Percy's *Reliques of Ancient English Poetry, collected in the Highlands* and was familiar with Sir Walter Scott's *Minstrelsy of the Scottish Border.* There are also influences of Italian and modern Greek folk songs in his later poetry. Twenty-seven free translations of modern Greek folk songs appeared in the group "Reime aus den Inseln des Archipelagus."

Textual comparisons between Müller's poems and the folk-song tradition are made in the study by Allen. Müller adopted the vocabulary, themes, imagery, and linguistic devices of the German folk song. His success showed that this folk tradition could enrich contemporary poetry. His son F. Max describes the characteristics which he feels had led to the popular acceptance of his father's poetry:

> Dies Erkennen des Schönen im Unbedeutenden, des Grossen im Kleinsten, des Wunderbaren im Alltäglichen, ja diese Ahnung des Göttlichen bei jedem irdischen Genuss, dies ist es, was den kleinen Liedern Wilhelm Müllers ihren eigenen Reiz verleiht und sie allen denen so liebgemacht, welche die Freude des Sich still der Natur Hingebens im Treiben des Lebens nicht verlernt und den Glauben an das Mysterium der göttlichen Allgegenwart im Schönen, Guten und Wahren nicht verloren haben. Man lese doch "Das Frühlingsmahl" oder "Pfingsten," und man wird sehen, dass auch im kleinsten Thautropfen sich eine ganze Welt, ja ein Himmel spiegeln kann.
>
> Und wie der Genuss an der Natur einen so hellen Widerhall in der Poesie Wilhelm Müllers findet, so auch der Genuss, den der Mensch am Menschen hat.[17]

Müller lives on a century and a half later in several popular "folk songs": "Am Brunnen vor dem Tore" ("Der Lindenbaum"); "Das Wandern ist des Müllers Lust"; "Im Krug zum grünen Kranze"; and "Ich schnitt' es gern in alle Rinden ein," a song so familiar that it has even been parodied:

> Ich ritzt' es gern in alle Rüben ein,
> Ich stampft' es gern in jeden Pflasterstein,
> Ich biss' es gern in jeden Apfel rot,
> Ich strich' es gern auf jedes Butterbrot,
> Auf Wand, Tisch, Boden, Fenster möcht' ich's schreiben:
> Dein ist mein Herz, und soll es ewig bleiben!

> Ich schör' es gern in jede Taxusheck',
> Graviert' es gern in jedes Essbesteck,
> Ich sät' es gern als lecker grüne Saat
> Ins Gartenbeet mit Kohlkopf und Salat,
> In alle Marzipane möcht' ich's drücken
> Und spicken gern in alle Hasenrücken
> Und zuckerzäh auf alle Torten treiben:
> Dein ist mein Herz, und soll es ewig bleiben!!

> Ich möcht' mir zieh'n ein junges Känguruh,
> Bis dass es spräch' die Worte immerzu,
> Zehn junge Kälbchen sollen froh sie brüllen,
> Hell wiehern hundert buntgescheckte Füllen,
> Trompeten eine Elefantenherde,
> Ja, was nur kreucht und fleucht auf dieser Erde,

Das soll sie schmettern, pfeifen, quaken, bellen,
Bis dass es dröhnt in allen Trommelfellen
Mit einem Lärm, der gar nicht zu beschreiben:
Dein ist mein Herz, und soll es ewig bleiben!!!
Nach   Wilhem Müller[18]

Perhaps the most striking evidence of the familiarity of a Müller "folk song" is Thomas Mann's laudatory references in his *Magic Mountain* to "Am Brunnen vor dem Tore," the "favorite song" of his "simple" protagonist Hans Castorp. Mann's use of this song (which is to be found in almost every contemporary collection of German "folk songs") is discussed in greater detail in Chapter 8.

Müller as a Poet of the Sea
In "Muscheln von der Insel Rügen" (1826) and "Lieder aus dem Meerbusen von Salerno" (1827), Müller was one of the first German poets to use the sea as a source of inspiration. Barthold Heinrich Brockes, Friedrich Leopold Stolberg, Karl August Varnhagen von Ense, Heinrich Christian Boie, Ewald Christian von Kleist, Salomon Gessner, Ludwig Tieck, Goethe, and several regional poets had all written at least one poem about the sea. Müller and Heine, however, were the first to write at length on the subject of the sea.[19]

Although Müller's "Vineta" (1826) and Heine's "Seegespenst" (in *Die Nordseebilder,* 1825) were composed independently of one another, they are similar in content and mood. Both poems describe a submerged city toward which the central character is drawn. In *Nordseebilder III* Heine quotes part of the Müller poem, crediting the Dessau poet:

> Man sagt, unfern dieser Insel, wo jetzt nichts als Wasser ist, hätten einst die schönsten Dörfer und Städte gestanden, das Meer habe sie plötzlich alle überschwemmt, und bei klarem Wetter sähen die Schiffer noch die leuchtenden Spitzen der versunkenen Kirchtürme, und mancher habe dort in der Sonntagsfrühe sogar ein frommes Glockengeläute gehört. Die Geschichte ist wahr; denn das Meer ist meine Seele—
>
> > "Eine schöne Welt ist da versunken,
> > Ihre Trümmer blieben unten stehn,
> > Lassen sich als goldne Himmelsfunken
> > Oft im Spiegel meiner Träume sehn."
>
> (W. Müller)

> Erwachend höre ich dann ein verhallendes Glockengeläute und Gesang heiliger Stimmen—"Evelina!"[20]

The sea in Müller's poems is peaceful; it is not the mysterious and demonic realm of Undine. "Müller grafted the sea-poem on to the German Volkslied, where the sea is rarely mentioned; he introduced the sea as background into poems modelled on the popular lyric, the shore taking the place of the green meadow, the white dunes of the mountains, the gull of the nightingale."[21]

Müller's Sources

Müller did not realize that the criticism contained in one of his epigrams could be applied to his own work:

> "Die Wiederkäuer"
> Ein Dichter, der nur dichten kann,
>   nachdem er erst sich voll gelesen,
> Ist wie ein wiederkäuend Thier,
>   das in der fremden Saat gewesen.[22]

The poet drew his inspiration not only from German and foreign folk songs, but also from the works of poets of different countries and centuries. Among the German authors whose influence may be traced in Müller's poetry are Johann Wolfgang von Goethe, Friedrich Schiller, Gottfried August Bürger, Ludwig Uhland, Ludwig Tieck, Johann Gottfried Seume, Wilhelm Ludwig Gleim, Max von Schenkendorf, Friedrich Baron de la Motte Fouqué, and Joseph von Eichendorff. The poems of the German baroque poets whose works Müller edited in his *Bibliothek deutscher Dichter des siebzehnten Jahrhunderts* were a rich source of forms and themes for him. From Friedrich von Logau he adopted the form and didactic nature of the epigram. There is a close relationship between Müller's "Geselligkeit" ("Ich bin nicht gern allein"), whose familiar melody was composed by Friedrich Schneider, and Martin Opitz's "Lebenslust" ("Ich empfinde fast ein Grauen"). Paul Gerhardt's poetry also influenced Müller, and some of Müller's motives and images strikingly resemble those of Joseph von Eichendorff.[23]

Müller, who had translated Marlowe's *The Tragical History of Doctor Faustus* and had written a poem ("Jägers Lust") reminiscent of "The Passionate Shepherd to His Love" (1599), also by Marlowe, was surprisingly conversant with Elizabethan literature. There is a strong parallel between Müller's "Ungeduld" from *Die schöne Müllerin* and a passage in Edmund Spenser's "Colin Clouts come home againe," published in 1595.[24]

> Her name in every tree I will endosse,
> That as the trees do grow, her name may grow:
> And in the ground each where will it engrosse,
> And fill with stones, that all men may it know.
> The speaking woods and murmuring waters fall,
> Her name Ile teach in knowen termes to frame:
> And eke my lambs, when for their dams they call,
> Ile teach to call for *Cynthia* by name.[25]

Müller adopted the rhymed iambic pentameter of the Englishman in his German version of the love confession made in nature.

> Ich schnitt' es gern in alle Rinden ein,
> Ich grüb' es gern in jeden Kieselstein,
> Ich möcht' es sä'n auf jedes frische Beet
> Mit Kressensamen, der es schnell verräth,
> Auf jeden weissen Zettel möcht' ich's schreiben:
> Dein ist mein Herz, und soll es ewig bleiben.[26]

Although the legend of the wandering Jew was a topic of many major and minor writers of German literature, there is evidence that Müller's "Der ewige Jude" was influenced in part by William Wordsworth's "Song for the Wandering Jew," which was first published in 1800 in the second edition of *Lyrical Ballads*.[27] One stanza of a Müller poem is a paraphrase of Henry Carey's (1693–1743) "Sally in Our Alley."[28]

There are other similarities between Müller and the English poets Thomas Moore and Sir Walter Scott (1771–1832).[29] Scott's "Maid of Isla" and Müller's "Die Mewe" have interesting parallels, and Moore's "Let Erin Remember the Days of Old" and Müller's "Vineta" are alike in several ways. Note the similarity between the following lines and those from "Vineta."

> On Lough Neagh's bank, as the fisherman strays,
> When the clear cold eve's declining,
> He sees the round towers of other days
> In the wave beneath him shining;
> Thus shall memory often, in dreams sublime,
> Catch a glimpse of the days that are over;
> Thus, sighing, look through the waves of time
> For the long faded glories they cover.[30]

> Und der Schiffer, der den Zauberschimmer
> Einmal sah im hellen Abendroth,
> Nach derselben Stelle schifft er immer,
> Ob auch rings umher die Klippe droht. . . .

> Eine schöne Welt ist da versunken,
> Ihre Trümmer blieben unten stehn,
> Lassen sich als goldne Himmelsfunken
> Oft im Spiegel meiner Träume sehn.[31]

Müller was very familiar with the life and works of Moore; in *Hermes, 1823*, he published a long essay, "Über die Gedichte des Thomas

Moore," which was reprinted in the Schwab collection. He had also written the articles about Moore in Brockhaus's *Konversationslexikon*.

The large number of similarities between Müller's poems and the poetry of others might lead one to discount Müller as a mere imitative poet. An examination of the parallel passages, however, reveals that Müller did not simply borrow or translate the poetry of others, but rather that he used single stanzas or individual lines or motifs as springboards for his imagination.

> Again and again in Müller the reader meets rhythms and verses and themes which bring at once to mind some dimly sensed and remembered places from the poems of other romanticists, and yet, often, when such correspondences are found and compared the mutual resemblance, though striking, does not necessarily imply plagiarism, either witting or unwitting. . . . So it comes, perhaps, that Müller seems compounded of all of them, while yet the pupil of none. He owes much to many and yet not all to any one, or any few.[32]

Müller's voracious reading of the literary efforts of his contemporaries provided material not only for his reviews but also for his poetry. He did not plagiarize, but rather he digested and used the lines of others as starting points; he reflected the literary themes and styles of his contemporaries, fashioning originals from borrowed materials.

A SURVEY OF THE POETRY BY COLLECTIONS

The organizational divisions in this section on Müller's poetry by collections are taken from the 1906 critical edition of the poetry by James Taft Hatfield, which was reprinted by Kraus Reprint in 1973 in the series *Deutsche Literaturdenkmale des 18. und 19. Jahrhunderts*.

Early Poetry Not Included in the Critical Edition
In 1902 Philip S. Allen published nine sonnets that Müller wrote during his military assignment in Brussels (1813–1814) as "Unpublished Sonnets of Wilhelm Müller."[33] Although these sonnets are of dubious literary worth, they are of biographical interest as expressions of the maturing poet's internal conflicts at a time when the Protestant youth was confronted with a passionate but painful love experience with a certain Thérèse. In his "Studien," Alfred Wirth lays great importance on this first significant love affair, maintaining that the hurt from this episode in Brussels caused Müller to hold back somewhat in his later relationships with women. For example, this could explain his shyness in expressing his admiration toward Luise Hensel.

The experience of love is the subject of the Brussels sonnet "Was sollten meine Lippen zu dir sprechen." In another sonnet, "Den alten Gott, den Ihr mit weissem Barte," the young poet rejects his childhood image of God. In the other sonnets he appears to view life as a battle—imagery which is not surprising considering the military campaign in which he was participating at the time. The hypocrisy of churchgoers, who think of God only on Sunday morning, is criticized in "Wenn Sonntags früh die Glocken laut erschallen." Müller largely avoided the sonnet form in his later works, writing only one other collection of sonnets, "Die Monate," during his brief stay in Florence in September 1818.

Müller's poetry appeared in the two landmark collections which brought together after Heinrich von Kleist's death in 1811 the poetry of both the older and younger Romantic authors in Berlin: "Seit Kleists Tode war Berlin der Romantik verfallen. Zwei Sammlungen erschienen am Anfange unseres Zeitraums, die Poesien Älterer und Jüngerer vereinigten: *Die Bundesblüthen* 1816 und *Die Sängerfahrt* 1818."[34]

Müller's four poems in *Die Sängerfahrt*, which has been called "one of the most significant documents of the entire Romantic movement,"[35] appeared beside the works of older, better-known writers. Among these were the brothers Grimm, Clemens Brentano, Achim von Arnim, Count Otto Heinrich Loeben, Adelbert von Chamisso, Helmina von Chézy, and Max von Schenkendorf. Müller's contributions were "Die Sage vom Frankenberger See bei Aachen," "Der blaue Mondschein," "Freie Glosse," and "Wechselreigen."

Although *Die Bundesblüthen* was published by five friends back from the War of Liberation (Müller, Wilhelm Hensel, Count Friedrich von Kalckreuth, Count Georg von Blankensee, and Wilhelm von Studnitz), Müller's work comprised a major portion of the collection. In addition to eighteen epigrams, he contributed nineteen longer pieces, among them patriotic poems, one dithyramb, anacreontic poems, and *Romanzen*. All of these reveal Müller as a poetic neophyte who imitated many: Bürger's "Leonore," the Scottish folk songs "Sweet Wilhelm's Ghost" and "Clerk Saunders," Goethe, Schiller, Gleim, Schenkendorf, Fouqué, and, of course, the German folk song. The youthful Müller was obviously trying his hand at various themes and poetic forms in an attempt to develop his own style. In the opinion of Philip S. Allen: "The chief value as regards Müller's later work which the *Bundesblüthen* songs possess is that they show conclusively how he passed through the stage of shallow copying of the external form of popular poetry, as did Uhland in his earlier ballads and Heine in the *Traumbilder*, to come finally to a true appreciation of the Volkslied spirit."[36]

The attempt to publish *Die Bundesblüthen* was the occasion of Müller's first difficulties with the government censor.[37] On January 6, 1816, an order was issued by the Prussian king forbidding not only the existence of secret organizations (previously forbidden on October 20, 1798) but also any mention of them in print. Offenders were subject to both financial and corporal punishment. The official censor, Renfner, after

glancing at the title *Die Bundesblüthen*, sent it back to the publisher with
the reprimanding question, "Doesn't the publishing firm Maurer know
the royal prohibition?" ("Ob die Maurer'sche Buchhandlung das Kgl.
Verbot nicht kenne?")[38] Müller and Hensel went personally to the cen-
sor about the matter. It was finally decided that permission to publish
the collection would be granted, but that the following dedicatory verse
would have to be censored:

> Fünf Sänger reichten einstens sich die Hand
> Zu ew'gen Bundes heil'gem Unterpfand.
> Sie hatten lang in frommer Glut gefochten
> Für Gott, die Freyheit, Frauenlieb und Sang,
> Und Eichengrün um ihre Stirn geflochten,
> Errungen in der Waffen wildem Drang,
> Und da sie nun die Freyheit siegen machten,
> Verbanden sie sich treu zu heitrem Klang:
> Und von den Blüthen, so der Bund getragen,
> Will Euch dies Buch die erste Kunde sagen.[39]

When pressed for a reason for this decision, Renfner replied that the
word "Freyheit" appeared too many times. Müller responded by asking
if the king himself hadn't asked his subjects to fight for freedom just
three years before. The censor's reply was a typical one for the govern-
ment at that time: "Ja, damals!"[40] The censor won, of course; *Die
Bundesblüthen* appeared without the offending dedication.

*Siebenundsiebzig Gedichte aus den hinterlassenen Papieren eines reisenden
Waldhornisten*
Müller's first collection of poems appeared in Dessau with the date
1821 on the title page. However, the copy of the volume which he
presented to his fiancée Adelheid bears the date October 28, 1820,
showing that the collection must have appeared before the date printed
on the title page. (This personal copy dedicated to Adelheid was exhib-
ited in Dessau by the family in 1927.) Earlier, it had been assumed that
the book had appeared in late November, because there is a record of
Müller's having sent Goethe a copy on November 30, 1820.[41]
   Ludwig Tieck was influential in persuading Müller to publish his
poetry. The memoirs of Karl Förster contain a description of an after-
noon Müller spent with Tieck in Dresden in July 1820:

> Am Nachmittag waren wir mit ihm [Müller] und Tiecks bei dem Graf
> Kalckreuth. Er las seine Müllerlieder, die zu einem kleinen Roman gespon-
> nen sind, vor; unter den Liedern ist viel Herrliches, vorzüglich unter den
> ersten; minder gefiel mir Prolog und Epilog. Tieck war mit dem tragi-
> schen Ausgange nicht zufrieden. Darauf las er: Johannes und Esther; er
> behandelt darin das Liebesverhältnis eines Freundes zu einer Jüdin; auch

darunter viel Schönes; überall in Müllers Poesien eine Freiheit und Leich-
tigkeit und Wohlklang der Sprache. Tieck sagte ihm viel Freundliches; nur
wünsche er der letzten Mittheilung mehr Scherz, worauf ihn Jener auf
seine Reiselieder verwies und Tieck ihm antwortete: "weil Sie dort so gut
zu scherzen wissen, vermisse ich es hier."[42]

In his long title, *Siebenundsiebzig Gedichte aus den hinterlassenen Pa-
pieren eines reisenden Waldhornisten,* Müller adopts a role typical of
many found in the poetry of the Romantic period. The *Waldhornist* is
a representative of the common people. The *Waldhorn* is a frequently
used symbol in the German literature of the early nineteenth century
and calls to mind that "Bible" of the Romanticists, *Des Knaben Wun-
derhorn,* published by Arnim and Brentano, with whom Müller was
acquainted. Since the *Waldhornist* of the poems is a traveling musi-
cian, the theme of wandering is infused into the entire Müller collec-
tion. The Romantic yearning to travel is expressed especially in a
grouping of sixteen poems, "Reiselieder," and in the famous "Das
Wandern ist des Müllers Lust." The quaint, archaic flavor of the
lyrics is explained by presenting them as the legacy of a man of an
earlier time.

The simplicity of these poems, their musicality, the unsubtle
rhythms, and their shortness (hence their amenability to memoriza-
tion), contributed to the considerable success of the *Waldhornistenlieder
I.* Although flawed in places with a superficiality of feeling or a too-
subtle, wry humor, the collection was well received. In August 1821
Müller reports to his friend Atterbom in Sweden that the collection has
found "excellent approval" and has received several favorable reviews
in leading journals, including the *Hallische Literaturzeitung.*[43]

The *Waldhornistenlieder I* not only added to Müller's literary reputa-
tion; it also sold copies. Müller writes in 1823 about the relatively good
sale of the collection: "Die 77 sind zu einer Zeit, wo ich so gut als ohne
Namen in der deutschen Litteratur war, als Kommissionsartikel, in
einer Handlung [Ackermann in Dessau], die den Vertrieb schlecht ver-
steht und wenig ausgebreitete Verbindung hat, erschienen und doch in
ca. zwei Jahren so gut wie vergriffen worden."[44] Due to the demand,
Müller published a second edition of this collection in 1826. The sec-
ond edition was dedicated to Tieck, who had originally encouraged
Müller to publish *Waldhornistenlieder I* in 1820.

The young poet received compliments from all quarters. The poets
Baron Friedrich de la Motte Fouqué and Friedrich von Matthisson
were generous with their praise. In a letter to Müller, Heinrich Heine
writes that he had been inspired by the collection, especially by the
meters, which he had imitated in his *Lyrisches Intermezzo.*[45] Müller felt so
secure in the success of the *Waldhornistenlieder I* that he took as a joke a
lampoon by Adolf Müllner, with whom he had debated in 1817 in *Der
Gesellschafter.* Müller went so far as to have embellished copies of

Müllner's review printed for his friends. In April 1821 he writes to Brockhaus: "Sie haben wahrscheinlich Müllners Pasquill auf meine Gedichte gelesen. Dennoch schicke ich Ihnen Spasses halber ein Exemplar der *Editio splendidissima* der Rezension, die ich für die Freunde des Buches habe abdrucken lassen."[46]

An unsigned review of the *Waldhornistenlieder I* in the *Heidelberger Jahrbücher* of 1821 praises the collection, but also criticizes it for its uneven quality. "Um die Hälfte weniger; und das Ganze wäre besser gewesen!"[47] Today, a century and a half later, many readers would probably agree wholeheartedly with that anonymous reviewer.

The collection *77 Gedichte aus den hinterlassenen Papieren eines reisenden Waldhornisten* is divided into six groups of poems, the first of which, *Die schöne Müllerin,* is discussed separately later in this chapter. The second group of poems, "Johannes und Esther," was a particular favorite of the poet Fouqué: "Sollte ich etwas aus dem Blütengarten ganz absonderlich lieb bezeichnen, so wären es die Estherlieder. So lieblich, so fromm, so keusch auch in Bezug auf das Höchste! Und vorzüglich das letztere Lob sagt aus meinem Herzen sehr viel."[48] The love of a young man for a Jewish girl is a theme that recurs in the novelette *Debora,* which is discussed in Chapter 6.

The theme of the third group of poems, "Reiselieder," is presented in the first poem, "Grosse Wanderschaft" with its refrain, "Wandern, wandern!" The nine poems following comprise a loosely connected cycle of Rollenlieder, "Wanderlieder eines rheinischen Handwerksburschen." Of these, two have found their way into the traditional song books: "Wenn wir durch die Strassen ziehen" and "Im Krug zum grünen Kranze."[49] The remaining six poems of the "Reiselieder" are spoken by various figures—a postilion ("Vivat, und in's Horn ich stosse!"), a musician from Prague ("Mit der Fiedel auf dem Rücken"), the musician's bride, and a sailor. These poems exhibit the influence of Uhland's "Wanderlieder," which appeared in *Deutscher Dichterwald* in 1813.[50] More than ten years later Müller refers to these "Wanderlieder" in his article "Über die neueste lyrische Poesie der Deutschen," which was published in *Hermes, 1827,* and reprinted in the Schwab collection.

The fourth group in *Waldhornistenlieder I,* "Ländliche Lieder," consists of seven poems supposedly spoken by such rustic figures as a shepherd, a reaper, and a hunter's wife. All but one of the poems are written in the four-line stanzas that Müller so often used. Although his rhyme schemes are simple, Müller practiced variety in his meter. The "Ländliche Lieder" are perhaps the weakest poems in *Waldhornistenlieder I;* the settings, costumes, and characterizations are wholly devoid of originality.

The next group of poems is "Die Monate," a series of sonnets written in Florence in 1818 and dedicated to the painter Ludwig Sigismund

Ruhl (1794–1887), in whose company Müller had left Rome. Each sonnet is written about a particular month and its appropriate "gift":

> Heiss' der zwölf Monde Schaar [*sic*] voraus dir eilen,
> Und was ein jeder Bestes kann erschaffen,
> Leg' er als Angebind' ihm gern zu Füssen.[51]

The personification of the months is mawkishly sentimental.

The sixth and final grouping in *Waldhornistenlieder I* is "Musterkarte," which contains one ballad and miscellaneous anacreontic poems. The ballad "Der Glockenguss zu Breslau" is the best work in the group and has often been included in poetry collections. The plot of the ballad is taken directly from the *Deutsche Sagen* published by Jakob and Wilhelm Grimm.[52]

Gedichte aus den hinterlassenen Papieren eines reisenden Waldhornisten II
The 172-page second volume to the *Waldhornistenlieder* appeared in 1824 and was dedicated to Carl Maria von Weber. The subtitle of the volume was "Lieder des Lebens und der Liebe." In 1828 Gustav Schwab wrote that he considered the second volume of the *Waldhornistenlieder* better than the first because he felt that Müller had learned from his editing of the poetry of baroque poets for his *Bibliothek deutscher Dichter des siebzehnten Jahrhunderts*. Furthermore, according to Schwab, the second volume had little of the "false folk song nature" of the first and exhibited a "nobler irony."[53]

The first and largest group of poems in this collection is "Tafellieder für Liedertafeln." In the tradition of Horace and Anacreon, Müller wrote a great many poems on the subjects of drinking and love. The simple structures and universal themes of these lyrics made them well suited to be set to music as drinking songs to be sung by singing groups.

Both Müller's first published drinking poem and the one which probably was his last were written in honor of Goethe. The first such poem, "Goethes Osterie in Rom," was written in March 1818, on the occasion of Müller's visit to the tavern which Goethe had depicted in his erotic "Fünfzehnte römische Elegie." "Goethes Osterie in Rom" and the story of Müller's visit to the tavern are included in *Rom, Römer und Römerinnen*.[54] Most probably, the last poem Müller wrote is "Hänschen und sein Herr," which was written for a competition sponsored by the Berlin "Wednesday Society" in honor of Goethe's birthday on August 28, 1827, less than a month before Müller's death. The poem is a reply to Goethe's "Offne Tafel."

Although Müller could not play a musical instrument, he loved to sing tenor in choral groups. As early as February 1816 he recorded in his diary his idea of organizing a glee club in Berlin. Later, as a Dessau resident, he associated occasionally with the Jüngere Liedertafel in Berlin, which had been founded in 1819 after his departure from Berlin. On October 15, 1821, the young librarian-teacher helped the newly appointed ducal Kapellmeister, Friedrich Schneider (1786–1853), in organizing a select singing group of twelve members—a Liedertafel. Müller was subsequently elected secretary of the group. Schneider's biographer reports that the composer-conductor was "brother and friend" to Müller.[55] Adelheid Müller performed the solo alto part for the first performance of Schneider's best-known composition, "Das Weltgericht"; she was also Schneider's soloist at the 1824 Klopstock festival in Quedlinburg. These amateur musical activities filled many enjoyable hours for Müller. The Dessau poet accompanied the Liedertafel on a trip in January 1823, to visit the comparable group in Berlin. In June of the same year, the Dresden Liederkranz honored the poet for the many drinking poems he had written. Shortly before his death, he was also honored by the choral society in Stuttgart.

Müller often wrote lyrics for the Dessau glee club. He writes his Swedish friend Atterbom about his activities: "Ich dichte auch mitunter *Trinklieder* für eine *Liedertafel*, die seit einem halben Jahre hier sich vereinigt hat, um zu singen und zu trinken. Unser Kapellmeister . . . Fr. Schneider . . . hat einigen von meinen Trinkliedern treffliche Weisen gegeben, in denen sie, denke ich, noch manchen braven Mann bei einem guten Glase ergötzen werden."[56]

There was, however, a more serious purpose behind the light, low-key topic of drinking songs: Müller spiked the seemingly frivolous Trinklieder with criticism of the government and the times. The wine was good, but the times were bad. For Müller, these songs were a way of attempting to circumvent the omnipresent government censor. Müller betrayed this intention to Brockhaus in 1823, when he referred to his Gesellschaftslieder as "political songs": "zum Theil politische Chansons, aber ohne Censuranstoss."[57] Müller puckishly addresses his drinking song "An die Ungünstigen" to the men in control of the times, begging their indulgence for his "childishness":

> Und lasst mir doch mein volles Glas,
> Und lasst mir meinen guten Spass
> Mit unsrer schlechten Zeit!
> Wer bei dem Weine singt und lacht,
> Den thut, ihr Herrn, nicht in die Acht!
> Ein Kind ist Fröhlichkeit.[58]

The youth who had fought in the War of Liberation became a man who was indignant at the reactionary policies of the times and who adopted the cause of the Greeks as his own. He hoped that his protesting voice might be heard between the lines of innocent-appearing songs of wine and fellowship. For Müller, the phrase "In Vino Veritas," the title of one of his drinking songs, was most meaningful:

> Die Wahrheit lebt im Wein.
> Lasst diesen Spruch uns ehren,
> Und von dem Heuchelschein
> Der Zeit uns nicht bethören.[59]

Müller's disguised political commentary did not always escape the attention of the censor, however. Some of the most vitriolic of these poems had appeared in the *Deutsche Blätter für Poesie, Litteratur, Kunst und Theater, 1823,* which was published in Breslau where the censor was more liberal. When Müller tried to include these poems in *Waldhornistenlieder II,* they were deleted because the publisher in Dessau did not dare to print them.[60]

Müller was pleased with the reception of his drinking songs, which had been quickly adopted into the repertoire of singing groups and students. As early as 1824 the drinking songs and their accompanying melodies were so popular that Heine in *Die Harzreise* mentions Müller's songs before those of Rückert and Uhland in his description of the carousing students in the inn on the Brocken: "An unserem Tische wurde es immer lauter und traulicher, der Wein verdrängte das Bier, die Punschbowlen dampften, es wurde getrunken, smolliert und gesungen. Der alte Landesvater und herrliche Lieder von W. Müller, Rückert, Uhland usw. erschollen."[61]

The popularity of Müller's "Tafellieder für Liedertafeln" continued after his death. The traditional collection of student songs, the *Lahr Kommersbuch,* contains several poems by Müller. This song book, which was first published in 1858 under the patronage of Moritz Arndt, was the most popular collection of its kind and had appeared in 151 editions as of 1953.[62] Several drinking songs in the collection are taken from Müller's "Tafellieder für Liedertafeln": "Meine Muse," "Schlechte Zeiten, guter Wein," "Die Arche Noäh," "Die schönsten Töne," "Tres faciunt Collegium," "Doppeltes Vaterland," and "Est Est."

The second group of poems in *Waldhornistenlieder II* is *Die Winterreise,* which is discussed in the section concerned with the musical settings of Müller's poetry. The third group, "Ländliche Lieder," is similar to the section of the same title in the first volume of the *Waldhornistenlieder.* The setting for these poems is the countryside; the themes are traditional and borrowed from the German folk song. Again, Müller uses stereotyped roles to create a ready-made environment; the shepherd and the hunter speak conventionally of the joys and sorrows of love.

The poet again plays upon the traditional German passion for hiking in the out-of-doors in his "Wanderlieder," the fourth group of the

Waldhornistenlieder II. The themes are the standard ones: the beauty of nature, the joy of wandering, and the pain of separation from the beloved.

The first poem in the group, "Der ewige Jude," has already been mentioned in connection with Wordsworth in the section about Müller's sources. The figure of the wandering Jew in Müller's poem becomes a symbol for every person, destined to wander through life until he dies:

> Ich wandre sonder Rast und Ruh',
> Mein Weg führt keinem Ziele zu;
> Fremd bin ich in jedwedem Land,
> Und überall doch wohlbekannt.
>
> . . . .
> Der müde Wandrer dieser Welt,
> Ein sicher Ziel ist ihm gestellt.
> Was klagt er ob des Tages Noth?
> Vor Nacht noch holt ihn heim der Tod.[63]

The homeless Jew shares the fate of the wanderer in *Die Winterreise,* who joins the old organ grinder on his journey to nowhere.

The final group in *Waldhornistenlieder II* is "Devisen zu Bonbons," which bore the following inscription when it was published in *Deutsche Blätter* in 1823: "Allen deutschen Konditoreien gewidmet. Die Bilder werden durch die Überschriften bezeichnet. Dem Dichter schwebten die bekannten grossen Pariser Bonbons vor, die auf diese Weise unter uns zu nationalisiren [*sic*] wären."[64] This unusual title, "Devisen zu Bonbons," was Müller's attempt to escape the notice of the censors, for some of these "confections" were sprinkled with "tacks." The majority of the poems deal with love; several contain the personification of love—Amor—in their titles ("Amor in der Vigne," "Amor in einer Rosenknospe," etc.).

Among these overly saccharine poems were a few which held political comments. In one of these "spiked confections," "Ein Kreuzchen in der neuesten Façon," Müller has the personified "Christian Cross" question the actions and policies of Christian political leaders.

> Ich Kreuz, mein eignes Kreuz euch klage,
> Wie man mir mitspielt heut' zu Tage. . . .
> Seitdem schweb' ich zwar wieder oben,
> Und werd' in Akten und Traktaten
> Geehrt von frommen Diplomaten;
> Allein im schönen Morgenlande
> Lässt mich, zu aller Christen Schande,
> Trotz allem Jammern, allem Beten,

Frau Politik mit Füssen treten.
Ich seufz' und muss darein mich finden:
Wer kann die Politik ergründen?[65]

The last six lines are Müller's reference to the "neutral" position European political leaders (especially Metternich) were taking on the matter of the Greek struggle for independence from Turkey. A white cross is depicted on the Greek flag.

Die Griechenlieder

The fourth section in the critical edition of the poetry is *Die Griechenlieder*. It consists of forty-seven poems that originally appeared in six separate pamphlets between 1821 and 1824. Along with these, the critical edition includes the poem "Byron" (1824) and the four poems on the Greek fortress Missolunghi (1826). These scattered poems were not published together during Müller's lifetime, although he had conceived the idea of bringing them together under one cover. It was not until 1830 that they were assembled together in the *Vermischte Schriften*. In 1844, more than a decade after the matter of Greek independence was finally resolved, the firm of Brockhaus still considered the *Griechenlieder* of enough interest to warrant a complete edition. The *Griechenlieder* are discussed here at greater length in Chapter 7, in connection with Müller's philhellenism.

Lyrische Reisen und epigrammatische Spaziergänge

This final collection of poetry published during Müller's lifetime appeared in July 1827, shortly before the poet left on his journey along the Rhine. It consists of eight groupings of poems and 200 epigrams. The collection is prefaced by a dedicatory poem to the childhood playmate of Adelheid, Alexander Baron von Simolin, who had traveled with Müller to Franzensbad during the summer of 1826.

The first group in the collection is "Lieder aus dem Meerbusen von Salerno," which contains poems published earlier in various journals. Müller here adopts some themes from the Italian folk songs that he had collected during his stay in Italy. Again he uses roles, such as a sailor and a fishermaid, in an attempt to convey an impression of the simple life of the Italian peasants living along the Mediterranean coast. The role-playing, however, often degenerates into affected posturing:

Ich armer Fischerbube,
Wo soll ich schiffen hin?
Es ist so klein mein Nachen,
So schüchtern auch mein Sinn.[66]

The second group in the collection is "Ständchen in Ritornellen aus Albano," which contains twenty-five nine-line poems, each divided into three stanzas—a type of Italian ritornello. Müller had studied this Italian form during his months in Italy and had discussed it in detail in his *Rom, Römer und Römerinnen*. His own first efforts in the form appeared in *Urania, 1824*. In the foreword to the ritornelli in *Urania, 1824*, the poet credits Friedrich Rückert as having been the first to import this Italian form into Germany in *Urania, 1822*. Müller explains that his ritornelli differ from those of Rückert: "Ich bin in der Form und im Ton meiner deutschen *Ritornelle* von den *rückertschen* Vorläufern abgewichen. Ich reime mit den Vocalen im ersten und dritten Verse (*Assonanz*), und mit den Consonanten im ersten und zweiten (*Allitteration*). Die Vereinigung dreier *Ritornelle* zu einem Gedicht giebt ihnen lyrischen Ton, und die italienischen Localfarben mögen an die Heimath dieser Form erinnern."[67]

Müller based his ritornelli on several Italian texts.[68] His German ritornelli are versions of some he had heard and written down in Italy. The first section of *Egeria*, the collection of Italian folk poetry begun by Müller and completed for publication by the Weimar professor O. L. B. Wolff, contains seventy three-line Italian ritornelli. Müller, however, expanded the Italian three-line stanzas into nine-line poems of three stanzas each. "Der Thränenbrief" is an example of this unusual form in German, which Theodor Storm and Paul Heyse later adopted.

> Mein Mädchen hat ein Briefchen mir geschrieben
> Wohl mit der schwarzen Feder eines Raben,
> Und hat mit Zwiebelschalen es versiegelt.
>
> Und wie ich nun das Siegel aufgebrochen,
> Da fühlt' ich in den Augen solch ein Stechen,
> Dass mir die Thränen auf die Wangen flossen.
>
> Ich trocknete die Augen, um zu lesen:
> Doch ist das Trocknen ganz umsonst gewesen—
> Denn ach, sie schreibt: Wir müssen Abschied nehmen.[69]

Müller's source for "Der Thränenbrief" is the following three-line poem, which was included in *Egeria:*

> Lo mio amore mi ha mandato un foglio,
> Sigillato con uno spicchio d' aglio,
> E dentro v' era scritto: non ti voglio.[70]

Translated into English, the Italian reads: "My lover has sent me a sheet of paper (a note) sealed with a clove of garlic; inside there was written: I don't want you." In his expanded version Müller has added the black feather of a raven to the imagery and has changed the garlic to the lacrimatory onion.

The third group of *Lyrische Reisen und epigrammatische Spaziergänge* is "Reime aus den Inseln des Archipelagus," which contains a total of thirty-eight poems. These poems are free versions of some neo-Greek folk songs which had not been included in Müller's translation of the Claude Fauriel collection published in 1825. The poems deal with love and its problems; for example, the lover tells the girl, who does not reciprocate his love, to sew him a shroud.

> Dein Herz von Eisen wird sich nicht,
> bis dass ich sterb', erweichen:
> Dann nähe mir ein Todtenhemd
> als erstes Liebeszeichen.[71]

The 1913 French study by Gaston Caminade on Müller as a philhellene contains a chapter on the "Reime aus den Inseln des Archipelagus," in which the Greek original, the German translation, and the imitation (free version) are given and discussed.

"Frühlingskranz aus dem Plauenschen Grunde bei Dresden," the fourth group of poems in *Lyrische Reisen,* was inspired by Müller's vacation from May 19 to June 13, 1824, at Villa Grassi, the estate of Count Kalckreuth outside of Dresden in the district known as Plauen. Nine of the thirteen poems appeared first in Brockhaus's important journal *Urania* in 1826. The other four poems now included in the group were first published in the *Taschenbuch zum geselligen Vergnügen auf das Jahr 1826.* Although the unifying theme in all of these poems is the common one of spring (the personified spring conquers winter), Müller uses unusual imagery and varied stanza patterns to create some of his best poetry. These poems show a depth of thought rare in Müller's often superficial poetry. Gustav Schwab considers the "Frühlingskranz" to be among Müller's best poems: "Die nach meinem Urtheile als die lieblichsten und zugleich schwungreichsten Produkte seiner Muse in unserer Sammlung glänzen." In his book on Müller's lyric cycles, Alan P. Cottrell provides a detailed textual analysis of these thirteen poems. He states: "A number of very beautiful poems stand out against a background of charming but conventional and dated material. The point is thus not simply to reject the work *en masse* because of its trite passages but to sift out those poems which have lasting artistic merit and set them against the background of the whole, for purposes of clarification."[72]

The next group of poems, "Muscheln von der Insel Rügen," has already been discussed briefly in the section on Müller and the sea. These poems date from his vacation in the summer of 1825 on the island of Rügen in the Baltic Sea off the coast of Pomerania. Müller enjoyed the unusual beauty of the island with its striking white cliffs and the company of the poet Adolf Friedrich Furchau (1787–1868), whom he was visiting. The poems were published in the fall of 1826 in Brockhaus's *Urania, 1827.* The poet's experiences while walking along the peaceful beach inspired poems about the island's unique landscape and the customs of the natives of Rügen. For those of his readers who were unfamiliar with the Baltic island, he included several notes explaining some geographical features and customs of the islanders. Of particular interest are the courting customs of the families on the peninsula of Mönchgut; the prehistoric burial mounds overlooking the sea; and the legendary city of Vineta, which supposedly sank off the island in antiquity.

The Vineta legend dates back to the *Acta Petri et Pauli,* and has recurred as a theme in many literary works, among them Johann Gottfried Herder's *Ideen,* Selma Lagerlöf's *Wunderbare Reise des kleinen Nils Holgersson mit den Wildgänsen,* and poems of Heinrich Heine, Wilhelm Meinhold, and Ferdinand Freiligrath.[73] Müller's poem "Vineta" was translated into English several times. In Germany it became such a familiar poem that in 1844 a reviewer in *Blätter für literarische Unterhaltung* poses the rhetorical question: "Wer kennt nicht W. Müllers schönes Lied 'Vineta'?"[74]

The sixth group of poems in *Lyrische Reisen* is "Lieder aus Franzensbad bei Eger," written during Müller's stay at the health spa in July and August 1826. Half of the poems appeared in *Zeitung für die elegante Welt* even before Müller returned from the trip. The second half appeared in print about a week after his arrival in Dessau. The poems are concerned with love and its problems and with the activities of the health resort (e.g., "Auf einem Zettel in der Badestube" and "Am Brunnen"). The first poem in the group, "Auf der Höhe von Schönberg," is dedicated to the poet's wife Adelheid.

The next group of poems, "Die schöne Kellnerin von Bacharach und ihre Gäste," was read to Tieck at New Year's, 1826, in Dresden. Tieck enjoyed the innocent humor of the poems; the pointed barbs characteristic of Müller's other drinking songs are not found in "Die schöne Kellnerin." The unifying and conventional theme in the group is the love of a young man for a pretty waitress:

> Du hast zum Trinker mich gemacht,
> Du schöne Kellnerin!
> Ei, ei, wer hätte das gedacht,
> Da ich so jung noch bin?[75]

The eighth group in *Lyrische Reisen* is "Berenice; ein erotischer Spaziergang," which was first published during the summer of 1826. Some of these love poems are related to the neo-Greek poetry that Müller had been studying and translating. Both the poem "Der Mond" and the verse "Ein Haar aus deinen Locken nur, die Augen zuzunähen," are based on a poem that he had earlier translated from the Fauriel collection.[76]

Lyrische Reisen und epigrammatische Spaziergänge closes with two groups of 100 epigrams each, entitled "Erster Gang" and "Zweiter Gang." The critical edition of the poetry also includes an additional collection, "Hundert Sprüche und Sinngedichte," and a small group of rhymed proverbs. Müller's epigrams had previously appeared in the *Zeitung für die elegante Welt* and the *Morgenblatt für gebildete Stände*.

Although Müller the classical philologist undoubtedly was familiar with the Latin epigrams of the first-century poet Marcus Valerius Martial, it was his study of the baroque poet Friedrich von Logau for the *Bibliothek deutscher Dichter* that drew his attention to the form. This debt to Logau, who had signed his *Deutscher Sinn-getichte Drey Tausend* with the anagrammatic pseudonym Salomon von Golau, was openly acknowledged by Müller in his original title: "Salomon von Golau Redivivus, oder: Deutscher Reimsprüche Erstes Hundert."

Müller's epigrams are mostly two- or four-line rhymed poems extolling the traditional virtues of moderation, love, humility, temperance, honesty, and truthfulness. The baroque theme of the transitoriness of life also appears frequently.

The epigrams are of uneven quality; the better ones exhibit Müller's ability to express a thought in a few words and to create an unusual image. Müller does not speak here through a role as he does in much of his other poetry; he speaks directly and openly. His purpose in the epigrams is didactic; he criticizes hypocrisy, society, the nobility, the organized church, religious intolerance, and human frailties. In his epigrams he reveals himself as a liberal: "Müller zeigt sich hier als ein handfester Liberaler und wird auch manchen heutigen Demokraten damit noch viel Freude bereiten."[77]

Perhaps because of their varying quality, the reception of the epigrams among Müller's contemporaries was either very positive or very negative. For example, shortly after Müller's death, August von Rode writes to the poet Friedrich von Matthisson of his low opinion of the epigrams: "Seine Griechenlieder werden seinen Namen erhalten. Seine Denksprüche und Epigramme möcht' ich aus den Journalen vertilgen." Gustav Schwab, on the other hand, views them as a statement of Müller's lofty moral philosophy. "In die 200 Epigramme endlich hat der hingeschiedene Dichter—an einen Ort wo man dies am wenigsten sucht—mitten unter Scherz und Spott den heiligen Ernst seiner sittlichen Lebensansichten niedergelegt, und viele dieser Sprüche lassen einen Blick in sein für das Wahre und Gute, nicht blos [*sic*] für das Schöne, begeistertes Gemüth thun, das aller Thorheit Feind und ein Schüler der himmlischen Weisheit ist."[78]

Vermischte Gedichte; Lieder aus unbekannter Zeit
Under this designation the critical edition includes sixty-four poems
which do not fit into any other category. The dates of the poems range
from 1815 to 1827, the year of the poet's death. In general, these
miscellaneous poems are translations from the Spanish, English, Ital-
ian, and neo-Greek; some ballads; several epigrams; drinking songs;
and a few pieces of occasional verse.

Written in 1815, the ballad "Der blaue Mondschein" is reminiscent of
Goethe's "Erlkönig." Müller's poem may have been an influence upon
Heine when he wrote "Die Wallfahrt nach Kevlaar."[79]

The censor forbade the publication of "Hymne auf den Tod Raphael
Riego's." The hero of the poem was the Spanish general and revolu-
tionary who was hanged on November 7, 1823. Müller had become
interested in the Spanish Revolution as early as January 1823, when he
wrote to Brockhaus that he was planning the composition of "Lieder
der Hispanier." Considering the repressive political situation, it is not
surprising that the censor objected to such lines as the following:

> Held der Freiheit,
> Schmählich gemordeter!
> Aber die Freiheit, wer kann sie morden?
> . . . .
> Held der Freiheit,
> Schmählich gemordeter!
> In Norden und Süden,
> In Westen und Osten
> Flamme sie lodernd empor
> Die Flamme der Freiheit,
> Aus deinen Adern,
> Aus jedem Tropfen
> Deines Blutes![80]

The poem was first published in the 1844 Brockhaus edition of the
Griechenlieder.

Müller also wrote poems for various special occasions. "Dem elter-
lichen Brautpaare," for example, was written on May 21, 1821, for
the dual celebration of his marriage to Adelheid von Basedow and the
silver anniversary of her parents. Müller's poem "An Friedrich
Schneider" was sung by a small group of the composer's friends after
the premiere of Schneider's oratorio "Die Sündflut" on November 2,
1824. The poem "Morgengruss aus Luisium," written in May 1826,
was dedicated to Duke Leopold Friedrich in gratitude for allowing
Müller to use his park Luisium as a place to recuperate from a bout
with whooping cough.

The Editions of Müller's Poetry

Although there is no critical edition of Müller's prose, there have been numerous editions of the poetry. The first collection of the main body of poetry in the *Vermischte Schriften* was edited in 1830 by Gustav Schwab, who described in a letter to Tieck his methods and goals in the editorial work.[81] The (well-intentioned, but inept) edition consists of five small volumes. The first two contain Schwab's inadequate and erroneous biography and the poetry with the order of the poems in accordance with Schwab's supposed "thematic" rearrangement. The remaining three volumes are devoted to the two Novellen, the Byron biography, the extensive article on Byron as a poet, and a selection of the most important critical writings.

In 1844 Brockhaus printed the first complete collection of the *Griechenlieder*. The following year a Berlin journalist, Arthur Müller, published in *Moderne Reliquien* an additional eighty poems and several selections of prose which had not been included in the Schwab collection. The additional material had been assembled from nine different journals from the years 1816 to 1827.

The *Miniatur-Ausgabe* of the poetry was published by Brockhaus in 1850. This edition combines the Schwab collection, the complete *Griechenlieder,* and the newly gathered material from *Moderne Reliquien,* but supplies no historical information or other critical commentary. This edition was reprinted without change by Brockhaus in 1858 under the rubric *Gedichte, Vierte Auflage.* The favorable review of the *Vierte Auflage* by Friedrich Hebbel is quoted at the beginning of this chapter. In 1864 Brockhaus published a new edition, *Ausgewählte Gedichte.* The 1868 edition for the series *Bibliothek der deutschen Nationalliteratur des achtzehnten und neunzehnten Jahrhunderts* contains a foreword by F. Max Müller and an abbreviated version of the Schwab biography, but is in other respects essentially a duplication of the *Miniatur-Ausgabe* of 1850.

Several later editions of Müller's poetry were based on the 1868 Brockhaus edition. In 1871 the series *Bibliothek deutscher Klassiker* included a collection of Müller's poetry published in Freiburg im Breisgau. An illustrated edition appeared in 1874 in Berlin with a four-page introduction by Ernst Hermann. The woodcut illustrations emphasize the rustic, folk-song settings of the poems. The *Bibliothek der Gesamtliteratur* published two volumes in 1889—a *Gesamtausgabe* and *Die Griechenlieder.* In 1894, in commemoration of the hundredth anniversary of Müller's birth, Reclam's *Universal-Bibliothek* published a *Gesamtausgabe* with a foreword and a short biography.

In 1906 James Taft Hatfield's critical edition of Wilhelm Müller's poetry was published in Berlin. It is still accepted today as the standard edition. The most recent edition of Müller's poetry was published in 1927, in honor of the hundredth anniversary of the poet's death, in the series *Die Freunde* in Leipzig. This collection was edited by Paul Wahl and introduced by Otto Hachtmann, both of whom also wrote articles about Müller. Hatfield's 1906 critical edition remains the definitive edition, which Kraus Reprint released in 1973 in the series *Deutsche Literaturdenkmale des 18. und 19. Jahrhunderts.*

WILHELM MÜLLER AND FRANZ SCHUBERT

A Poet for Many Composers
Although Müller's poetry is read infrequently today, several musical settings of his poems are still popular. In 1815 the Dessau poet had written: "Aber, getrost, es kann sich ja eine gleichgestimmte Seele finden, die die Weise aus den Worten heraushorcht und sie mir zurückgiebt." The Austrian composer Franz Schubert was by far the most talented "kindred spirit" to "hear the melody" in Müller's words and to set them to music. Otto Erich Deutsch calls attention to another statement by Müller which indicates that the poet was aware of the attraction his poetry held for composers. On December 15, 1822, Müller wrote a letter to the Berlin song composer Bernhard Josef Klein (1793–1832) on the occasion of the publication of two sets of Klein's settings of Müller's poetry. Speaking of the "musical animation" of his verses, Müller writes that his songs lead but half a life, a paper life of black and white, until music breathes life into them. He also maintains that it is the composers who penetrate most deeply into his poems.[82]

Again and again, Müller calls his poems "songs": "Reiselieder," "Wanderlieder," "Tafellieder," "Griechenlieder," "Ländliche Lieder," and so on. He was pleased that composers set his poems to music. In 1821 he proudly writes his friend Atterbom of the fine reception that the *Waldhornistenlieder I* had enjoyed, and about the large number of settings to the poems that he was receiving daily: "Sie finden in Deutschland ausgezeichneten Beifall und ich freue mich besonders über die vielen Kompositionen derselben, die mir täglich zukommen. Maria v. Weber, Methfessel in Rudolstadt, Kapellmeister *Schneider* in Dessau (der Komponist des *Weltgerichts*) haben sehr viele davon in Musik gesetzt, unbekannterer Namen nicht zu gedenken." During the summer of 1822 in Dresden in the Tieck home, Müller was honored by a performance of songs set to his poems by Ludwig Berger, Bernhard Klein, and Eduard Devrient. The bass soloist was Devrient, who was a leading performer in Dresden. Müller writes Adelheid: "Abends wieder bei *Tiecks*, wo viel gesungen wurde—aber nicht so gut wie du.—Unter andern sang mir der Bassist *Devrient* die Compos[itionen] meiner Lieder von *Berger, Klein* u[nd] von sich selbst vor, u[nd] die Sängerinnen unterstützten ihn."[83]

Long after Müller's death, his poems were still popular with composers. This attraction of composers to his poems was the subject of a 1924 study by Richard Koepke, in which several standard German song collections were examined for settings of Müller poems. Surprisingly,

Koepke documents 123 poems by Müller set to music by no fewer than 241 composers 530 times: "Höher als das Urteil des gelehrten Literaten steht uns das Denkmal, das ihm Schubert, der Poet unter den Komponisten, der 'König der Sänger,' gesetzt hat. Dazu gesellt sich die Tatsache, dass 123 Gedichte [von Müller] von nicht weniger als 241 Komponisten 530x vertont worden sind. Die Musiker als Vermittler zwischen Dichter und Volk haben damit ihr Urteil über den Wander-Müller gesprochen."[84] This study also contains two tables—one listing each Müller poem and the composers who set it to music, and another alphabetical listing of the composers with the total number of settings of Müller poems set by each. Among the composers one finds the names of Johannes Brahms, Hugo Wolf, Fanny Mendelssohn, Ludwig Berger, Bernhard Klein, Heinrich Marschner, Carl Loewe, Ludwig Spohr, Friedrich Schneider, Albert Methfessel, Conradin Kreutzer, and Giacomo Meyerbeer.

When Müller is remembered today, it is usually in connection with Schubert's settings of *Die schöne Müllerin* and *Die Winterreise*.

> Noch vor wenigen Jahren wäre es fast selbstverständlich gewesen, eine Betrachtung über Wilhelm Müller mit etwa folgenden Worten zu beginnen: "Wir wüssten wohl kaum mehr etwas von Müller, wenn nicht Franz Schubert kurz vor seinem Tode diesem bescheidenen Dichter durch seine Komposition der 'Schönen Müllerin' und 'Winterreise' Unsterblichkeit verliehen hätte." In der letzten Zeit sind verschiedene Versuche gemacht worden, Wilhelm Müller grössere Gerechtigkeit auf seinem eigenen und eigentlichen Gebiet widerfahren zu lassen und diese Verdienste mit dem Hinweis auf positive Eigenschaften seines dichterischen Werkes sichtbar zu machen.[85]

Twentieth-century critics now seem to give more consideration to Müller's contributions to the Schubert song cycles. One reads, for example: "Er [Müller] war für ihn [Schubert] doch nicht nur blosser 'Textdichter,' sondern ein starkes Inspirationszentrum, das seine frischesten, lieblichsten und tiefsten Melodien zum Erklingen weckte."[86]

In addition to *Die schöne Müllerin* and *Die Winterreise*, Schubert set a third Müller work to music, "Der Berghirt" ("Wenn auf dem höchsten Fels ich steh' "). Schubert's *Der Hirt auf dem Felsen* (Opus 129, D. 695), written originally for soprano, clarinet, and piano, is often heard today in chamber music recitals. This work, written for the soprano Anna Milder, was composed after *Die Winterreise*, shortly before Schubert's death in 1828. Schubert had found the poem (one of the "Ländliche Lieder") in *Urania, 1822*, but, to please the soprano, he had the middle part of the poem rewritten by Helmina von Chézy. Milder, who was the first singer to make Schubert's songs known in Germany, premiered the work in Riga in March 1830, when both the poet and the composer were deceased. The excellent article by Günther Eisenhardt, which was published in the Dessau commemorative booklet honoring the one hundred and fiftieth anniversary of Müller's death in 1977, summarizes the compositions of Müller's poetry, with emphasis on the three Schubert works.[87]

Baritone Dietrich Fischer-Dieskau, the world-renowned interpreter of Schubert's songs and song cycles, states in his *Auf den Spuren der Schubert Lieder: Werden, Wesen und Wirkung* that one cannot be a lover of Schubert and completely reject Müller, who for Fischer-Dieskau brings back the times in which the music and poetry were written, when there was a mixture of strong sentimentality and increasing skepticism:

> Man kann nicht Schubertianer sein und Müller ganz ablehnen. Die Feindseligen meinen, Müllers Situationen und Gefühle seien billig wie schlechtkolorierte Postkarten. Solche Beurteilung wird dem Dichter nicht ganz gerecht. Die Verse haben Form, Phantasie und vor allem die Qualität der Singbarkeit. Man führe sich auch die Zeit vor Augen, in der es nichts zu belachen gab, wenn einer weichen Herzens war und schnell in Tränen geriet. Müller verkörpert den Prototyp seiner Zeit, in jener Mischung von ungebrochener Gefühlsseligkeit und aufkommender Skepsis.[88]

Die schöne Müllerin

This lyric cycle differs from the other works of Müller in that it was written over a relatively long period of time. As a rule Müller worked very rapidly; poems and prose articles were often the work of a day or two. *Die schöne Müllerin*, however, was written over a period of four years (1816–1820).

During 1815 and 1816, a small group of friends gathered weekly in the Berlin home of the privy councillor Friedrich August von Stägemann. In November 1816 the group decided to write a series of poems and to recite them together in a dramatic playlet. The main source for their dramatic structure was the popular opera of Giovanni Paisiello, *La Molinara* (1788), which was named *Die schöne Müllerin* in the German version. The amateur poets also drew from the German folk-song tradition. Each participant wrote poems for his own role. Rose, the lovely maid of the mill, was played by the hostess, Hedwig von Stägemann. Rose's suitors were the gardener boy (Luise Hensel), the hunter (Wilhelm Hensel), the country squire (Friedrich Förster), and the miller lad, who was played by his namesake Wilhelm Müller. The miller lad, rejected by his beloved in favor of the hunter, drowns himself in the brook. After realizing that she has been the cause of the suicide, Rose follows the miller lad in death. Following a general dirge, the playlet closes with the hunter's lament beside the two graves.[89]

According to the minor Berlin poet Ludwig Rellstab, the song composer Ludwig Berger persuaded Müller to rework his contributions to this playlet into a cycle. Berger then composed settings for the poems, which were published in 1818 under the title *Gesänge aus einem gesellschaftlichen Liederspiel "Die schöne Müllerin."*[90] Before his trip to Italy

Müller revised this version of the cycle. Then, after his return to Dessau, he made new additions and read a polished version to Tieck in Dresden. Although the older writer did not especially like the tragic ending, he encouraged Müller to publish the cycle. The final version appeared at the end of 1820 in *Waldhornistenlieder I*.

On October 17, 1826, Müller writes Tieck on the occasion of the publication of the second edition of *Waldhornistenlieder I*:

> Bei dem neuen Abdruck meiner ersten Gedichtsammlung erinnerte ich mich lebhaft des schönen Nachmittags in Kalckreuths Sommerwohnung an der Elbe, wo ich Ihnen, kurz nach unsrer Bekanntschaft, meine Müllerlieder vorlas, und von Ihrem Urtheil aufgemuntert, den Entschluss fasste, damit in die Welt zu treten. Von diesem Tage an, wieviel verdanke ich Ihnen, mein verehrter Freund! Darum nehmen Sie meine Dedikation, die einfach ist, wie ich selbst, nicht für eine formelle Redensart, sondern für den wahren Ausdruck meiner Dankbarkeit.[91]

Schubert used the 1820 version of Müller's twenty-three poems (plus a prologue and epilogue) as the text for his song cycle. The composer omitted three of Müller's poems and the "frame"—the prologue and the epilogue. *Die schöne Müllerin*, Opus 25 (D. 795), was in print by August 1824. Schubert dedicated the cycle to the young Baron Karl von Schönstein (1797–1871), a friend of Count Esterházy.

In the song cycle several themes and images from the German folksong tradition have been combined to form a playlet dramatizing the theme of unrequited love. The simple figures are identified only by their occupation or social status (hunter, miller boy, daughter of the miller). These figures are surrounded by standard folk-song motifs such as wandering, the lute, the rushing water, and flowers. Alan P. Cottrell summarizes his detailed discussion of the song cycle: "The uniqueness of Müller's creative talent reveals itself in the manner in which he employs the conventional material, recasting it in his own mold."[92]

In addition to studies of the poems and their settings (such as the one published by Breitkopf and Härtel in 1928),[93] two recent studies of the cycle as an independent literary work have appeared. Cottrell devotes a chapter of his book on Müller's Liederzyklen to a detailed stanza-by-stanza analysis of the cycle. In an article on Müller's song cycles, Klaus Günther Just emphasizes the expansion of the "lyrical I" to represent every person. He argues that the whole cycle should be considered an example of romantic irony, and in support of his argument he calls attention to the ironic tone of the prologue and epilogue. The prologue, which Schubert did not set to music, begins:

> Ich lad' euch, schöne Damen, kluge Herrn,
> Und die ihr hört und schaut was Gutes gern,

> Zu einem funkelnagelneuen Spiel
> Im allerfunkelnagelneusten Styl;
> Schlicht ausgedrechselt, kunstlos zugestutzt,
> Mit edler deutscher Rohheit [sic] aufgeputzt,
> Keck wie ein Bursch im Stadtsoldatenstrauss,
> Dazu wohl auch ein wenig fromm für's Haus:
> Das mag genug mir zur Empfehlung sein,
> Wem die behagt, der trete nur herein.[94]

Just summarizes his point: "Der Hinweis auf den tragischen Schluss ist nun allerdings noch kein Beweis dafür, dass die Lust des Wanderns, von der zu Anfang die Rede ist, zwanghaften Charakter trägt, zumal es durchaus möglich ist, den gesamten Liederzyklus einschliesslich des Schlusses als Produkt romantischer Ironie zu deuten. . . . So akzentuiert gerade die Ironie der Rahmengedichte letztlich den tiefen Ernst des Liederzyklus."[95]

The familiarity of the Schubert cycle has tended to result in a lack of recognition for the poet. The recent interpretations of Just and Cottrell call for a reassessment of Müller's poems as a work of literary merit, rather than a mere "text" for the Schubert melodies.

Die Winterreise

Schubert's *Die Winterreise* is generally held in musical circles to be the greatest masterpiece of the song cycle genre. Famous singers such as Hermann Prey and Dietrich Fischer-Dieskau occasionally perform the cycle as the entire program on a solo recital and have competed in recording its "definitive" interpretation.

The composition is so familiar that Thomas Mann used a song from the cycle ("Am Brunnen vor dem Tore") as a musical reference in the closing scenes of his *Magic Mountain* (1924). Russian Nobel Prize winner Alexander Solzhenitsyn used the opening song ("Gute Nacht") as a kind of musical Leitmotiv in his 1960 drama *Candle in the Wind*. These twentieth-century literary uses of Müller lyrics made famous by Schubert's settings are discussed in greater detail in Chapter 8.

The story of the creation of Schubert's magnificent *Die Winterreise* is a complicated one, since Müller's cycle of poems did not originally appear as a unit. In January 1822 Müller sent twelve poems to Brockhaus for inclusion in *Urania, 1823*. Then, in March 1823, additional poems were published in Breslau in Schall and von Holtei's *Deutsche Blätter für Poesie, Litteratur, Kunst und Theater*. The completed cycle, *Die Winterreise*, was published in the *Waldhornistenlieder II*. Müller had added another two poems to the original twenty-two, bringing the total to twenty-four.

Schubert became acquainted with *Die Winterreise* in an old copy of *Urania, 1823*, and set the twelve poems to music in February 1827. Only after he had already completed this first group of songs did

Schubert discover the completed cycle in Müller's collection *Waldhorni-stenlieder II*. Late in the summer of 1827 Schubert set the additional twelve poems in the order that he found them. Schubert's use of the two texts thus explains the discrepancy between Müller's own sequential arrangement of the poems and the order in which they appear in the Schubert cycle. The printer's proofs of the second part of *Die Winterreise* were corrected by the composer on his deathbed. Schubert died on November 19, 1828, at the age of thirty-one. His friend Josef von Spaun maintains in his memoirs that the excitement generated by Schubert's feverish composition of the beautiful but melancholy songs hastened the composer's early death.

Six weeks later on December 30, 1828, *Die Winterreise* appeared as Opus 89 (D. 911). The success of the union of poetry and music was recognized early by a reviewer for the *Theaterzeitung* on March 29, 1828, when Schubert published the first half of the cycle:

> *Winterreise* by Wilhelm Müller, set to music for voice with pianoforte accompaniment by Franz Schubert, op. 89, no. I. Property of the publisher Tobias Haslinger, Music Publisher in the building of the Savings Bank, Am Graben, Vienna. To recommend a successful work is the most pleasing task that a lover of the arts can undertake. We therefore speak with great pleasure of the present work whose publication does honour to the poet, the composer and the publisher. Schubert has displayed his genius in his interpretation of the poet. He has truly appreciated the emotions expressed in these poems and reproduced them in music which none can sing or hear without being deeply moved. Schubert's spirit soars so boldly that he carries along all who approach him and we are borne through the immeasurable depths of the human heart into worlds beyond, where the promise of the infinite opens up longingly in the radiance of the setting sun, but where also the gentle confining hand of the present joins with the fearful bliss of an inexpressible premonition to define the boundaries of human existence. Herein lies the very essence of the Romanticism of German culture and in such a genuine union of external and internal harmonies lies the main achievement of both the poet who speaks and the poet who sings. Since this paper is not concerned with theory, this is not the place to discuss the technical beauties but rather to point out how this beautiful and noble work can be most deeply and completely enjoyed, an urgent need in our time, since it has become almost a mania to give one's self up solely to material impressions in music.[96]

Die Winterreise is a simple story of a rejected lover who leaves the town where his love resides and sets out in winter on an aimless journey. Modern literary interpreters, however, have seen in this simple plot an allegory of modern man's loneliness.

> The unhappy lover assumes the tragic aspect of man himself, the wanderings become man's bewildered progress through life, tossed by winds of emotion, frozen by grief. "Fremd bin ich eingezogen, fremd zieh' ich

wieder aus . . . " sings the lover at the start: "A stranger I came hither, a stranger I depart. . . . " The opening words of the little verse-tragedy, in Schubert's hands, take on the import of man's advent into this world, and his departure from it: the mystery unexplained.[97]

Die Winterreise may also be interpreted in psychological terms. In this case, attention is focused not upon the outward plot of the unhappy love affair, but rather upon the steadily increasing inward loneliness of the wanderer, a symptom of schizophrenia. In his 1950 article "Das Problem der *Winterreise*," Günther Baum writes: "Die stetig zunehmende Vereinsamung eines Menschen und das allmähliche Erkalten seines Gefühlslebens, ausgelöst durch eine schwere seelische Erschütterung, kennt die heutige Psychologie als hervorragendes Symptom drohender Schizophrenie."[98]

Eight years later in 1958, Hans Brandenburg published an article in which he praises Müller's inventiveness:

> Was sich da nun dichterisch bietet, das muss zunächst einmal durch seine Erfindungskraft Bewunderung erregen. Nirgendwo ist das an sich monotone Motiv hoffnungsloser Liebe bloss ausgesagt, was ohne Wirkung bleibt und wie es doch meist geschieht, sondern es wird an immer neue Situationen geknüpft, die es erst wahrhaft verlebendigen, die zugleich Stationen der Wanderschaft und des inneren Passionsganges sind, wie in Eisfacetten die ganze Landschaft des deutschen Winters und sinnbildlich den ewigen Winter des Herzens spiegelnd.[99]

In his detailed literary analysis of *Die Winterreise,* Alan P. Cottrell finds that the cycle has a symbolic existential meaning: "It is this compressing of a 'path through life' (from youth to the inner experience of old age) into a series of characteristic psychological states which allows the cycle to symbolize the whole sweep of a particular destiny. It is a destiny permeated with suffering and pain."[100]

The existential meaning of the cycle is seen by Just in a religious context—the "stations of a passion," in which man faces the sorrows of earthly existence: "*Die Winterreise* ist, im direkten wie im übertragenen Sinne, als Passion strukturiert. Erscheint das lyrische Ich in der *Schönen Müllerin* als Sinnfigur für den unbehausten Menschen, so in der *Winterreise* als Erdensohn in seinem abgründigen Leiden an der Welt schlechthin. Liebesleid spielt zwar eine Rolle, hat aber letzten Endes lediglich auslösende Funktion. Es wird vom Weltleid absorbiert."[101]

Wolfgang Stechow honors the musical composition of *Die Winterreise* by showing how Schubert's music reflects the meaning that the Austrian composer found in the poetry: "Der grosse Komponist fühlte sich dem kleinen Dichter auch in seinen Kunstmitteln tiefer verbunden und verpflichtet als man anzunehmen geneigt ist."[102]

There is no question that the song cycle *Die Winterreise* has held a special fascination over the past 150 years for the performer and listener alike. Numerous musicologists and literary historians have analyzed various aspects of the cycle to explain the unusual effectiveness of this composition. However, no scholar has previously drawn attention to the similarity of Müller's poems to the so-called stages of dying as categorized by Elisabeth Kübler-Ross. In her book about the terminally ill, *On Death and Dying* (which has been translated into German), she outlines and describes five "stages" through which most terminally ill patients pass: unwillingness to accept the fact of approaching death and isolation from others (denial); anger; bargaining; depression; and acceptance.

Müller's "stranger," who begins his "winter's journey" by leaving behind the village of his beloved, experiences these same emotions. The poet depicts the protagonist's "stream of consciousness" by having him react to the desolate winter landscape around him. The traveler on this "one-way journey" away from society (symbolized by the village and the houses) into an endless winter scene, alternates erratically and seemingly irrationally between depression (reflected in images of burning heat contrasted with ice and cold); blissful reminiscences of happier days with his beloved; vain hope of word from his love in response to the sounding of that Romantic symbol, the *Posthorn;* seeming indifference with an "I don't care" tone; bravado ("Into the world then merrily, / Braving wind and weather! / If there is no God on earth / Then we ourselves are gods!"); to peaceful acceptance of symbolic death, as he joins the eerie barefoot hurdy-gurdy man ("Strange old man! / Shall I go with you? / Will you grind away on your hurdy-gurdy / to my songs?").

It is hard to believe that these melancholy lyrics were written by a twenty-six-year-old, happily married father-to-be with a reasonably secure and comfortable existence in his hometown. In the extant materials about Müller, there are few clues as to the reason for these strikingly melancholy lyrics, which stand out among his other sentimental and patriotic poems. The lack of biographical information explaining *Die Winterreise* has long puzzled scholars working on Müller, since, from outward appearances, this should have been a relatively happy period in his short life.

It may have been that Müller sensed that he would not enjoy a long life and that he expressed his emotions in the accepted literary styles of the times. Examination of Müller's letters shows that the first twelve poems of *Die Winterreise* were sent to Brockhaus on January 16, 1822, and that he made no mention of them either in the cover letter or in letters written during the previous months. It is known that Müller had been ill and that he was depressed and bitter about the European political situation. He was emotionally involved in the Greek War of Independence and was experiencing much difficulty with political censors. Perhaps the dreary winter weather in Dessau was depressing him; his letters give little basis for speculation. Müller simply sent the twelve *Winterreise* poems to Brockhaus, commenting only that he was sending "poetical contributions to *Urania, 1823*"; the poems were not mentioned by title. Ten more poems appeared in Breslau in *Deutsche Blätter für Poesie, Litteratur, Kunst und Theater* on March 13 and 14, 1823. The complete cycle, with the addition of "Die Post" and "Täuschung," appeared in 1824 in *Gedichte aus den hinterlassenen Papieren eines reisenden Waldhornisten II*. Again, in regard to the remaining twelve poems in the completed cycle, Müller remained silent about the genesis of the finished work. But the fact that *Die Winterreise* in its final form developed over a period of at least two years may be an indication that Müller (who did not usually alter works after publication) was more personally involved with the cycle than his correspondence indicates.

After considerable study of the materials available, it is this author's opinion (as previously discussed) that Müller probably was in "delicate health," perhaps suffering from tuberculosis. Perhaps Müller decided not to write about his health for professional reasons; or it may be that written evidence was among the "missing" papers supposedly lost in the undocumented "fire" reported by the poet's son F. Max. At any rate, Müller's sense of joie de vivre and carpe diem, as well as his business acumen in dealing with his employers, may have led him to try to conceal his ill health. Chronic illness would likewise help explain Müller's unusually privileged position of ducal librarian with limited school duties and his frequent "vacation trips" away from his family to Berlin, Leipzig, Dresden, Rügen, the spa at Franzensbad, the ducal villa Luisium, the Rhine trip, and other destinations. Müller's frantic work pace, which produced thousands of pages of publications in less than a decade, and his concern about earning money for his family (as expressed frequently to Brockhaus) may reflect a desire to use well the time remaining to him. Further, Müller was known for his congeniality and hospitality, which were reflected in his drinking songs and in the lively level of entertaining described later by F. Max.

Perhaps Müller's emotions expressed more than 150 years ago in *Die Winterreise* are the same ones experienced by the terminally ill, and which have become today a widely discussed topic of medical, psychological, and social concern. Kübler-Ross's books, lectures, and television appearances have resulted in wide public interest in the "process of dying" and its implications for today's society.

Whatever Müller's thoughts may have been as he wrote *Die Winterreise* in cold and dreary Dessau, it is a historical fact that his poems struck a responsive chord in the terminally ill Franz Schubert. There is no record that Müller ever became aware of the existence of Schubert's *Die schöne Müllerin*. In the days before the passage of copyright laws, a composer could set to music any poem he selected without requesting permission from the poet. It has been observed that Schubert, who set to music the works of some ninety different poets, did not make it a practice to send copies of his songs to the writer of the lyrics. Apparently he had sent a collection of settings of Goethe's poems to Weimar, but had received no reply.[103] The settings of *Die Winterreise* appeared more than a year after Müller's death (1827). Ironically, Müller never heard the musical compositions which have kept his name alive.

CHAPTER THREE

The Translator

Ein guter Übersetzer ist von Natur vielseitig; denn eine vorherrschende und überwiegende Richtung oder Eigenthümlichkeit des Geistes hindert das Eindringen und Untergehen in eine fremde.[1]

BLUMENLESE AUS DEN MINNESINGERN

The Translations

While studying ancient classics and philology at the University of Berlin, Müller became interested in the *Nibelungenlied* and began experimenting with the translation of Middle High German poetry. His first efforts were solely labors of love, but soon friends had persuaded him to publish his translations, with the idea that the Middle High German poetry would thus be rendered more accessible (and certainly more enjoyable) for interested readers not as well versed in the older language as Müller, a student of philology. At the beginning of the nineteenth century interest in the German past was great; young people wore "old German" attire; the brothers Grimm were collecting fairy tales. Müller and his friends pursued with missionary zeal the task of restoring to Germans their cultural heritage.

Müller's philosophy of translation was, by his own admission, one of *Nachahmung*—literally "imitation." For him, fidelity to the original lay not in presenting a slavish word-for-word translation, but rather in the re-creation of the "spirit" of the older literature. "Hiemit [*sic*] habe ich auch schon das Hauptaugenmerk meiner Bearbeitung angedeutet, ich meine, den alten Geist in der neuen allgemeinverständlichen Sprache und in der gängen [*sic*] Form des heutigen Liedes aufzufassen und wiederzugeben. Ich habe dabei keines Weges auf Wörtlichkeit gesehen, aber wohl auf innere Treue."[2]

In the introduction to the *Blumenlese*, Müller explains his method of translation. First he would read a poem through several times. Then he would lay aside the original text and "sing" the poem to himself. "Jetzt wird es auch Keinen mehr befremden, wenn ich erkläre, dass ich die meisten Lieder so übersetzt habe, dass ich die Urschrift drei bis vier Mal aufmerksam durchlas, dann das Buch weglegte und das Gedicht aus meinem Innern wieder heraussang."[3]

Blumenlese aus den Minnesingern appeared at Easter 1816. Besides explaining his method of translation in his introduction, Müller describes the work of previous translators of Middle High German poetry, discusses the Manesse manuscript collection, and presents his theory of the origin of the *Nibelungenlied*.

Müller believed that the German epic had had its origin in an old Scandinavian saga, and that the first version—the work of a single poet—had been written in the Frankish dialect around A.D. 900. Subsequently, the Frankish poem had undergone two translations, first into the Saxon dialect and then (finally) into the Swabian. Thus far he was in general agreement with the Schlegel brothers, who had also decided that the epic was the work of one man, and who had dated the epic around A.D. 900. Müller, however, went to great pains in an attempt to prove his own theory that the original epic in the Frankish dialect had been composed of eight-line stanzas, whose original end rhymes lay buried (but still were discernible) within the four-line stanzas of the current version. He even reconstructed his own version of several stanzas as they might have appeared in the original, supplying his own (hypothetical) rhymes where the text failed him. The theories of Müller and others were later discounted by Karl Lachmann, who published a critical edition of "Manuscript A" of the *Nibelungenlied* in 1826. By thus using the introduction to the *Blumenlese* as a vehicle for prematurely publishing his "scholarly" ideas, Müller unwisely left himself open to criticism that, by association, detracted somewhat from an otherwise favorable reception of the translations themselves.

The fifty translations are representative works of thirty different poets,[4] with the original text and Müller's New High German rendering of it on facing pages. The volume closes with thirty-four pages of notes—a commentary on the original texts and earlier translations of them, together with biographical information about each poet. Musical settings by Theodore Gäde round out the volume. The "Falcon Song" by "Der von Kürenberg" is reproduced here in Müller's nineteenth-century orthography:

Ich zoch mir einen valken	Ich zog mir einen Falken
Mere danne ein jar;	Wohl länger als ein Jahr,
Do ich in gezamete,	Und als ich ihn gezähmet
Als ich in wolde han,	Und er mir freundlich war,
Und ich im sin gevidere	Da flocht' ich um die Schwingen
Mit golde wol bewant,	Ihm manches goldne Band;
Er huop sich uf vil hohe	Doch ach, bald lernt' er fliegen
Und floug in anderiu lant.	Und flog in andres land!
Sit sach ich den valken	Wohl sah' ich oft ihn schweben
———schone vliegen:	Und rief ihm weinend zu,
Er fuorte an sinem fuosse	Doch er will mich nicht hören

————sidine riemen,
Und was im sin gevidere
Alrot————guldin.
Got sende si zesamene,
Die geliep wellen gerne sin.

In seinem stolzen Flug.
Er trägt viel seid'ne Riemen
Und glänzt von rothem Gold:
O Gott, gieb mir ihn wieder
Und mach' sein Herz mir hold![5]

The Reception of the Translations

Although Jakob Grimm disagrees with Müller's theories about the *Nibelungenlied* and the Manesse manuscript, he admits in a review of *Blumenlese* that young Müller's translations are "more readable" than those in Tieck's *Minnelieder aus dem schwäbischen Zeitalter* (1803): "Herr W. Müller verdient dagegen lob, in sofern er sich von einer manierierten nachahmung frei zu erhalten wusste; auch gebührt dieses seiner bescheidenheit und aufrichtigen neigung zu den alten minneliedern, die er gern wieder unter die 'schöne lesewelt' einführen möchte. seine [Müllers] umdichtungen lassen sich beinahe durchgehends leicht und flieszend lesen; man kann ihm zugestehen, dasz sie viel lesbarer sind, als die Tiekischen bearbeitungen."[6]

Later critics have praised Müller's translations. Lohre writes: "Die Erneuerungen sind liedhaft schwebend, rhythmisch klingend." Rudolf Sokolowsky, the author of a detailed study on the *Minnesang* in the Classical and Romantic periods of German literature, finds Müller's work exact and tasteful. "Kann man diesen Versen eine genaue und doch geschmackvolle Wiedergabe absprechen? Sinngetreu übersetzt er fast überall."[7]

THE TRAGICAL HISTORY OF DOCTOR FAUSTUS by Christopher Marlowe

The Translation

In order to provide models for the national German theater which they hoped to create, several nineteenth-century German writers studied and translated the masterpieces of foreign dramatists—especially those of England and Spain. August Wilhelm Schlegel and Ludwig Tieck, who was later assisted by his daughter Dorothea and Count Wolf Baudissin, translated the dramas of Shakespeare. Tieck, a good friend of Müller, also published *Das altenglische Theater*, and Schlegel translated dramas of Calderón de la Barca and *Blumensträusse italienischer, spanischer und portugiesischer Poesie*.

Müller's 1818 German edition of Christopher Marlowe's *The Tragical History of Doctor Faustus* (1588 or 1589) was his contribution to the growing body of such translations into the German language. Young Müller's translation with its introduction by Achim von Arnim has special significance because it introduced Goethe to the Marlowe drama.

Neither the manner in which Müller became acquainted with the Marlowe drama nor his reason for translating it is known. His studies of older English literature under Benjamin Beresford at the University of Berlin may have led him to the collection *Old English Plays* by C. W. Dilke (London, 1814), which he used as his source.[8] Another possibility is that Achim von Arnim, who had been in England, had persuaded the translator of the *Blumenlese* to try his hand at the Elizabethan drama. Arnim wrote the introduction to the volume and apparently looked after the final details of publication and advertising after Müller's sudden departure for Italy with Baron von Sack.

In his introduction to the translation, Arnim mentions an "unpleasant coincidence" which had required the translator to repeat his work and which had resulted in the published translation's being "a second improved version." This vague reference was clarified by Reinhold Steig in 1906 after he examined Berlin journals of the period. Steig explains that, as advance advertising for his soon-to-be-published translation, Müller had allowed the opening and closing scenes to be printed in the Berlin journal *Der Freymüthige* in August and early September 1816. One of the editors of the journal, Garlieb Merkel, probably had the entire manuscript in his possession. Unfortunately for Müller, Merkel became involved in an unpleasant controversy and had to leave Berlin overnight. The manuscript was lost, and the entire work had to be duplicated.

After examining the sections of Müller's original translations in *Der Freymüthige,* Steig agrees with Arnim that the second version was indeed better than the first; Müller had stayed closer to the original in his second version. In the *Gesellschafter, 1818,* Arnim announces the publication of the translation, praising Müller's work: "Die Übersetzung ist ebenso treu als ungezwungen."[9]

The opening speech by the chorus shows how Müller preserved Marlowe's meter as it appeared in the 1814 Dilke edition:

Chorus:
Not marching in the fields of Thrasimen
Where Mars did mate the warlike Carthagen:
Nor sporting in the dalliance of love,
In courts of kings where state is overturn'd:
Nor in the pomp of proud audacious deeds,
Intends our muse to vaunt his heavenly verse;
Only this, gentles, we must now perform,
The form of Faustus' fortunes, good or bad:[10]

Der Chor tritt auf.
Nicht schreitend durch die Thrasimener Felder,
Wo Mars sich mit dem tapfern Punier mass,
Nicht tändelnd in dem losen Spiel der Liebe
An Königshöfen, im verkehrten Staat,

Nicht in dem Glanze stolzer Heldentaten
Will unsre Mus' auf hehren Versen prangen:
Ein andres woll'n wir heut, ihr Herrn, euch spielen,
Das Spiel von Faustus Schicksal, gut und schlecht.[11]

Achim von Arnim's Introduction

Arnim's twenty-five-page introduction to Müller's translation (dated November 19, 1817, in Berlin) begins with a summary of the known facts about Marlowe's life and works taken from English sources. Then comes a discussion of the Faust legend in German literature, followed by Arnim's theory about the relationship between Marlowe's *Faustus* and the German puppet play. (Arnim was convinced that an English translation of the *Faustbuch* published in Frankfurt by Johann Spies in 1587 had been Marlowe's source. Subsequent studies by others indicate that Marlowe's source was indeed most probably an English translation of the Spies *Faustbuch* by one "P.F., Gent.")[12] Arnim suggests further that the Marlowe drama had in turn influenced the German puppet play. Although Lessing and Tieck had previously noticed a resemblance between the puppet play and the English tradition, it is here in Arnim's introduction to Müller's translation of *Faustus* that the thesis is first directly stated. "Arnim aber bleibt das Verdienst, ausdrücklicher als diese Vorgänger den Satz ausgesprochen zu haben, den die deutsche Faustforschung des 19. Jahrhunderts trotz neuerer Einwendungen übernommen und anerkannt hat: Marlowes Faust ist als Quelle des deutschen Puppenspiels vom Doktor Faust zu betrachten."[13]

Goethe and Müller's Translation of Marlowe's Faustus

Arnim sent a copy of the translation to Goethe in June 1818. Since Goethe first acknowledged acquaintance with the drama via Müller's translation, a controversy has arisen as to whether Goethe knew Marlowe's *Faustus* at the time he was writing *Faust I*. Several scholars argue that Müller's version was the first of the Elizabethan drama Goethe had seen. On the other hand, Otto Heller contends that textual similarities demonstrate Goethe's familiarity with Marlowe's version long before 1818.[14]

It has long been the author's opinion that Goethe did discover Marlowe's *Faustus* through Müller's translation. The detailed records of Goethe's library, readings, and correspondence do not show that he had seen any version of Marlowe's drama before 1818. This opinion is shared by the professional staff of the Goethe Archives, the Nationale Forschungs- und Gedenkstätten der klassischen deutschen Literatur in Weimar. In a letter addressed to the author, an official of the Goethe Archives, Dieter Görne, confirms the importance of the Müller translation:

Ob Goethe bereits vor dem 11. Juni 1818 Christopher Marlowes Drama "The Tragical History of Doctor Faustus" gekannt habe, können wir unter Berufung auf das uns im Goethe- und Schiller-Archiv zur Verfügung stehende Material eindeutig negativ beantworten. Wir haben darüber hinaus recherchiert und festgestellt, dass Goethe weder in seinen Werken noch in seinen Briefen und Gesprächen vor 1818 auch nur den Namen Marlowes erwähnt. . . .

Wir haben selbstverständlich auch Otto Hellers Buch geprüft. Tatsächlich gibt es Parallelen zwischen Marlowes "Faustus" und Goethes "Urfaust" und "Faust I." Daraus kann spekulativ auf eine Bekanntschaft Goethes mit dem Werk Marlowes geschlossen werden—wissenschaftlich belegbar sind diese Vermutungen nicht.[15]

Critical Response to the Translation
Several of Müller's contemporaries praised his translation. Clemens Brentano refers to Müller's "masterfully translated" *Faustus* in a letter to Tieck: "Den *Titurel* bin ich leider nicht im Stande Ihnen jetzt zu senden, da ich ihn dem jungen Dichter und Philologen Wilhelm Müller, der den alten englischen Faust meisterhaft übersetzt hat, auf einige Zeit eben bei Erhalt Ihres gütigen Briefes mitgetheilt." The Berlin journalist and editor August Kühn praises both the translation and the translator: "Die Übersetzung selbst ist treu und fliessend, wie man sie aus der Hand des Bearbeiters der Minnelieder erwarten durfte." The Berlin editor Garlieb Merkel writes: "Nach einer freundlich gestatteten Ansicht der Übersetzung, darf ich ihr das Zeugnis geben, dass sie Klang und Leichtigkeit eines Originals hat."[16]

Later critics of Müller's *Faustus* have differed in their evaluations of its overall quality. Lohre finds that blank verse was not Müller's forte: "Der Blankvers lag Müller nicht; er klingt bei ihm an nicht wenigen Stellen hart und gestopft. Als erster Versuch kann die Arbeit immerhin bestehen. Ein Nachfolger, Bodenstedt, hat noch manche Zeile daraus wörtlich übernommen." In his 1948 study of the history of the Faust figure, Karl Theens is more complimentary: "Es war dem Übersetzer gelungen, die Kraft und den Gehalt der Dichtung ganz im Sinne seines Schöpfers wiederzugeben, so dass man in Deutschland damit die Möglichkeit hatte, sich mit der Urfassung des nur verstümmelt überlieferten Dramas vertraut zu machen."[17]

Almost one hundred years after the appearance of the translation, the reviewer Max Förster writes that although "no drop of Faustian blood flowed in Müller's veins" and Müller was unsuccessful in duplicating the power of Marlowe's language, Müller, nonetheless, had a good ear for poetry. Förster maintains that Müller had matched the sharp rhythm of Marlowe's blank verse better than any of the translators who followed him: "Wilhelm Müller, dem Übersetzer, das muss zugegeben werden, floss wohl kein Tropfen Faustischen Blutes in seinen Adern; und so ist es ihm auch nicht gelungen, das Markige und

Wuchtige der Marloweschen Sprache wiederzugeben. Immerhin besass er aber Ohr: den scharfen Rhythmus des Marloweschen Blankverses hat er besser getroffen, als irgendeiner seiner Nachfolger."[18] Förster also praises Müller's talent for replacing English idioms and jokes with aptly chosen German equivalents.

Berta Badt, the editor of the 1911 edition of the Müller translation, argues that even though Müller's German blank verse does not do justice to the original, his version nevertheless comes closer to conveying the power of Marlowe's language than any other. "Es ist nicht zu leugnen, dass der häufend malerischen Sprache Marlowes auf diese Weise nicht immer Genüge getan wird. Aber eins gewann Müller dadurch: den scharfen Rhythmus, die strenge Gewalt des Marloweschen Verses fühlt man eindringlicher bei ihm als in den treueren Umschreibungen der andern Übersetzer. Der Hauptwert dieser Übersetzung liegt nicht eigentlich in ihrer Tiefe noch in ihrer Treue: sondern im Klange."[19]

Müller's translation of the English drama was the subject of a study by Joseph C. Blair in 1960. Giving excerpts of the original English side by side with Müller's translation, Blair discusses the good aspects of the translation, potential pitfalls that he avoided, and the few mistakes that he did make. Blair concludes that Müller's translation of the drama is quite good, especially when one considers the difficulties of translating from Elizabethan English into the German of two centuries later. He also finds that Müller faithfully reproduced Marlowe's metrical structure, even the shifts in meter made for emphasis, and that most of the German translation is accurate and clear. Müller's attempt to retain the exact meter of the original, however, did result in some awkward passages. The main deficiency of the translation really lies not in his work, but rather in the inaccuracies in the English edition he used. Although Müller may have been aware of the inaccuracies and inconsistencies of Dilke's edition, no other text was available to him.[20]

The Editions of the Translation

Müller's translation of 1818 was reprinted in no fewer than seven different editions between 1847 and 1970. In 1949 another translator of Marlowe's *Faustus*, Adolf Seebass, writes that he considers Müller's version "die klassisch gewordene Übersetzung."[21]

In 1847 the translation and the original introduction by Arnim were reprinted in Scheible's *Das Kloster*. Heine read this edition but was apparently more interested in the original Faust book and in Simrock's version of the puppet play. Müller's translation next appeared in Reclam's *Universal-Bibliothek* in 1879. This edition in Reclam did not include Arnim's introduction and was marred by printing errors. In 1911 Rudolf Frank chose Müller's translation for his collection of Faust literature. A scholarly and accurate edition introduced by Berta Badt also appeared in 1911; again, Arnim's introduction was included. A 1913 collection of the literature on Faust, edited by Karl Georg Wendriner, included Müller's translation, as did Horst Geissler's 1927 compilation. As recently as 1970 another collection of Faustian literature edited by Margret Dietrich includes Müller's translation.[22] It may be noted that the editors of these various collections of the literature on Faust selected Müller's translation of Marlowe's text over the translations of those who followed him: Adolf Böttger (1857), Friedrich von Bodenstedt (1860), Kühne (1868), and Alfred Van der Velde (1870). Later translators of the drama into German include Adolf Seebass (1949) and Klaus Udo Szudra (1964).

In 1967 Müller's translation was the subject of a laudatory article by Hans Henning, who described it as the most effective, most impressive, and stylistically most natural translation: "Wir können die Vorsicht ebenso für die Form der Übersetzung anführen, die zu ihrer Zeit nicht besser geleistet werden konnte. Sie hat jedoch auch für einen langen Zeitraum den Anforderungen entsprochen, indem sie sich als die wirkungsvollste, einprägsamste und stilistisch nicht gekünstelte Fassung präsentierte."[23]

CHAPTER FOUR

The Literary Critic, Editor, and Scholar

Schreiber, was bemühst du dich,
immer gut zu schreiben?
Liest dich denn ein Jeder gut?
Treib's, wie's Alle treiben![1]

Although Wilhelm Müller is remembered today as a poet, the major portion of his writing time was spent on critical entries and articles for several journals and reference books and on editorial duties for the *Allgemeine Enzyklopädie der Wissenschaften und Künste* and for his *Bibliothek deutscher Dichter des siebzehnten Jahrhunderts*. Müller's studies in philology and classics at the University of Berlin led to his sole contribution to the field of classical philology, *Homerische Vorschule*.

As a critical writer Müller possessed the ability to take the measure of his audience and to tailor his material accordingly; he altered his style to suit the particular publication for which the article was intended. There is also evidence that he was well aware of the shortcomings of his own hastily executed reviews and those of others. At the end of his review "Taschenbücher für das Jahr 1826" in *Literarisches Konversationsblatt*, Müller includes a rhymed critique of criticism: "Wir schliessen hier unsere letzte Anzeige der Taschenbücher für 1826 mit einer Kritik unserer Kritik selbst."

Mit grosser Lust und grossem Glück
Hält ihr Serail hier Frau Kritik.
Ein Jeder, er sei gross oder klein,
Wird ihr gar sehr willkommen sein.
Sein Zimmer ist ihm gleich bereit,
Sein Essen auch zu rechter Zeit;
Er wird genährt und verwahrt
Nach seiner Art und seinem Bart.
Doch lässt aus Furcht vor Neidesflammen
Sie ihre Freunde nie zusammen.
Sie hat zwar weder Leut' noch Land,
Auch weder Capital noch Pfand,
Sie bringt auch selber nichts hervor,
Und lebt und steht doch gross im Flor:

Denn was sie reich macht und erhält,
Das ist eine Art von Stempelgeld;
Drum sehen wir alle neue Waaren
Zum grossen Thor hineingefahren.[2]

THE LITERARY CRITICISM

The Beginning of His Journalistic Career

Müller's first articles were a series, "Oper und Schauspiel, nebst einigen Bemerkungen über das Theater im Allgemeinen und das Berliner Theater im Besonderen," for the influential Berlin journal of Friedrich Wilhelm Gubitz, *Der Gesellschafter, oder Blätter für Geist und Herz, 1817.* As a result of these articles, Müller became involved in an extended literary quarrel with the dramatist-critic Adolf Müllner. Müller, the newcomer on the Berlin literary scene, apparently held his own in the debate. The older Müllner was not quick to forgive and forget. Not until 1826, when Müller's reputation was well established, did Müllner invite him to contribute to his *Mitternachtsblatt für gebildete Stände.* Müller responded by submitting a few poems. These first articles of the young Müller are worthy of more than a historical note; Gubitz republished the literary duel between the then well-known dramatist and the young critic forty years later in 1857.

After returning from his protracted stay in Italy, Müller was asked by the liberal publisher Friedrich Arnold Brockhaus in December 1819 to write a survey of the most important books about Italy for his literary journal *Hermes.* This survey, which appeared as an extended series of reviews, was widely read. (Nine years later, in 1829, Heine mentions the series of Müller's reviews in *Reisebilder III: Reise von München nach Genua.*) Thus began Müller's lifelong connection with the firm of Brockhaus in Leipzig, during which he maintained a close working relationship with both F. A. Brockhaus and later Heinrich Brockhaus, who assumed control of the firm upon his father's death in 1823. The letters of Müller addressed to the two publishers number more than 150 and date from December 20, 1819, to the very evening of Müller's death—September 30, 1827. These letters were not released by the Brockhaus firm until 1927, when they were published by Heinrich Lohre under the title *Wilhelm Müller als Kritiker und Erzähler: Ein Lebensbild mit Briefen an F. A. Brockhaus und anderen Schriftstücken.*

Müller's Increased Involvement in Critical Writing

Müller's successful debut in literary criticism in *Hermes* marked the beginning of a constant exchange of letters, journals, books, reference books, manuscripts, and proofs between Leipzig and Dessau. Soon he was contributing to several Brockhaus publications: *Hermes, Urania,*

Zeitgenossen, Konversationslexikon, and *Literarisches Wochenblatt* (which later became *Literarisches Konversationsblatt* and ultimately, in 1826, *Blätter für literarische Unterhaltung*).

Müller's success in this type of writing was reflected in an ever-increasing demand for his work; the more Müller wrote for Brockhaus, the larger his circle of literary and journalistic acquaintances became. Editors of journals in several cities invited Müller either to submit his poetry to them or to join their editorial staffs. During his brief career Müller saw his prose and poetry published in twenty-five different journals and reference works in Leipzig, Berlin, Vienna, Stuttgart, Halle, Breslau, Nuremberg, Mannheim, Ilmenau, Aarau, Braunschweig, and Göttingen.[3]

Brockhaus kept increasing the amount of work assigned to Müller. His ability to grasp quickly the important aspects of a work to be reviewed, his excellent knowledge of contemporary literature and writers, his familiarity with reference materials, and his ability to write an article speedily in the particular style demanded by the occasion made Müller a valuable worker for Brockhaus, despite the problem created by the distance between Leipzig and Dessau.

Early in their collaboration Müller writes Brockhaus that the publisher will have it on his conscience if he, Müller, should become a speedy writer for every taste: "Wenn ich ein Allerwelts-Geschwindschreiber werde, so haben Sie mich auf Ihrem Gewissen." Unfortunately, Brockhaus's insistence that Müller accept so much work proved to be detrimental to the quality of much of his journalistic critical writing, with the exception of the longer articles he wrote for *Hermes*. It would appear that the relationship between Müller and Brockhaus was one of mutual need. Müller's letters reveal that he became dependent upon the additional income from this free-lance work to support his growing family and to finance his travels outside of Dessau. Occasionally he was even forced by his tight budget to request an advance payment from Brockhaus. Müller apparently lived from hand to mouth; this is shown by a letter to F. A. Brockhaus when the publisher had been ill, and the firm's payment had been delayed: "Meine kleine Ökonomie ist von der Art, dass ich von dem, was ich verdiene, nichts zurücklege, und selbst leicht derangirt [*sic*] werde, wenn mir Posten ausbleiben."[4] Although Müller needed the additional money, the letters to Brockhaus do record several instances of Müller's rejecting suggestions for articles, either because he recognized that he was not well informed about the subject (e.g., *The 1001 Nights*) or because he preferred to spend extra time on the more important articles, such as the biography of Byron.

The prodigious amount of material which Müller produced as a critic becomes even more impressive when one learns that he suffered from very poor eyesight, an affliction which sometimes made it impos-

sible for him to read and write by artificial light. As early as 1815, in his
Berlin diary, he mentions his weak eyes. In 1822 he writes Brockhaus
to explain why his reviews of the year's popular anthologies are slow in
coming; the small print in the journals made it necessary for others to
read them aloud to him: "Dass meine Anzeigen nicht so schnell einlau-
fen, wie Sie wünschen, liegt an meinen schwachen Augen. Die kleine
Almanachsschrift nöthigt mich, bei Lichte die Büchlein einem Andern
zum Vorlesen zu geben, und das geht denn doch nicht so schnell, als
wenn ich selbst lese." Two years later he writes Brockhaus: "Sie wissen
ja, dass ich im Winter nur halb so viel arbeiten kann, wie im Sommer,
da ich meiner Augen wegen bei Licht fast gar nicht schreiben darf, ja
kaum lesen."[5]

Müller's Method of Criticism
As a critic Müller was respected. Willibald Alexis, for instance, com-
mends Müller's method of critical writing: "Die allgemeine Achtung
durch Deutschland trug ihn, und glänzte wieder, ohne Arroganz, auf
seiner offenen Stirn. Er war ein glücklicher Mann, jeder sah es ihm an;
auch seine Stimme als Kritiker war hoch geachtet, und er recensirte
[*sic*] viel, oft scharf, aber mit sicherm Takt und ohne Gehässigkeit." In
a study written eighty years later, Aloys Becker praises him as both
poet and critic: "Wilhelm Müller ist nicht bloss ein gottbegnadeter
Sänger und Dichter, . . . sondern auch wie viele Romantiker ein Kri-
tiker, der wie wenige dazu berufen war, das Feld der Poesie, das er als
Dichter mit Erfolg bebaute, auch von der Höhe der Theorie zu
überschauen."[6]

In 1975 a piece of Müller's critical writing was praised by Karl S.
Guthke in his *Literarisches Leben im achtzehnten Jahrhundert in Deutschland
und in der Schweiz*. He characterizes Müller's article on Thomas Chatter-
ton in the encyclopedia published by Ersch and Gruber as one of the
best character portraits of the English author the nineteenth century
produced. Furthermore, Guthke maintains that Müller's evaluation of
Chatterton's spurious medieval writings served to increase the literary
myth surrounding the English author.[7]

Müller was a conscientious critic who did not hesitate to reprimand
others—even his friends—when he felt it necessary. ("Ich habe, nach
meinem Grundsatze, die Rezension mit meinem Namen unterzeichnet.
Das hindert mich nicht, freimüthig und rücksichtslos zu sprechen, wie
auch hier gegen meinen Freund *Büsching* geschehen ist.") In turn, he
accepted criticism of his own work gracefully, so long as it was just and
impersonal. ("Dass meine Beiträge eine *strenge* Kritik erfahren haben, ist
mir lieb, da ich selbst einen strengen Ton angestimmt habe—
Persönlichkeit und Ungerechtigkeit habe ich in einem Blatte, das unter
Ihrer [Brockhaus's] Redaktion erscheint, nicht zu fürchten, und sehe
daher der nächsten Sendung, die ich erst Mittwochs erhalte, erwartungs-

voll entgegen.")[8] It was this principle of impersonal, justified criticism, based on the text, which Müller tried to apply in his own critical writings. He insisted that his identity as reviewer be made known, whenever this was in keeping with the editorial policy of the particular journal. ("Ich halte überhaupt, wo es das Gesetz des Instituts nicht bedingt, meine Autorschaft als Kritiker nicht geheim und nenne mich überall, wo es erlaubt ist, z.B. im *Hermes*.")[9]

Müller was also insistent that he be able to view the final proofs of important works before publication because he was concerned with details. ("Meine Handschrift ist zwar deutlich und Ihre Druckerei korrekt, aber dennoch wäre es mir lieb, die letzte Korrektur zu besorgen. Es pflegt nämlich oft zu geschehn, dass eine Kleinigkeit, die man im Lesen eines Manuskripts übersieht, einem erst im Drucke bemerklich wird, und ich bin im Styl sehr skrupulös und ein ängstlicher Silbenstecher. Ich werde keinen Bogen, den Sie mir senden, aufhalten.")[10]

The Problem of Censorship

The policy of stringent censorship which was in effect during the Restoration was a constant source of annoyance to Müller, who had both poems (especially his Trinklieder and *Griechenlieder*) and entire pieces of critical writing kept from publication. Most often, however, his writing simply appeared in abridged form, with unmarked deletions—even alterations of meaning. Several times Müller requested that Brockhaus at least note the deletions of the censor with an indication of ellipsis. Müller accepted the censor as a fact of life that had to be reckoned with; he tried several different means to circumvent censorship, including having his works published in cities where the censor was known to be more liberal than in Leipzig. Müller pleads with Brockhaus to allow some of his opinions to be heard:

> Es ist in der That abscheulich, wie es mit der Zensur hergeht—sie hat nicht einmal Courage, zu verbieten und zu verbrennen, wie die Neapolitanische, sondern schleicht und lauert, das Freie und Rechtliche allmählig [*sic*] und in aller Stille zu unterdrücken, und schneidet dabei noch ein liberales Gesicht. *Auf jeden Fall* hoffe ich, etwas über meine Lieder [*Griechenlieder*] in dem Conv. Bl. [*Literarisches Konversationsblatt*] zu hören. Lassen Sie doch die politische Ansicht, die ich ausspreche, angreifen—ich nehme es nicht übel—aber lassen Sie nur von meiner Meinung etwas durchhören.[11]

Censorship during this period took various forms: official actions of the government censor; editing by publishers like Brockhaus, who did not want to irritate the government too much; and self-censorship by writers who knew that certain topics or statements would not pass the censor. It is difficult to determine how much of his own work Müller censored. Several instances of self-censorship are mentioned, however, in his letters. Once he did not translate an article in an English journal because he knew that doing so would be wasted effort. ("Den ange-strichenen Aufsatz über Russland in der Lit. Gaz. [*Literary Gazette*] bringen wir nicht durch die Censur. Daher spare ich die Mühe des Übersetzens.")[12]

Another source of irritation for Müller (and Brockhaus) was the delay involved in sending packages of materials and books across the border between Prussia and Anhalt. The Prussian customs officials at the town of Delitzsch (nineteen miles north of Leipzig) often delayed packages and mail for indefinite periods. Müller frequently urged his many correspondents to send materials in several small packages instead of one large one, because the smaller ones seemed to pass through customs faster.

The Various Types of Articles Müller Wrote

Müller's journalistic prose may be divided into five groups: well-written, thoughtful reviews of recent publications, such as the one on Rückert's "Östliche Rosen"; surveys of the contents of various popular literary anthologies, for example, *Das Frauentaschenbuch* and *Urania;* excerpts from English magazines, edited and translated into German; essays on Italy and Greece, such as "Bilder aus dem neugriechischen Volksleben"; and biographical articles like "Byron."

In his longer reviews Müller followed the practice of the English journals *Edinburgh Review* and *Quarterly Review,* providing information that would enable the reader to better understand and interpret the work being reviewed, rather than merely summarizing its contents. Excerpts from the work were included when they were pertinent to the discussion. Most of Müller's articles of this type were written for Brockhaus's *Hermes.* Among the works discussed in detail were editions of the works of Hans Sachs, Paul Fleming, and Thomas Moore. New translations of Homer, Alphonse de Lamartine, Torquato Tasso, Lodovico Ariosto, Dante Alighieri, William Shakespeare, and Calderón de la Barca received the same thorough treatment, as did published works of Lord Byron, Sir Walter Scott, Count August von Platen, Friedrich Rückert, Willibald Alexis, Justinus Kerner, and many others. Although these reviews represent some of Müller's best critical writing, all too often they are overburdened with insignificant details, too much background information, or too many excerpted passages from the work under discussion. The reason for this was probably a very mundane one: Müller was paid for his reviews by the column inch! He complained to Brockhaus more than once about the reduced size of the type used to print his articles. When the publisher ignored his pleas, Müller responded by increasing the length of his contributions, sometimes sacrificing quality for quantity.

Writing the second type of article—the reviews of the year's popular literary anthologies—was an onerous chore for Müller. To prepare them he was forced to wade through countless pages of insignificant material in such publications as *Penelope, Cornelia, Frauentaschenbuch, Urania, Minerva, Taschenbuch zum geselligen Vergnügen, Orphea, Taschenbuch der Liebe und Freundschaft, Aglaja, Berliner Calender, Rheinblüthen,* Cotta's *Damenalmanach,* Becker's *Taschenbuch,* and Gleditsch's *Taschenbuch.* His successful attempt to bring a bit of originality to the task is reflected in some of his titles: "Streifereien durch die Almanachsliteratur von 1821," "Briefe an eine Dame über die Almanachsliteratur des Jahres 1825," and "Literarische Abendunterhaltungen auf dem Lande" (this last article is written in dialogue form). Müller felt that these reviews were a misuse of his valuable time, and he objected (in vain) to Brockhaus, who kept assigning them to him each year. ("Alle Taschenbücher zu lesen und beurtheilen, dazu reicht meine Zeit und Geduld nicht hin, und ich habe Ihnen auch nichts der Art versprochen. Was ich hie und da durchblättert habe, ist auch in der That zu unbedeutend und alltäglich, dass man Ihnen nicht zumuthen kann, über alle diese Bücherchen zu sprechen.") He expresses his low opinion of the popular anthologies more candidly in a letter to Atterbom. ("Die Almanachsfluth hat uns überströmt. Blasen und nichts als Blasen.")[13] In the end, however, Müller always gave in and wrote the survey of the anthologies of the year, rather than jeopardize his valued (and lucrative) association with Brockhaus.

The third group of articles is represented by such titles as "Literarische Stadtgespräche aus London," "Literarische Notizen aus England," "Englische Zeitungen," and "Literaturbriefe aus Paris." These summaries and translations from foreign journals were also Brockhaus's idea; Müller viewed them simply as tedious tasks to be performed for money. ("Jene Berichte aus London und Paris sind mir sehr undankbare mühselige Arbeiten, und wenn ich die Materialien Stossweise [*sic*] erhalte, kann ich sie gar nicht zwingen.") Müller often referred to these foreign reviews as "fodder" for the *Literarisches Konversationsblatt,* which had originally been a weekly publication before Brockhaus increased the number of issues to one each weekday. ("Anbei auch einiges Futter für das *Konversationsblatt.*")[14] Müller's essays on Italy and Greece include "Erinnerungen aus Toskana," "Bürgers 'Leonore' und ein neugriechisches Volkslied," and "Bilder aus dem neugriechischen Volksleben." Here Müller found good use for his memories from his Italian months and for his knowledge of modern Greek.

The fifth type of article—biography—is represented by those about Lord Byron, Otto von der Malsburg, Otto Heinrich Graf von Loeben (pseudonym Isidorus Orientalis), and Leopold Friedrich Herzog von Anhalt–Dessau. In addition to these longer biographies, Müller wrote or revised numerous articles for the *Konversationslexikon* and the *Allgemeine Enzyklopädie der Wissenschaften und Künste.* Although Brockhaus had tried to persuade Müller to take an editorial position with the *Konversationslexikon,* Müller declined the offer, which would have made too great a demand upon his time. Because of the remuneration, however, he did agree to write some articles for the publication. Eighty-three articles were written by Müller in the sixth (1824–1826) and seventh (1827) editions of the reference work. The variety of subjects on which Müller wrote shows the breadth of his knowledge; he used materials sent to him by Brockhaus, library holdings in Dessau, and, in the case of some contemporary writers, personal letters.

Among the men whose biographies Müller wrote were Daniel Amadeus Atterbom, Samuel Taylor Coleridge, George Crabbe, Thomas Moore, Friedrich Rückert, Gustav Schwab, Bernhard Thiersch, Ludwig Uhland, Walter von der Vogelweide, Simon Dach, Georg Rudolf Weckherlin, Gottfried von Strassburg, the brothers Grimm, Georg Phillip Harsdörffer, Heinrich von Kleist, Hrabanus Maurus, Max von Schenkendorf, and Julius Wilhelm Zincgref. In addition to the biographical entries in the *Konversationslexikon,* Müller wrote more extensive articles on "Deutsche Poesie," "Literaturgeschichte," "Schwedische Literatur," and "Italienische Reisen." He also advised Brockhaus on which subjects to include and which reference works and materials to consult for information.

Allgemeine Enzyklopädie der Wissenschaften und Künste
In 1821 Müller began writing for the encyclopedia founded in 1818 by Johann Samuel Ersch (1766–1828) and Johann Gottfried Gruber (1774–1851) in Leipzig. From 1821 until 1825 he wrote fifty-six articles, mainly on Italian topics and German and English writers. Then, at the end of 1825, Müller accepted the joint editorship with Georg Hassel, a teacher in Weimar, of the second section (H–M). Hassel proved to be a less than skilled editor, however, and Müller found himself making most of the major decisions and doing most of the work. In addition to writing approximately 275 articles for the B's and C's, Müller prepared 143 separate articles for his own section, H–M. He also handled all of the correspondence for the encyclopedia, requesting articles from different writers, reminding them of deadlines, and editing the contributions after they had been submitted. He alone read the final printer's proofs before the section went to press.

In a letter to Enoch Richter, owner of the firm that published the encyclopedia, Müller shows that he understood how to handle the diplomatic tasks of an editor. He advises Richter on the manner of dealing with a delinquent contributor:

> Sie werden also Ihren Brief bei allem strengen Ernst der Mahnung doch so stellen, dass er dadurch nicht beleidigt werde. Unter einer höflichen und schmeichelhaften Form lässt sich viel Ernstliches sagen. Hoffmann hat mir schon unsägliche Schreiberei gemacht, wie ich nun aus der Berech-

nung meiner Korrespondenz sehe, wo fast der vierte und fünfte Brief nach oder von Jena ist. . . . Aber nochmals bitte ich um eine recht höfliche Form: Sie können ihm auch dabei einige Komplimente über seine (wirklich) vortrefflichen Arbeiten machen.[15]

In the fifth part of the second section (1829) of the encyclopedia, the frontispiece is a copper engraving of Müller. In his foreword the new editor, A. G. Hoffmann (Hassel died soon after Müller), praises Müller's work on the encyclopedia. Wahl devotes four pages of his *Wilhelm Müllers Rheinreise von 1827* to a list of all of Müller's contributions to the encyclopedia.

BIBLIOTHEK DEUTSCHER DICHTER DES SIEBZEHNTEN JAHRHUNDERTS

Müller's Intentions in Preparing the Collection
As early as June 1820 Müller approached F. A. Brockhaus with his idea of publishing a collection of seventeenth-century poetry. He explained that copies of the older editions of this poetry were rare, and that the archaic orthography and many typographical errors made them difficult to read. He envisioned a collection of several volumes, each devoted to an individual poet or a group of poets. Brockhaus liked the idea and approved the project.

The collection was not intended for scholars, but rather for the educated reading public. In the foreword to the first volume, Müller explains for whom he has prepared the collection:

> Unsre *Bibliothek deutscher Dichter des siebzehnten Jahrhunderts* unternimmt es, das grössere Publikum, das freilich in Deutschland nicht grösser zu sein pflegt, als das kleinste in England und Frankreich, mit dem Besten aus der genannten Periode in einer gedrängten Auswahl bekannt zu machen. Als Masstab des Werthes oder Unwerthes eines Stückes musste nothwendiger Weise, bei einer für das grössere Publikum bestimmten Sammlung, der herrschende *Zeitgeschmack* dienen, zu dem jedoch die *Mode* nicht einfliessen durfte.[16]

Müller believed that educated Germans should have the opportunity to read the poetry of the seventeenth century, because he was aware of the influence it had had upon contemporary German literature: "Sie sind die eigentlichen Gründer der gegenwärtigen Form der deutschen Poesie, die Bildner der Sprache, die bis auf unsre Zeiten die gebundene Rede von der Prosa unterscheidet, und die Schöpfer unsrer Metrik und Prosodie."[17] He also hoped that this limited collection would spark the public's interest in these poets, thereby creating a demand for critical editions.

Müller's publication of the series spoiled the plans of his friend Gustav Schwab, who had published an extensive collection of Fleming's poetry in 1820 and had toyed with the idea of publishing a series of similar editions of seventeenth-century poets. When Müller's plans were announced, Schwab and his publisher Cotta inquired of Brockhaus and Müller as to whether the two enterprises might be combined. Müller and Brockhaus felt that the price that Schwab was demanding was too high. Also, the form and method of the two proposed collections differed in concept; Müller intended to be more selective than Schwab. Despite the rejection of his offer, Schwab remained friendly toward Müller and Brockhaus.

Also in connection with the *Bibliothek deutscher Dichter des siebzehnten Jahrhunderts,* Müller was accused of "ruining the market" of an aristocratic connoisseur of sixteenth- and seventeenth-century German literature, Karl Gregor Hartwig von Meusebach (1781–1847) of Berlin, who had spent much time researching the subject and who possessed many original manuscripts and first editions. However, those who criticized Müller for his "interference" in Meusebach's plans forgot that it was undoubtedly accidental on Müller's part. The two men first met in the summer of 1825, five years after Müller had first proposed the idea to Brockhaus and three years after the publication of the first volume of the series. If Meusebach was originally annoyed about the publication of a series that conflicted with his unfulfilled plans, he does not seem to have held a grudge against the young man he had never met. The correspondence which grew out of the meeting in 1825 was extremely cordial. Müller joked about being a "market spoiler." Meusebach offered him the use of some rare manuscripts for the eighth volume of the series, a favor which was graciously acknowledged in Müller's introduction to the volume. Meusebach's protégé, Hoffmann von Fallersleben, recorded a detailed description of Müller's first visit in the Meusebach home and printed Müller's first letter to the aristocratic dilettante.[18]

The Contents of the Series
Between 1822 and 1827 Müller published ten volumes: I—Martin Opitz; II—Andreas Gryphius; III—Paul Fleming; IV—Georg Rudolf Weckherlin; V—Simon Dach, Robert Roberthin, Heinrich Albert; VI—Friedrich von Logau, Hans Assmann von Abschatz; VII—Julius Wilhelm Zincgref, Andreas Tscherning, Ernst Christoph Homburg, Paul Gerhardt; VIII—Johann Rist, Daniel Georg Morhof; IX—Georg Philipp Harsdörffer, Johann Klaj, Siegmund von Birken, Andreas (Scholtz) Scultetus, Justus Georg Schottel, Adam Olearius, Johannes Scheffler (Angelus Silesius); X—Johann Christian Günther. Each volume contains a foreword giving information about Müller's method of editing, his sources, and his reasons for publishing the work of a particular poet. A fairly detailed biography of each poet follows, together with a commentary on his writings. The poetry selections themselves

are restricted to shorter poems, which would appeal to the audience for which Müller was writing. For the reader interested in a deeper study of a poet, Müller indicates the best sources and manuscripts available.

Karl August Förster, a teacher in the Cadettenhaus in Dresden and a friend of Tieck and Weber, completed the series after Müller's death. Volume XI appeared in 1828 with Jakob Schwieger, Georg Neumark, and Joachim Neander represented. Volumes XII (Friedrich Spee von Langenfeld) and XIII (Zacharias Lund, David Schirmer, Philipp von Zesen) appeared in 1831 and 1837, respectively. The final volume (XIV) appeared in 1838 and contains the poetry of Christian Hofmann von Hofmannswaldau, Daniel Casper von Lohenstein, Christian Wernicke, Friedrich Rudolf Ludwig von Canitz, Christian Weise, Johann von Besser, Heinrich Mühlpfort, Benjamin Neukirch, Johann Michael Moscherosch, and Nikolaus Peucker.

The Reception of the Series
The collection found a large enough public to convince the firm of Brockhaus to complete the series after Müller's death. Müller's successor, Karl Förster, admits that he had had reservations about the original idea, but that the success of the first ten volumes had caused him to change his opinion. "Der Beifall, den das von der Verlagshandlung mit Liebe gepflegte Unternehmen gefunden, hat jene Bedenklichkeiten daniedergeschlagen [*sic*]; die Sammlung hat sich ihr Publicum gemacht, und so durfte sie . . . nicht unvollendet bleiben."[19]

In his biography of his father, Heinrich Brockhaus writes about the collection:

> Ein zweites grösseres Verlagsunternehmen, dem Brockhaus in den letzten Jahren seines Lebens besondere Aufmerksamkeit widmete, war eine *Bibliothek deutscher Dichter des siebzehnten Jahrhunderts,* herausgegeben von dem mit ihm schon länger befreundeten Dichter Wilhelm Müller. . . . Die Sammlung suchte das Beste aus den deutschen Dichtungen des 17. Jahrhunderts darzubieten und leistete auch, was bei dem damaligen Stande der Textkritik möglich war; jedenfalls hat sie wesentlich dazu beigetragen, das Interesse für die Literatur der genannten Periode im deutschen Publikum zu beleben.[20]

Some forty years later, the firm replaced Müller's collection with an updated version edited by Karl Goedeke and Julius Tittmann, under the title *Deutsche Dichter des 17. Jahrhunderts.*

HOMERISCHE VORSCHULE

The Explication of the Theories of F. A. Wolf
The title *Homerische Vorschule* was intended to bring to mind Jean Paul Friedrich Richter's *Vorschule der Ästhetik.* The subtitle identifies the con-

tents more exactly: *Eine Einleitung in das Studium der Ilias und Odyssee.* The book was very important to Müller, and he spent a year of hard work on it. The study was intended to explicate the theories of his former professor at the University of Berlin, Friedrich August Wolf (1759–1824). Müller had been a favorite student of Wolf; the Berlin diary notes about a dozen extracurricular meetings between the two, often over meals.

In a letter to Brockhaus requesting publication of *Homerische Vorschule,* Müller calls it his "most meaningful prose work":

> Das vorliegende Werk biete ich aber um so unbefangener an, da ich es für das Bedeutendste halten muss, was ich—die nicht in Vergleich tretenden poetischen Versuche abgerechnet—als Schriftsteller bisher geleistet habe. Es verdankt seinen Ursprung der Aufforderung und Anregung des grössten Philologen unserer Zeit, F. A. Wolf's, meines ehemaligen Lehrers, mit dessen Urtheile über meine homerischen Studien ich Sie jedoch nicht bestechen will. . . .
>
> Meine Arbeit ist die Frucht jahrelanger Studien, und ich weiss wohl, dass diese nicht von dem Verleger belohnt werden können. Auch trägt jede wissenschaftliche Arbeit ihren Lohn in sich.[21]

Brockhaus readily accepted the work.

F. A. Wolf, who came to Berlin in 1807 from Halle, was the author of one of the most significant works of classical studies, *Prolegomena ad Homerum* (1795). Wolf also distinguished himself as a translator of Homer. Müller observed that his former professor's theories, which had been published only in the difficult Latin volume, were not readily available to the educated public. After discussing his idea of writing an explication of the ideas expressed in the *Prolegomena* with Wolf himself in 1823 and being encouraged by him, Müller devoted much time to the study. It appeared in June 1824, only weeks before the much-admired professor died in Marseilles. The work is dedicated to Duke Leopold Friedrich of Anhalt-Dessau in gratitude for the freedom allowed Müller in his positions in Dessau and for permission to utilize the ducal library for his own research.

In his introduction Müller gives two reasons for his having decided to write the book, after having carried the idea around in his head ever since his student years in Berlin. First, his teaching obligations had brought the texts of Homer into his hands "almost daily." Second, recent publications in the field had shown that the theories of Wolf had been largely misunderstood or ignored. Müller hopes to bring the attention of scholars back to the fundamental considerations stressed by Wolf in his *Prolegomena.*

Homerische Vorschule is filled with detailed arguments about the contradictions in the external unity of the epics and about recent Homeric scholarship. Müller shows that he is familiar with the works of Friedrich Schlegel (*Geschichte der epischen Poesie*), August Wilhelm Schlegel

(*Briefe über Poesie*), Bernhard Thiersch, Payne Knight, Robert Wood, and Karl Böttiger, as well as those of the classical Greek and Roman authors.

In a lengthy letter to the historian Friedrich von Raumer, who was professor and rector at the University of Berlin, Müller summarizes what he has tried to achieve in his study, explaining that he has emphasized the external evidence (in plot, character confusion, anachronisms, etc.) which belies the idea that the epics had been created singlehandedly by one Homer:

> An ein ursprüngliches zusammenhängendes Episches Ganzes der Ilias u[nd] Odyssee kann ich also durchaus nicht glauben, ja, ich kann es mir nicht einmal vorstellen. *Einen* Dichter als Verfasser der beiden Gedichte oder auch nur eines derselben anzunehmen, erlauben die inneren u[nd] äusseren Widersprüche in denselben nicht. . . . Ich habe von *innern* u[nd] *äussern* Widersprüchen in den beiden Gedichten geredet. Mein Buch handelt aber fast nur von den äussern, ich meine denen, die im Stoffe liegen (Personenverwechselung, Zeitwirrwar pp) [*sic*]. Die *innern* habe ich nur angedeutet, und nur in so weit sie die poetische Behandlung angehn, etwas näher ausgeführt.[22]

The Reception of the Study

About four months after the publication of *Homerische Vorschule*, Müller writes to Brockhaus that the praise he has been receiving about the book has exceeded his expectations: "Über meine *Homerische Vorschule* erhalte ich von vielen Seiten her (z.B. von Raumer, von Manso) Urtheile und Lobsprüche, die über alle meine Erwartungen gehn."[23]

Müller's scholarly book was successful enough to warrant a second edition, which was issued by Brockhaus twelve years later in 1836. The 1836 editor, Detlev Carl Wilhelm Baumgarten-Crusius, states in his introduction that Müller's work had been so "successful" and "highly recognized" that he has found it necessary only to write a historical introduction and to add footnotes on recent scholarship; the main body of Müller's work remains untouched. Baumgarten-Crusius explains that Müller's work had appeared at the right time for those who wished to know more about Wolf's ideas but who found the Latin of the *Prolegomena* too difficult. Müller's enthusiastic explanations of his professor's ideas had convinced many. The 1836 editor explains that Müller had not only achieved his purpose of popularizing Wolf's theories, but had also inspired some scholars to undertake new research. The late 1820s saw a revival of interest in Wolf's theories that reached across the Atlantic to the United States. In 1827 and 1828 extensive articles explicating Wolf's ideas appeared in English in the *American Quarterly Review*.[24]

CHAPTER FIVE

The Promulgator of Folk Songs

Volkslieder sind Stimmen der Völker. Und so möge auch die kraftvolle, aus tiefster Brust empor klingende Stimme des griechischen Volkes in die Ohren derer tönen, die Ohren haben zu hören.[1]

NEO-GREEK FOLK SONGS—THE FAURIEL COLLECTION

Müller's Translations
Beginning in 1815 Jakob Grimm and Goethe encouraged the German nobleman Werner von Haxthausen (1780–1842) to publish the first collection of neo-Greek folk songs. Haxthausen procrastinated, however, and the Frenchman Claude Fauriel (1772–1844) published the first such collection. Fauriel's original Greek texts and his French translations appeared in two volumes in Paris in 1824 and 1825. Upon receiving these volumes, Müller enthusiastically began to write German translations of Fauriel's Greek texts. The two volumes of the German translations appeared in Leipzig in May and November 1825. A second edition was reprinted in 1828 in Bremen.

In his version, Müller edits Fauriel's extensive introduction and notes, eliminating repetitive details and adding geographical information, which he found lacking in the French original. As a teacher and philologist, Müller intended the translations not only for those who could not otherwise read the original Greek, but also for those readers who knew classical Greek but needed assistance with the modern Greek. The German translations face the Greek originals, thereby assisting the comparison of the two languages. "Was diese Übertragung betrifft, so hoffen wir, dass sie nicht allein dem der neugriechischen Sprache Unkundigen das Original so weit ersetzen möge, als eine Übersetzung das überhaupt vermag, sondern auch dem Leser, welcher zu dem Verständniss [*sic*] des Textes zu gelangen strebt, ein philologisches Hülfsmittel zu diesem Zwecke abgebe."[2]

Müller was an avid supporter of the cause of the Greek people in their struggle against the Turks. The philhellene Müller thus had a political purpose for translating modern Greek poetry. In his introduction he calls folk songs "voices of the people" (an allusion to Herder's well-known collection *Stimmen der Völker in Liedern*). He emphasizes that the spirit of the Greek people—the direct descendants of those upon whose culture Western civilization is based—finds voice in these poems. Müller challenges those who are sympathetic to the Turkish cause (i.e., the supporters of the Austrian statesman Prince Metternich and his theory of legitimism) to listen to the voices of the modern Greeks. ("Wer aber seine Sinne durch türkisches Opium umnebelt und erschlafft hat, der schone seines Trommelfelles. Es möchte diesen Stentor wohl nicht ertragen können.")[3]

Müller was convinced that true folk songs are the expression of the spirit of the people who sing them—the naïve, unspoiled creation of the unconscious poetic talent of people who might not even know how to read or write. He expresses these ideas in the introduction to the collection:

> Es ist eine Eigenthümlichkeit aller ächten Volkspoesien, dass die Verfasser derselben in der Regel unbekannt sind, indem sie sich weder selbst nennen, noch auch dafür sorgen, von Andern genannt zu werden. Die Eitelkeit und Ruhmsucht haben also keinen Einfluss auf ihre poetische Thätigkeit geübt; sie dichten und singen zu ihrer und Andrer Ergötzung, und das Hervorbringen gewährt ihnen einen schönern Genuss, als das Hervorgebrachte.
>
> So sind auch die griechischen Volkslieder die Früchte eines unbewussten, anspruchslosen und ungeregelten poetischen Talents, die Kinder der Begeisterung, des Schmerzes, der Freude oder der Andacht eines Hirten, eines Landbauers, eines Handwerkers, einer alten Frau oder eines jungen Mädchens; und vielleicht haben die Verfasser der schönsten Gesänge unsrer Sammlung weder zu lesen, noch zu schreiben verstanden, geschweige denn eine Idee gehabt von den Regeln der Dichtkunst oder des Versmasses.[4]

Both in the introduction to his translation of Fauriel's collection and in the *Allgemeine Literatur-Zeitung* of Halle (January 1825), Müller criticizes the unidentified translator of several neo-Greek folk songs in *Kunst und Alterthum, 1823*. The author of these very free translations was none other than Goethe himself, who had worked on them in the summer and fall of 1822.[5] Later writers agree that Müller was justified in criticizing the accuracy of Goethe's translations. Nevertheless, F. Max attributed the cool manner in which Goethe had greeted his father in 1826 and 1827 to annoyance over Müller's criticism of the translations in *Kunst und Alterthum, 1823*.[6]

The Reception of Müller's Translations
In a letter to Leopold Voss, the publisher of his translation of Fauriel's collection, Müller indicates that he never intended to make money from the book, but rather thinks of his work as a service for a small (but interested) audience: "Ein schneller Absatz unseres Artikels war freilich kaum zu erwarten, jedoch wird ein solches Buch auch *nie* Makulatur und bleibt, wenigstens durch den Text, ein stehendes

Bedürfnis für ein kleines Publikum."[7] Müller was correct; his translation was not a best seller. Nevertheless, the work aroused a surprising amount of interest and received much praise for the effectiveness of the translations. In his extensive and well-documented study (1966) of Claude Fauriel, Miodrag Ibrovac describes Müller as the "first and best emulator of Fauriel in Germany": "Le premier et le meilleur émule de Fauriel en Allemagne, après Haxthausen, Wilhelm Müller (1794– 1827), le 'Griechen-Müller,' . . . avait réussi très jeune à acquérir une triple réputation de savant, de poète et d'idéologue."[8]

Müller's translations enjoyed a favorable reception in several literary journals.[9] They also inspired a number of additional collections of neo-Greek poetry. During the next twenty years a dozen collections appeared that borrowed some of their poems from the Fauriel-Müller collection. Both collectors and scholars were drawn to the modern Greek poetry; eleven books and numerous journal articles on the subject had appeared by 1847.

Fauriel's Greek texts were quite accurate, and Müller's German translations were likewise faithful to the Greek originals. Critics have praised Müller's success in keeping the spirit of the originals in his literal translations: "Toujours est-il que le traducteur de Fauriel est exempt de tels reproches: tous les historiens ont loué sa conscience, 'un respect presque religieux de l'original.' Le poète avait déjà chanté la Grèce au combat. Pour rendre maintenant la voix même de ses fils, l'érudit y apporta sa ferveur. Le souci d'exactitude ne lui fait pas oublier la beauté suave ou austère de ces chants."[10] Müller's translations reflect both the literal meaning of the Greek texts and their austere beauty.

Müller's volumes were reviewed in Boston in 1842 by the American transcendentalist Margaret Fuller in *The Dial*. The lengthy review gives much material from the introduction of the collection, describing the customs of the modern Greeks and giving English translations of the ballads. The reviewer compliments the conciseness of Müller's introduction and recommends it to her American readers: "These extracts are abridged from the German, not without injury, and a risk of confusion, for there are no superfluous words or details in the book. It should be read; considering that it has been published so many years, very few, in proportion to its merit, can have had the benefit of it, or allusion to its subjects would be more frequent." Fuller sees parallels between the Greeks and the American Indians: "This pleasure in details marks the reality of their existence; whatever they had or did was significant. In this, as in so many other respects, they represent our Indians, softened by the atmosphere which a high civilization, though mostly forgotten, does not fail to leave behind, and a gentler clime. Whatever we can obtain from our aborigines has the same beauty as these ballads. Had we but as complete a collection as this!"[11]

The Influence of Fauriel's Collection upon Müller's Critical Writing and Poetry
It is to Müller's credit that he was the first to point out similarities
between Greek and Serbian folk poetry.[12] Müller had met personally
"Madame Talvj" (*Therese Albertine Luise Robinson*, née *von Jakob*,
1797–1870) and Jernej-Bartholomé Kopitar (1780–1844) and knew
their publications of Serbian folk poetry. He was the first to draw atten-
tion to the parallels between Bürger's "Leonore" and both a Greek folk
song in Fauriel's French collection ("Voyage Nocturne") and a Serbian
one translated by Mme. Talvj ("Die Brüder und die Schwester"). In his
1825 article "Bürgers 'Leonore' und ein neugriechisches Volkslied,"
Müller also discusses parallels between the German ballad and two Eng-
lish poems, "The Suffolk Miracle" and "Fair Margaret and Sweet Wil-
liam," and the Scottish poem "Sweet William's Ghost."

Müller's interest in the folk poetry and customs of the modern
Greeks is reflected also in the critical writing he did for several jour-
nals. For example, he published "Bilder aus dem neugriechischen
Volksleben—Die Kinderwelt, Brautwahl, Verlobung und Hochzeit" in
Morgenblatt für gebildete Stände in 1825. Müller reviewed not only the
Fauriel collection, but also French, English, and German translations of
modern Greek folk poetry.

The Greek texts inspired the poet in Müller; he freely drew upon
some of the untranslated neo-Greek poems, especially the two-line dis-
tichs, and created his own German versions, which he published in
several journals. These were collected under the title "Reime aus den
Inseln des Archipelagus" in his *Lyrische Reisen und epigrammatische
Spaziergänge* of 1827. Müller first translates the Greek text literally and
then re-forms it into his own German version. His literal translation of
one distich reads:

Hohe Zypresse, neige dich, damit ich zu dir spreche,
Zwei Worte nur hab ich für dich, nach diesen will ich sterben.[13]

These lines ultimately become the following:

Neige dich herab, Zypresse, nur zwei Worte sag' ich dir.
Sage dir: Ich lieb', und sterbe dann zu deinen Füssen hier.[14]

ITALIAN FOLK SONGS—*EGERIA*

Early Studies
During his stay in Italy (1817–1818), Müller studied the customs and
language of the Italian people. He transcribed the songs he heard in
the streets of Rome and in the Roman countryside. Several sections of
his Italian book *Rom, Römer und Römerinnen* are devoted to detailed

descriptions of Italian folk poetry and chapbooks. For the reader unfamiliar with the subject, Müller reproduces numerous Italian folk songs to clarify the meaning of his comments.

Müller writes of the "folk improvisers" (Improvisatoren des Volkes), who sing in the streets to anyone who will listen. Their themes are mainly those of love—courtship, rejection, separation, and the like.

> Die meisten Volkslieder verdanken ihren Ursprung solchen Improvisatoren. Es ist ein natürlicher und gerechter Vorzug der mündlichen Mittheilung, dass das Gedächtnis sie leichter auffasst und fester hält, als Geschriebenes und Gedrucktes, das ihm ja auf keine Weise entlaufen kann. . . .
>
> Wenn also ein Lied des Improvisators zu einer beliebten Melodie oder auch mit einer neuerfundenen dem Volke frisch und herzlich zusagt, so wird es flugs wiederholt und der Improvisator hilft wohl ein wenig nach. So klingt es im Munde der Leute fort, wächst und schmilzt zusammen, krümmt und wendet sich, bis es endlich seinen letzten Hauch in ein fliegendes Blatt verathmet. Ein gedrucktes Volkslied ist ein Leichenstein des erstorbenen Gesanges. So wird auch nie ein Lied durch den Druck zu Leben und Liebe unter dem Volke gelangen, aber der Gesang ist der Seelenwecker, der göttliche Bote, der das gefesselte Wort aus dem Reiche des Todes heraufführt an das himmlische Licht.[15]

Dante, Petrarch, Tasso, and others had been translated into German by the beginning of the nineteenth century, but the folk poetry of Italy had been neglected by both the Germans and the Italians themselves. At the time of Müller's Italian travels, there had been only three German publications on the subject. The song composer Johann Friedrich Reichardt had published several Italian folk melodies in his musical journal. Ritornelli and two short Italian poems had been included in *Altdeutsche Wälder* by the brothers Grimm. Johann Gustav Büsching had published articles about Italian folk songs and chapbooks.

In *Rom, Römer und Römerinnen* Müller writes: "Die eigentliche Volkspoesie der Italiener ist von Einheimischen und Fremden bisher mit Stolz und Gleichgültigkeit übersehen worden. Goethe regte zu genaueren Forschungen vergebens an, in seinen Fragmenten über italienischen Volksgesang. (S. Fragmente eines Reisejournals in Italien.)"[16]

It fell to Müller himself to produce the first significant collection of Italian folk songs, *Egeria*—the first in a long series of Italian and Italian-German collections which appeared during the nineteenth century.

Müller's Collection

Müller began his collection during his stay in Italy, with the intention of enlarging it into a supplement for his *Rom, Römer und Römerinnen*. While in Berlin during the spring of 1825, Müller met O. L. B. Wolff, who in 1826 was appointed professor at the Gymnasium in Weimar on Goethe's recommendation. Müller discussed Italian folk poetry with Wolff and was excited when Wolff promised to send him copies of some Roman ritornelli. Death prevented Müller from fulfilling his plans to publish his collection of Italian folk poetry. Wolff subsequently used Müller's manuscripts to publish the collection, enlarging it somewhat with songs that he had collected himself.

The 262 pages of *Egeria* contain six large sections of Italian folk poetry, eight pages of accompanying melodies, and a chart showing the major characteristics of the several Italian dialects. The first section of poetry, "Lieder in der Büchersprache und den unbedeutend von derselben abweichenden Mundarten des römischen und toskanischen Landvolks," contains thirty-two poems in various forms, including sestine, ritornello, ottaverime, canzonetta, and villanelle. The second section, "Geistliche Lieder," and the third section, "Politische Lieder," are grouped thematically as the titles indicate. The next section is very specific in content: "Römische Haus- und Lebensregeln für Stadt und Land." Chapbooks written in verse are found in the next section. The last and most extensive section includes poetry in dialects which differ greatly from the standard written Italian. One finds representative poems from Venice, Piedmont, Naples, Sardinia, and Sicily.

Reception of Egeria *and Its Place in the History of the Study of Italian Folk Poetry*

A reviewer in *Kunst und Alterthum, 1828,* expresses the hope that *Egeria* may inspire additional work in the field:

> Aus dieser mitgetheilten Übersicht nun lässt sich ersehn, dass ein Hauptzweck der Herausgabe darin bestand, durch treffende Beyspiele zu zeigen, welche Richtung der poetische Geist bey dem lebhaften italienischen Volke nahm, wie er sich nach den Eigenthümlichkeiten der verschiedenen Provinzen richtete und von denselben modificirt wurde, und welchen Einfluss die verschiedenen in den einzelnen Theilen Italiens vorherrschenden Lebensansichten darauf hatten.
>
> Und so möge sich denn diese Sammlung ähnlichen Bestrebungen anderer Völker bescheiden anschliessen.[17]

The reviewer's hope was fulfilled; the collection by Müller-Wolff was indeed only the first of many such collections and studies.

Nine years after the publication of *Egeria*, August Kopisch published his *Agrumi: Volksthümliche Poesien aus allen Mundarten Italiens und seiner Inseln* (1838), in the introduction of which he acknowledged the influence of Müller's *Egeria*. The first significant collection by an Italian did not appear until 1841, when Niccolo Tommaseo published a collection of Tuscan, Corsican, and Illyrian folk songs. In 1889 Paul Heyse writes in his *Italienische Dichter seit der Mitte des achtzehnten Jahrhunderts:* "Was wir besassen, verdankten wir zum grössten Theil zwei deutschen Dichtern [Müller and Kopisch], die das Volk in Italien lieb gewonnen hatten. Zunächst hatte Wilhelm Müller, der in seinen eigenen Liedern oft so glücklich den Volkston traf, auf einer Reise durch Italien überall auf den Volksgesang gelauscht und eine werthvolle Sammlung aus den verschiedenen Dialekten mit nach Hause gebracht." Other German scholars whose collections of Italian poetry appeared during the nineteenth century were Paul Heyse, Eduard Dorer-Egloss, Ferdinand Gregorovius, Georg Widter, Eduard Engel, and Woldemar Kaden.[18]

CHAPTER SIX

The Prose Writer

Italien wird mir auch in der Heimath unvergesslich bleiben. . . . Aber,
werd' ich darum mein Vaterland weniger lieben? Werd' ich es nicht im
Gegensatze desto tiefer erkennen und ergründen?[1]

Müller's prose was enriched by the months he spent in Italy, and his
memoir of this time, *Rom, Römer und Römerinnen*, was largely responsi-
ble for establishing his reputation as a writer. Near the end of his life,
Müller was encouraged by Ludwig Tieck to try his hand at the novel-
ette (*Novelle*) form. His first such attempt, *Der Dreizehnte*, uses the de-
parture of a young artist for a lengthy stay in Italy as the "frame" for
the story. Much of his second (and last) Novelle, *Debora*, is also set in
Italy. Although Müller was attracted to the "land where the lemons
bloom," he remained faithful to his own country; Italy was for him a
springboard for the imagination, not a utopia.

ROM, RÖMER UND RÖMERINNEN

Form and Content
Immediately upon returning to Dessau in January 1819, Müller began
working on a book about Italy. He wrote down his recollections in the
form of letters addressed to an imaginary friend in Germany. The Latin
motto from Horace (*Epistles* I, xi, ll. 20–30) on the title page expresses
the attitude of the young Italian visitor: "Quocunque loco fueris, vixisse
libenter Te dicas!" ("In whatever place you shall have been, may you say
that you have lived happily!") Müller certainly could say that he had
"lived happily." Not content to live in the German artist colony, he
sought out "his own Rome" among the Italian people. ("Gerade so geht
es den Reisenden aller Lande und aller Charaktere mit dem Zauber, der
sie unwiderstehlich an die Siebenhügelstadt fesselt. Jeder empfindet ihn
auf eigene Weise und sucht ihn sich danach zu erklären, und man
könnte sagen, dass Rom eben deswegen, trotz allen guten und
schlechten Beschreibungen und Abbildungen, ewig neu ist und bleiben
wird, weil wir alle gleichsam *unser eigenes Rom in Rom* finden.")[2]
  Müller devoted much time to observing the "living" Italy; he experi-
enced Italian daily life and customs firsthand. Friedrich Noack, the

German author of two books on German life in Italy, views Wilhelm Müller and some of his contemporaries as "modern spirits," who saw Italy through eyes different from those of casual tourists: "Diese modernen Geister beschäftigten sich nicht nur mit Ruinen, malerischen Lumpen und der Kunst vergangener Zeiten, sondern auch mit der politischen und sozialen Lage, mit den nationalen Bestrebungen und Freiheitshoffnungen des zerrissenen und geknechteten italienischen Volkes." Müller's "Rome book" was not intended to be an ordinary Italian travel guide (which often reads like a classical art catalogue). Instead, his introduction promises the reader a glimpse into "hidden" sides of Italian life and customs: "Meine Nachrichten sollen zunächst einer genauen Darstellung des italienischen Lebens und Webens gewidmet seyn. . . . Ich will mich bemühen, der viel gezeichneten und gemalten Stadt manche versteckte Seite abzugewinnen, oder doch den bekannten Gegenständen in neuer Verbindung und Beleuchtung den Reiz erster Überraschung zu leihen." Müller makes no promise of completeness, for he is describing a "living people" from his own observations—a job with no end: "Auf Vollständigkeit und Erschöpfung mache ich keinen Anspruch: die Darstellung eines lebenden Volkes ist an und für sich unendlich. . . . Wo aber zu berichtigen ist, will ich lieber erzählen, was ich gesehen und gehört, als mit Anderer Augen und Ohren rechten."[3]

Volume I of *Rom, Römer und Römerinnen* is dedicated to Count Friedrich von Kalckreuth (1790–1873) and Ludwig Sigismund Ruhl (1794–1867) with whom Müller spent time in Rome. Volume II is addressed to the Swedish scholar and writer Per Daniel Amadeus Atterbom (1790–1855), with whom he had shared living quarters in Albano during the summer of 1818. Müller also mentions a friend (the poet Friedrich Rückert [1788–1866]), who lived in Ariccia and who collected ritornelli.

In *Rom, Römer und Römerinnen*, Müller discusses everything from the courting customs of the Italians to government censorship. The German colony in Rome, the artists known as the Nazarenes, Italian rhymed jokes, the notorious Roman summer humidity, sexual mores, the various folk festivals, street robbers, escorts of married women, Italian marketplaces, Italian theater and opera, superstitions, religious customs, gardens, Italian chapbooks, and folk songs—all are among the numerous topics discussed in a light, entertaining style. The following description of a boisterous evening at the tavern where Goethe's "Fünfzehnte Elegie" was set is an example of that style. Müller opens his anecdote with two lines from the Goethe elegy:

> Und von heut' an seyd mir noch schöner gegrüsset,
> > ihr Schenken,
> Osterieen, wie euch schicklich der Römer benennt!

Eine Tradition unter den deutschen Malern hat den Namen der Osterie aufbewahrt, in welcher Goethe das anmuthige Abentheuer erlebte, das er in der fünfzehnten römischen Elegie beschrieben hat. Die Osterie trägt das Zeichen einer *goldenen Glocke* und liegt auf dem Platze am *Theater des Marzellus*, unfern dem *Ghetto degli Ebrei*. Heute wanderte eine Gesellschaft fröhlicher Deutscher nach dieser Schenke, vielleicht mit so klassischer Begeisterung, als ob ihre unscheinbaren Mauern die Überbleibsel einer antiken *Popina* oder *Taberna* wären. Der Oste hatte eine Normalgestalt und stand mit eingestemmten Armen neben dem grünen Baume vor seiner Halle, die uns mit ihren nackten schwarzen Steinwänden und unbehobelten Tafeln und Bänken nicht abschreckte. Wir ordneten uns nach Burschenbrauch an einem Tische, der Präses las die römischen Elegieen, und der Wein mundete köstlich auf die Gesundheit des grossen, lieben Meisters. Wer uns den Ort gezeigt hätte, wo er gesessen, und den Fleck, wo der verschüttete Wein hingeflossen, der wäre uns heute *magnus Apollo* gewesen.[4]

The poem which Müller composed to commemorate the occasion follows the above passage and is his first known "drinking song"—"Goethe's Osterie in Rom."

Müller's Political Motivation for Writing the Book

Müller explains that the tense political situation in Europe is a strong motivation for him to write a book about the more carefree life in Italy. Müller sees the ruins of Rome as a lesson in world history. The past should serve as a warning for the present and the future: "Woher diese traurig ernsten Betrachtungen in dem lustigen Rom? Die Ruinen lehren Weltgeschichte, mein Freund, und die Vergangenheit beleuchtet Gegenwärtiges und Zukünftiges mit warnender Fackel."[5]

Müller believes that in such bad times one must either act or mourn. Müller's actions are his writings, specifically *Rom, Römer und Römerinnen*, the second volume of which is introduced with a bold statement addressed to Atterbom: "Und somit grüsse ich Sie in Ihrem altheiligen Vaterlande [Sweden], nicht wie das Buch, dessen Schreiber mir fremd geworden ist, scherzend und spielend; nein, ernst und kurz; denn die grosse Fastenzeit der europäischen Welt, der Marterwoche entgegensehend und harrend auf Erlösung, verträgt kein gleichgültiges Achselzucken und keine flatterhaften Vermittelungen und Entschuldigungen. Wer in dieser Zeit nicht handeln kann, der kann doch ruhen und trauern."[6]

The Reception of the Book

Müller's *Rom, Römer und Römerinnen* was widely reviewed and sold many copies. Müller writes Atterbom: "Mein Büchlein über *Rom* findet viel Beifall, und wie ich höre, auch Absatz."[7] Favorable reviews appeared in several journals including one in Vienna. An unfavorable review was written by Adolf Müllner, who was still annoyed about the literary debate he had had with Müller in 1817.

Although the book was successful, some readers objected to Müller's light and playful descriptions of Roman customs, especially those relating to courtship, marriage, and sex. It was felt that such matters should be treated only in a lofty, moralizing tone, or (better still) should not be discussed at all.[8]

While he was in Florence, the poet Friedrich von Matthisson read a copy of the newly published *Rom, Römer und Römerinnen* (which a traveler had brought with him over the Alps from Germany) and found it both interesting and accurate. "Ebenso wüsste ich auch ausser Goethe Niemand, der die römische Volkswelt lebendiger und naturgetreuer (wie aus dem Spiegel) dargestellt hätte als der Verfasser des mit allgemeinem Beifall gekrönten Werks über *Rom, Römer und Römerinnen*. Ich las es mit lebhaftem Interesse zuerst in Florenz, wohin es ein Reisender mit über die Alpen gebracht hatte."[9]

The New Editions (1956 in Bremen and 1978 in East Berlin)
Christel Matthias Schröder edited and revised *Rom, Römer und Römerinnen* for a new edition which was published in Bremen in 1956— 136 years after the first edition appeared.[10] This new Bremen edition contains detailed notes which explain Italian terms and references to classical literature and obscure nineteenth-century figures. Drawings by Franz Catel (1778–1856) depicting scenes of nineteenth-century Italian life and customs are also included.

The Bremen edition is not a scholarly version, nor was it so intended; the book was prepared with a wider audience in mind. Much of Müller's supplementary material is therefore omitted. The editor explains: "Im Hinblick darauf, dass die Erneuerung von Wilhelm Müllers Italienbuch nicht literarhistorischen Zwecken dienen, sondern einem aufgeschlossenen weiteren Leserkreis zugute kommen soll, konnte auf diese Beigaben durchaus verzichtet werden."[11] Schröder finds the book historically valuable as a record of a perceptive young German's impressions of Rome in 1818 and believes that a modern tourist will acknowledge Müller's success in describing many of the timeless characteristics of the country and its capital city. "Auf der anderen Seite jedoch wird der Italienreisende unserer Tage, wenn er tiefer einzudringen sich bemüht, erkennen, dass Wilhelm Müller bei seinen Schilderungen mit glücklicher Hand eine Fülle bleibender Wesenszüge getroffen und dass vor allen Dingen die Ewige Stadt, trotz ihrem äusseren und inneren Anders-geworden-Sein [*sic*], nichts von jenem Zauber eingebüsst hat, der damals den Dichter so überwältigend und nachhaltig gefangennahm."[12]

In addition to the Bremen version of the work, another edition appeared in the German Democratic Republic in 1978 during the one hundred and fiftieth anniversary of Müller's death. This version, which was edited by Wulf Kirsten, includes a portrait of the author and thirty-two engravings from the period when young Müller recorded his impressions of Rome and the Romans (1818).

DER DREIZEHNTE

Conception, Publication, and Reception

During his student days Müller had experimented briefly with writing fictional prose in his retelling of the story of the troubadour Geoffrey Rudel. He showed a copy of his story to Luise Hensel, who was pleased by the work. Then for several years he lost interest in this type of writing and devoted his efforts to poetry and critical writing. His conversations with Ludwig Tieck, however, revived his interest in writing fictional prose. On October 20, 1824, Müller informed Brockhaus that in several months he would like to submit a Novelle, a work which he had been contemplating for some time and which he had often discussed with Tieck: "Dann möchte ich aber auch eine Novelle liefern, mit der ich mich schon lange herumtrage, und über deren Ausarbeitung ich mit Tieck schon oft verhandelt habe. Diese könnten Sie aber freilich erst im April oder Mai nächsten Jahres erhalten. Der Titel ist: *Der Dreizehnte*."[13]

The work, of which Müller was openly boastful, was submitted to Brockhaus over a year later on December 7, 1825. It appeared in Brockhaus's popular literary anthology *Urania, 1827,* which (according to the usual practice) appeared in 1826. *Der Dreizehnte* was an instant success. Müller writes Brockhaus that the editor of almost every literary anthology has requested Novellen from him. ("Fast alle Redaktoren von deutschen Taschenbüchern haben sich Novellen bei mir bestellt.")[14] Wilhelm Hauff, the editor of *Das Morgenblatt* and a representative of the Cotta publishing firm (Brockhaus's competition), promised to better any offer Müller had for a future Novelle: "Sie erhalten bei mir stets einen Dukaten mehr, als Ihnen irgendwo anders geboten wird."[15]

Der Dreizehnte pleased the readership of *Urania*. The Novelle shows the influence of Tieck in its structure and of E. T. A. Hoffmann in its mood and characterizations. But, although there are some effective moments in the story, it is by modern standards melodramatic and contrived.

The Plot

Der Dreizehnte opens with a scene reminiscent of the *Serapionsbrüder* of E. T. A. Hoffmann: a group of young intellectuals is gathered in a Berlin tavern late on a humid, stormy July evening. The occasion is a farewell party for a young artist, Sölling, who is to depart that evening for Italy as the twelfth passenger in the post chaise. The topic of conversation turns to various superstitions surrounding the number thirteen, and the artist relates the sad story of his brother Bernhard—the un-happy thirteenth child in the family. From childhood the unusual boy had been a troublemaker. Every time the number twelve was mentioned, Bernhard would scream, "And I am the Thirteenth!" This habit soon became part of his nature and led to an unfortunate incident in which Bernhard's young friend was wounded in the head when a teacher threw a Bible at Bernhard, hitting instead the younger pupil, the teacher's own son. As a result of this incident, the elderly teacher suffered a heart attack, and Bernhard disappeared without leaving a trace.

The "fate" motif common during the first decades of nineteenth-century German literature plays a role in Müller's Novelle. After relating his story, the artist boards the post chaise. Out of the darkness materializes a thirteenth passenger—the long-lost brother, who tells the story of his flight from the superstition he himself has helped to perpetuate. In a small coastal town Bernhard had been engaged to a lovely girl, but a fortuneteller had warned the girl to avoid the "Thirteenth." Bernhard departed without explanation. The artist-brother advises Bernhard to return to his beloved. He does so. Unfortunately, his financée has since become ill, and Bernhard's unexpected return precipitates her death. In his despair, Bernhard falls from a bell tower just as it strikes the hour of twelve.

The "frame" of the Novelle is completed as it ends back in the tavern with Sölling relating to his friends the last details of his brother's unhappy fate.

DEBORA

Conception, Publication, and Reception

After his success with *Der Dreizehnte*, Müller soon began a second Novelle—one which was much better written. Müller submitted *Debora* to Brockhaus on February 14, 1827, but it did not appear until after his death, in *Urania, 1828*. (Müller thought it wiser to have Brockhaus publish it than to accept higher payment from another firm, thereby jeopardizing his cordial relationship with Brockhaus.)

The characters' actions in *Debora* are better motivated and more natural than in *Der Dreizehnte*, and their speech mannerisms more clearly reveal them as individuals. Paul Heyse decided to include *Debora* in his *Deutscher Novellenschatz*, because he felt that, despite its weaknesses, the work showed promise:

Auf der Neige seines kurzen Lebens versuchte sich Müller auch in der Novelle, aber die Frist war ihm nicht gegönnt, sich zu der vollen Selbstständigkeit zu entwickeln, die er auch auf diesem Gebiete zu erringen der Mann gewesen wäre. . . . Die jüngere der beiden Novellen, die er hinterlassen hat, . . . weist trotz eines ungemeinen Fortschritts Elemente auf, die ihrem Dichter nicht eigen sind: zu Anfang begegnen Züge, die man kaum anders als trivial nennen kann, . . . und weiterhin zeigt sie sich von dem romantischen, katholisierenden Geiste der Zeit beherrscht. Allein dessenungeachtet verräth das ganze Gefüge der Erfindung eine immer bedeutender hervortretende Kraft, die den künftigen Meister ankündigt; und so glaubten wir es nicht bloss dem schönen Dichternamen, den sie vertritt, sondern der Erzählung selbst in ihren Hauptbestandtheilen schuldig zu sein, sie dem Kreise auserlesener Novellen einzureihen.[16]

The Plot

The structure of *Debora* is complicated. The "frame" story surrounds a mysterious tale of love, intrigue, murder, and religious intolerance, told through a series of flashbacks and letters interspersed in the narrative. Arthur, a young Berlin medical student, accompanies a wealthy, old, eccentric Marquis on a trip to Rome.

Upon arriving in Rome, the travelers hear of the discovery of the strangled corpse of a young Spanish Catholic near the Jewish ghetto. Leaflets containing a ballad are being circulated in Rome. The ballad tells how the murdered youth had converted a beautiful Jewish girl to Christianity, thereby incurring the wrath of her murderous father. It gradually comes out that this recent murder in Rome is connected to the secret story of the Marquis's past. The forced recollection of the sad memories causes the Marquis to suffer a fatal heart attack in the street during the Roman carnival. Arthur subsequently learns that as a young man the Marquis (who was in Spain during the French Revolution) had loved Debora, the wife of a Jewish merchant. A Spanish noblewoman in love with the Marquis had betrayed the beautiful Debora to the Spanish Inquisition, causing her death. Profound feelings of guilt led the Marquis to become a recluse, dedicating his life to the memory of the woman he had loved.

Fate again plays a role in Müller's second Novelle. The murdered youth was the son of the Spanish noblewoman who had betrayed Debora. The young Jewish girl (also named Debora) is none other than the daughter of the first Debora, reared in isolation by her father after her mother's death. The old Jew murders the youth upon learning of his despised parentage. Later, discovering his daughter in prayer before a crucifix, he fatally stabs her, causing a noise which brings the police, who apprehend him. The daughter dies in a Catholic hospital after receiving the last rites of the Catholic Church. Arthur, deeply moved by the whole experience, ultimately converts to Catholicism and enters a monastery.

Autobiographical Aspects of Debora

Arthur, the young hero of the Novelle, resembles Müller himself on his journey to Rome with Baron von Sack. Both Arthur and Müller were gifted students at the University of Berlin who appeared unwilling to specialize in one particular field of endeavor. Professors advised both to seize the opportunity of the Italian journey, since the likelihood that their studies would lead to the completion of the academic program was not great.

Müller's description of Arthur's childhood also matches his own: "Arthur, von seinen frühesten Jahren an, als einziges von mehreren Geschwistern übrig gebliebenes Kind, verzogen und gelehrt sich zu überschätzen, hatte einen hartnäckigen Sinn, wenn es darauf ankam, seine Ansichten, Grundsätze und Urtheile über Gegenstände des Lebens und der Kunst geltend zu machen, und so leicht sein Herz sich rühren liess, eben so schwer hielt es, seinen Kopf zu bewegen."[17] The headstrong Müller and the equally determined Arthur also had differences of opinion with their older traveling companions.

There has been speculation as to whether the love of the young Christian Arthur for a Jewish girl reflects a personal experience in the life of Wilhelm Müller, whose childhood home was located within sight of the Dessau synagogue. Such a relationship might also have inspired the cycle "Johannes und Esther" in *Waldhornistenlieder I*.[18] H. W. Behrisch, a calligraphy instructor at the Dessau school that Müller attended, has been cited as the model for the unusual figure of the Marquis.[19]

Müller's avid interest in the life and writings of Lord Byron is reflected in Arthur, who reads *Childe Harold*. Also visible in *Debora* are Müller's fascination with Italian customs, the Roman carnival, and Italian folk poetry. Finally, both Arthur and Müller lived in the Via Sistina in Rome.

CHAPTER SEVEN

The Philhellene

Ohne die Freiheit, was wärest du, Hellas?
Ohne dich, Hellas, was wäre die Welt?[1]

The Philhellenic Movement
After Napoleon's defeat the reactionary policies of Austria's Prince
Metternich were the model for other European political leaders. Met-
ternich's principle of "legitimacy"—the support of rule by hereditary
right—was used as an excuse to impose stringent codes of censorship
upon any who would advocate the principle of "national self-determi-
nation." When the nationalistic uprising of the Greeks against their
Turkish rulers began in March 1821, repercussions were felt all over
Europe. "Thus the policies of Metternich's European 'Concert' of
powers were shattered by the combined forces of Liberalism and Na-
tionalism. The principle of 'legitimacy' received its deathblow when
Metternich, in the course of the Greek War of Independence (1821–
1829), expressed his sympathies for the cause of the Turkish sultan,
condemning the Greeks for their rebellion against their 'legitimate'
ruler."[2]

European sympathizers with the Greek cause had various motivations.
Among the most common were a desire for political freedom in all of
Europe; religious fervor aroused by the "heathen" Muslims' oppression
of Christians in Greece; and a love of the ancient Greek culture.

The philhellenic movement in Europe has been examined in several
thorough studies. The author of one such work explains his own attrac-
tion to the subject: "The philhellenism of the early nineteenth century
deserves detailed investigation because it is one of the very clear in-
stances of a meeting-point between literature and action. Impressions
derived from literature (which we can easily study) provoked certain
sentiments and opinions (which can be clearly defined), and these senti-
ments and opinions prompted actions (which can be a matter of direct
historical investigation)."[3]

The author of the entry "Philhellenismus" in the *Reallexikon der
deutschen Literaturgeschichte* views the lyrics of Müller and other German
philhellenes as a bridge between the poetry of the War of Liberation
and the July Revolution of 1830: "Am augenfälligsten und zugleich am
besten durch Wilhelm Müllers 'Lieder der Griechen' (1821–1824) ver-
treten, erscheint sie [die Lyrik] geschichtlich als eine nicht unwichtige

Phase im Werdegang unserer politischen Dichtung zwischen den . . . nationalen Liedern der Befreiungskrieger, Burschen, Turner und der durch Polenkult und die ganze Stufenleiter oppositioneller Gesinnung gekennzeichnete Lyrik diesseits der Juli-Revolution."[4]

Müller's Role in the Movement

Like many of his idealistic countrymen, the volunteer Müller had fought against Napoleon, only to be bitterly disappointed later by the political policies adopted during and after the Congress of Vienna. From Italy he observed the political developments in Germany with a growing feeling of despair. Upon returning to Germany, Müller saw that the "times were moving backwards" and that the ideals for which he and his comrades had fought were being betrayed. He writes candidly to the conservative aristocrat Baron de la Motte Fouqué:

> Was geschehen ist, kann nicht ungeschehen gemacht werden, und der Kongress von Laibach wird eine Seite der künftigen Weltgeschichte füllen, von der der freie, fromme Mann seufzend zurückblicken wird, ob auch das Wort *heilig* oft darauf vorkömmt. So mein' ich's, *ich kann nicht anders!*—Was sagen Sie zu Österreich? Da will man, wie es scheint, die Welt *retour schrauben*, wie es in *Prinz Zerbino* mit dem Schauspiel geschieht. Geht es mit dieser Maschinerie so rüstig fort, wie man anfängt, so kommt man nächstens zu der Inquisition und den Autodafé's etc. zurück. Und der Kaiser gab seine Stimme zur Verbannung seines Schwiegersohnes nach St. Helena—weil—ei, wesswegen [sic] doch?
>
> Seyn Sie mir nicht böse, weil ich *bitter* bin. Ich wollte lieber ein Loblied, als eine Satyre auf die Zeit schreiben. Aber—*ich kann nicht anders.* Ich habe mit *gekämpft*, drum steht's mir zu, auch mit zu *klagen* und zu *zürnen.*—Ich weiss, Sie haben ein festeres Vertrauen auf die Machthaber der Zeit, und ich möchte Sie darum beneiden.[5]

One reason that Müller could be as vocal as he was about politics was that he enjoyed the favor of the Duke of Anhalt, whose rule was not as oppressive as that in other duchies and countries. Although Müller felt fortunate to be a citizen of Anhalt, he was depressed by the backsliding of a Germany to which he felt an allegiance: "Wenn das kleine Anhalt meine Blicke beschränkt, so kann auch ich mich glücklich preisen, unter der Regierung eines guten, lieben Fürsten zu stehn, der seine Unterthanen leicht übersehen kann und daher ihre Bedürfnisse und Wünsche versteht und nach Kräften erfüllt. Aber ich fühle freilich nur zu oft, dass ich nicht bloss *Anhaltiner*, sondern auch *Deutscher* bin—und da seufz' ich!"[6]

Müller supported the Greeks in the hope that their struggle for freedom might help turn the tide of European politics.

> Von den Welthändeln will ich schweigen. Unwille und Wehmuth ergreift mich, wenn ich an sie denke. Gen Morgen nur schau' ich. Sollte auch die Sonne der griechischen Freiheit wieder untergehen, so ist doch ihr

Emporflammen, wenn es auch das letzte ist, für die Menschheit erhebend. Auch viele deutsche Jünglinge ziehen aus, um für die grosse Sache der Griechen mit zu kämpfen. Wer weiss aber, ob die Fürsten ihnen freien Abmarsch gestatten werden. Pfui! über die hundsvöttische Zeit![7]

Although activities on behalf of the Greeks were officially forbidden by the government, isolated voices called out for the German people to adopt the cause of the beleaguered Greeks. The voice of Wilhelm Müller was, if not the first, certainly one of the loudest and most effective to be heard. When the tide of battle seemed to have turned against the Greeks, others became silent. Müller, however, continued to write enthusiastically for the cause. Many wrote about the Greek War of Independence, but Müller is the only one whose works survived past the occasion of their conception (e.g., "Der kleine Hydriot" and "Alexander Ypsilanti"). The nickname "Griechen-Müller" bears testimony to the degree to which his name came to be associated with the cause. One authority on German philhellenism writes:

Wilhelm Müller . . . steht unter den Philhellenen wie Gleim unter den militärisch-patriotischen Dichtern, wie Gerstenberg unter den Barden, als Charakterkopf unter Durchschnittsgesichtern, als beinahe einzige Erhöhung auf unbegrenzter Steppe. Mit dem reichen Erbgute klassischer und romantischer Dichtung ausgestattet, hat er doch mit eigenstem Gesang den Besten seiner Zeit wie dem Volke genuggethan, als politischer Dichter bestimmend auf den Lauf der Literaturgeschichte eingewirkt.[8]

Müller's sympathy for the Greeks, which was largely predicated upon his own desire for personal freedom and his liberal political views, was reinforced by his extensive training in classical philology and his acquaintance with leaders of the Greek independence movement, the Philikí Etairía (Hetaireia), in Vienna in 1817. Müller's letters to friends reveal his dedication to the Greek cause. For example, in a letter to Matthisson on April 13, 1822, he enthusiastically calls the revolt a "holy matter" to which he is committed with his "entire soul":

Ihre innige Theilnahme für meine Griechenlieder ist mir um so erfreulicher, da Sie mir auch Ihre Theilnahme für die heilige Sache, der sie gewidmet sind, verbürgt, eine Sache, der ich mit ganzer Seele angehöre, die Sache des Christenthums, der Humanität, der Freyheit, gegen Heidenthum, Barbarey und Tyranney. Wenn ich je den Beystand der Muse mit Inbrunst angerufen habe, so ist es jetzt, und ich könnte wol [sic] das Shakespearische Motto über meine Griechenlieder setzen: *O for a Muse of fire, that would ascend!* [Shakespeare, *Henry V*, Prologue, line 1][9]

A year later, at a low point in the Greek struggle, Müller writes Fouqué that he will remain true to the Greeks, even though all others may waver (and the cause may be in vain): "Meinen Griechen bleibe ich treu, ob Alle wanken."[10]
Another example of Müller's sincerity is to be found in a letter writ-

ten to his Swedish friend Atterbom in May 1822, in which Müller
declares that if he weren't married (and the father of a two-week-old
baby), he might well have joined those Germans who sailed to Greece
to participate in the fighting. ("Wär' ich ledig, vielleicht ständ' ich jetzt
bewaffnet in Griechenland.")[11]

Müller's fifty-two *Griechenlieder* appeared in several pamphlets be-
tween 1821 and 1826. Their publication was complicated by constant
difficulties with government censorship. Despite the problems with the
censors, Müller persisted in publishing these stirring calls for support
of the Greek cause against the Turks.

Die Griechenlieder

The change in tone from the *Waldhornistenlieder* to the *Griechenlieder* is
striking. Müller's verse prologue to the first pamphlet, *Lieder der
Griechen* (1821), makes his motive for writing the poems clear: he is
challenging the "friends of the Greeks" to respond to the plight of the
descendants of the greats of antiquity. The prologue bears the title
"Die Griechen an die Freunde ihres Alterthums":

> Sie haben viel geschrieben, gesungen und gesagt,
> Gepriesen und bewundert, beneidet und beklagt.
> Die Namen unsrer Väter, sie sind von schönem Klang,
> Sie passen allen Völkern in ihren Lobgesang;
> . . . .
> Was schwärmt ihr in den Fernen der grauen Heldenzeit?
> Kehrt heim, ihr Hochentzückten!—der Weg ist gar zu weit.
> Das Alt' ist neu geworden, die Fern' ist euch so nah,
> Was ihr erträumt so lange, leibhaftig steht es da,
> Es klopft an eure Pforte—ihr schliesst ihm euer Haus—
> Sieht es denn gar so anders, als ihr es träumtet, aus?[12]

As time passed Müller grew more bold; his cautious pleas for sup-
port of the Greeks became unqualified demands. In "Meine Muse"
(1823) Müller explains why he has laid aside the shepherd's flute and
taken up the "war trumpet" (Roman *tuba*) of battle.

> "Und willst du, meine Muse, denn gar zur Megära werden?
> Du sangst noch jüngst im stillen Hain den Hirten und den
>   Heerden,
> Und nun schwingst eine Geissel du laut durch die lauten
>   Gassen,
> Und sprühest Flammen um dich her—Ich weiss dich nicht
>   zu fassen."
> Du fragst? Siehst du die Hirten nicht nach scharfen Eisen
>   greifen?

Siehst statt der Lämmer Wölfe nicht Arkadien durchstreifen?
Siehst in Epirus Felsen nicht die Weiber Schwerter wetzen?
Siehst du auf Sparta's Fluren nicht die Kinder Tiger hetzen?
Da musst' ich Hirtensängerin mein Haferrohr zerbrechen,
Und, wie's die scharfe Zeit gebeut, in scharfen Tönen
    sprechen.
Der Freiheit Tuba hab' ich hell durch Stadt und Land
    geblasen:
Lass meine Geissel nun um's Haupt der Pharisäer rasen![13]

Müller's Greek poems were the product of strong emotions. Once he wrote Brockhaus that he could concentrate on nothing else for three days: "Endlich hat sich die Griechenmuse bei mir eingestellt, und zwar mit solchem Empressement, dass ich in drei Tagen nichts Anderes habe denken, fühlen und schreiben können—als Hymnen der Freiheit. Heute bin ich gerade so weit gediehen, dass zu einem Hefte (wie die bei Ackermann) Materialien zum Druck bereit liegen. . . . Da dergleichen Poetisch-Politische Waare warm genossen werden muss, so eile ich Ihnen eins zur Probe zu schicken."[14]

The majority of the *Griechenlieder* are supposedly spoken by representatives of the Greek people. Just as he used roles in his poetry in the folk-song style, Müller now puts his words in the mouths of Greek patriots. He does not hide behind these roles, however; there is never any doubt that Müller is here expressing his own liberal political opinions. In a letter to Atterbom Müller writes that he hopes his own voice will be heard in the poems: "Auch halte ich die beiden Hefte meiner *Griechenlieder* . . . gewisser Massen für eine Unterhaltung mit Ihnen, und zwar für eine Unterhaltung über eine Angelegenheit, die uns Beide jetzt tiefer und kräftiger berührt, als Alles, was sonst wohl der Gegenstand unsrer gegenseitigen brieflichen Mittheilungen war. Meine Muse ist keine Heuchlerin, und so hoffe ich, dass Sie in meinen Griechenliedern nicht allein die *Griechen*, sondern auch *mich* vernehmen werden."[15]

The several pamphlets and individual printings of Müller's Greek poems sold many copies in Germany and Austria. They were even carried to Greece by German philhellenes who had joined the Greek forces. "Einer meiner Landsleute und Schulkameraden ist jetzt in *Navarino*. . . . Neulich ist ein Brief von ihm nach *Dessau* gelangt, der auch die Nachricht enthält, dass meine *Griechenlieder* unter den deutschen Kreuzfahrern in Griechenland nicht unbekannt sind, und also wohl auch den *Griechen* selbst zu Augen und zu Herzen kommen werden."[16]

Schwab describes the emotional reception of the *Griechenlieder* in Germany: "Die *Griechenlieder* wurden in ganz Deutschland mit einem Jubel aufgenommen, mit welchem man in der Poesie nur ein Kind der Unsterblichkeit begrüsst."[17] From Stuttgart Müller received comments from the poet Friedrich von Matthisson about the enthusiastic reception of the poems.

> Empfangen Sie meinen wärmsten Dank für das köstliche Geschenk Ihrer Griechengesänge, über die es im Publicum und in den Zeitschriften nur Eine Stimme gibt, nämlich die des gerechtesten Beifalls. Zum Beweise, welche Sensation die "Lieder der Griechen" hier in Stuttgart hervorbrachten, nur Folgendes: Am Morgen nach der Ankunft der ersten Exemplare in unsern Buchhandlungen, lagen gegen zwanzig Abschriften von dem herrlichen "Empor! empor!" auf dem Lesetisch unsers Museums. Von den tiefen Eindrücken, welche diese Gesänge voll Kraft, Feuer und Leben beim Vorlesen hervorbringen, haben mich mehrere Erfahrungen überzeugt.[18]

Reviews in journals were favorable. One reviewer in the *Literarisches Konversationsblatt, 1821,* describes the language of the poems as that of "holy anger": "Nur aus der reinsten und würdigsten Gesinnung können Lieder hervorgehen wie diese, herzzerreissend, gross, tief und herrlich, frei und kühn, wie der Bergstrom sich die Bahn bricht, nach dem Lichte gewendet wie der Aar, der die Sonnenbahn durchwogt. . . . Sprache des heiligen Zornes und der tiefsten, glühendsten Wehmut."[19]

Ludwig Tieck, a personal friend of Müller's, writes enthusiastically to him in Dessau upon receipt of the stirring patriotic poems:

> Mein geliebter Freund; mit dem innigsten Dank, und mit Rührung erfüllt, sende ich Ihnen diese Lieder [*Die Griechenlieder*], ein rühmliches Denkmal eines eben so schönen Herzens, als Talentes zurück. So müssen in diesen bedrängten Zeiten, Dichter, Priester, Redner, Theater, alle zusammentreten, und die bedrohte, noch freie kleine Welt durch Wort und Kraft begeistern. Sie haben schon das Ihrige beigetragen, und es wird gewiss nicht ohne Erfolg sein. Ich habe die schönen Lieder nicht ohne Thränen lesen können, der ich sonst nicht zu den Leichtgerührten gehöre.

Another friend and poet, Gustav Schwab, felt that Müller had invented something new in the *Griechenlieder,* whereas he had borrowed much from others in the *Waldhornistenlieder.*[20]

The bombastic rhetoric of the *Griechenlieder* did not appeal to everyone, however. Some critics felt that poets should not enter the political arena. Others objected on purely aesthetic grounds to the monotony of theme found in the poems. Another criticism of the *Griechenlieder* was made by the noted dramatist and poet Friedrich Hebbel, who turns Müller's own imagery of the flute and tuba against the rhetoric of the Griechen-Müller: "Wilhelm Müller hat viel eigenthümlicher von Wein und Liebe, als von der Befreiung Griechenlands gesungen, ja er verwandelt sich fast augenblicklich in einen Rhetoriker, wenn er die Flöte bei Seite legt und nach der Tuba greift, und redet dann, statt zu blasen."[21]

Despite their faults (or perhaps even because of some of them),

Müller's *Griechenlieder* contributed to the rise of nationalistic feeling and the eventual downfall of the Metternich philosophy of government based on "legitimacy." The words of Müller and others called forth actions; Germans joined the Greek forces. Money was raised by the educated and aristocratic; political pressures were brought to bear. In "Die neuen Kreuzfahrer" Müller states clearly his purpose in writing:

> Hervor, ihr Ritter allzumal! Hervor aus allen Ecken!
> Mein Lied soll eurer Thaten Ruf mit hellem Klang erwecken.
> Hervor, der du mit frechem Mund die Freiheit nennst Empörung,
> Und der Hellenen Heldenkampf bejammerst als Bethörung![22]

Wilhelm Müller on Lord Byron

The critic Wilhelm Müller was as much a philhellene as Müller the poet. His critical writings were to a great extent responsible for Byron's enthusiastic reception in Germany and had a marked influence upon subsequent German "Byronic literature." Müller wrote four works about Byron: a critique of the English poet's poetry (*Urania, 1822*); a eulogy published after his death in 1824; a review of the literature published about him (1825); and an extensive biography (1826). A noticeable change in Müller's attitude toward the English philhellene took place during the five years (1821–1826) in which these articles were written.

In 1821 Müller wrote a lengthy article on the poetry of Lord Byron, "Kritik Lord Byrons als Dichter," in which he expressed some ambivalence in his evaluation of him. While Müller recognized Byron's genius, he was repelled by the scandals in the poet's private life. He pointed out several weaknesses in Byron's poetry and admonished those who worshipped him blindly. Müller writes: "Lord Byron ist vielleicht das grösste und fruchtbarste, aber auch das gefährlichste Dichtergenie unsers Zeitalters."[23]

Much of the *Urania, 1822* article was based on materials from English sources, which Müller either reworded or simply translated. He indicated his sources to make his indebtedness clear, but Brockhaus deleted the acknowledgment without Müller's consent, much to the author's distress. One phrase in the article on Byron caused a long battle with the Austrian censor. Müller's English source had described Marie Louise (the daughter of Emperor Francis I of Austria who became the second wife of Napoleon) as "proud Austria's mournful flower." Müller repeated the metaphor. The result was that the 1822 volume of *Urania* was banned throughout Austria. When Brockhaus objected, he was informed that he should be thankful that only the *Urania, 1822* had been banned and not all Brockhaus publications. The prohibition remained in effect for more than a year. When it was finally lifted, *Urania, 1823* was already on the market.[24]

Müller's reservations about Byron were forgotten in his admiration for the poet's actions in behalf of the Greek cause. The news of his death (April 19, 1824) affected Müller greatly; his elegy on the "martyred" Byron, "Siebenunddreissig Trauerschüsse? Und wen haben sie gemeint?" eulogizes the poet as a fighter against the hypocrisy of the political leaders of Europe. Within the year Müller's moving poem had been translated into English (by Lord Francis Leveson Gower, the second son of the Duke of Sutherland) for Byron's English admirers. It was published in 1826 and 1833 in England.

In the 1825 article in the *Allgemeine Literatur-Zeitung* of Halle (no. 206), Müller reviewed eight English works about Byron. The article did much to publicize in Germany the English materials about the life of the poet.

When Müller accepted the assignment to write an extensive biography of Byron for *Zeitgenossen* on June 20, 1824, he made it clear to Brockhaus that the article would take considerable research and time. ("Die Biographie kann aber nicht übereilt werden. Nach dem Vielen, was schon über Byron geschrieben ist, kann nur eine mit Benutzung aller Quellen sorgfältig gearbeitete Biographie Werth haben.")[25] During the next eight months Müller worked industriously, rejecting other writing assignments. He wrote Brockhaus that a less conscientious author might well take a shorter period of time to complete the task, but that he wished to do a thorough job. Materials from England were slow in arriving. He finally submitted the work on March 1, 1825. It appeared in *Zeitgenossen, 1826* (Vol. 5). Müller's biography (which is reprinted in Volume III of the Schwab edition) was the first German biography of Byron.[26]

The facts about the poet's life are derived from English sources, but the interpretation of the facts is Müller's own. "So war sein ganzes Leben ein unaufhörliches Zerstören und Wiederaufbauen, ein Ringen nach dem Fernen und oft Unerreichbaren, ein trotziges Wegwerfen des Nahen und Gewöhnlichen; und was er von Thaten ausgeführt und von Werken hinterlassen hat, sind Kinder dieses Kampfes, Funken, herausgestoben aus dem Zusammenprallen seiner Kräfte. Und welche Funken!"[27]

Greek Recognition of Müller's Philhellenism

The Greek people did not forget that Müller's poetry had aroused support for their cause in Germany. When the Greek Parliament voted to send marble to England for a monument to Lord Byron, they also dispatched a shipload of Pentelic marble for a monument to Müller in Dessau. The idea of erecting such a monument found enthusiastic support in Dessau and subsequently became a national project to which admirers of Müller in Germany, Greece, and England contributed. The fourteen-foot monument was unveiled on the sixty-fourth anniversary of the poet's death, September 30, 1891. The Greek inscription reads: "A grateful Greece gives the singer of Greek freedom this stone from Attic and Laconian quarries."[28] Among the contributors to its construction were King George of Greece, the Greek government, the University of Athens, and the poet A. R. Rhangawis. The bust of Müller was modeled after one done by the Dessau court sculptor Ludwig Nikolaus Friedemann Hunold (1772–1840). The monument is displayed prominently today in Dessau in a central park area surrounded by new high-rise apartment buildings.

On the hundredth anniversary of Müller's birth (in 1894), celebrations were held both in Germany and Greece. Commemorative events also honored the poet in both countries on the centennial of his death (1927). Articles about Müller have appeared in Greece during this century. A modern Greek encyclopedia published in Athens contains a 3,000-word entry on Müller, illustrated with a picture of the poet.

The Greeks have not forgotten the German poet who rallied others to support their struggle for independence against the Turks. In March 1979 a delegation, "Free Greece," under the leadership of Kostas Chrissomalos, paid an official visit to Müller's hometown. The wreath the group laid at the foot of the Müller monument bore the following dedication: "Dem grossen deutschen Dichter—der für die Freiheit Griechenlands kämpfte." ("To the great German poet who fought for the freedom of Greece.")[29]

A Forerunner of Junges Deutschland
Because of Müller's liberal political opinions and activities as a philhellene, John G. Robertson in his well-known *History of German Literature* calls Müller a forerunner of Junges Deutschland:

> The poetry of several young writers whose sympathies were with the Greeks in their struggle for independence can hardly be included under the rubric of Romantic decline; they are forerunners rather of the political and revolutionary poets of the 'forties. Of the poets who, as admirers and imitators of Byron, were inspired by the Greek revolt, the most gifted was Wilhelm Müller. . . . Müller's *Lieder der Griechen* (1821–24) were Germany's chief contribution to the literature inspired by the Greek struggle.[30]

At the end of his biography of Müller, Heinrich Lohre, the editor of the correspondence between Müller and the liberal publishers Friedrich Arnold and Heinrich Brockhaus, also sees in Müller's life the transition from the Romantic period to Junges Deutschland: "Denn das rückt nun deutlicher in den Blick: wie sich der Übergang von der Romantik zum jungen Deutschland innerhalb von Müllers Leben selbst vollzieht, des Mannes, der als Student in altdeutscher Tracht einhergeht, im *Gesellschafter* Blumen deutet, und als Mann an die Seite eines politisch-literarischen Kämpfers wie Brockhaus tritt."[31]

Like other individualistic writers (such as Georg Büchner, Ferdinand Freiligrath, Christian Dietrich Grabbe, Karl Gutzkow, Heinrich Heine, and Georg Herwegh) classified as members of Junges Deutschland by contemporary literary historians such as Herbert A. Frenzel and Elisabeth Frenzel,[32] Müller strongly criticized government policies. He, like others, also used a journalistic career to express his political opinions. His Italian "travel book," *Rom, Römer und Römerinnen*—like the lively and satirical travel descriptions of Heine—contains considerable political and social commentary. Like the writers of the 1830s and the 1840s, Müller decried the hypocrisy of organized religion and satirized the excesses of the nobility.

The life and works of Lord Byron, whose reputation and popularity in Germany Müller helped to establish, influenced the members of Junges Deutschland. Wilhelm Ochsenbein, the author of a study of Byron's reception in Germany, sees Müller's emotional eulogy as the beginning of the characterization which Junges Deutschland later gave him: "Soviel wir wissen, wurde Byron hier zum erstenmal in Deutschland auch als Kämpfer gegen die politischen Restaurationsversuche und gegen Heuchelei auf sittlichem und religiösem Gebiet dargestellt. Was hier nur schüchtern durchklingt, sollte bald dem 'Jungen Deutschland' als der Grundzug von Byrons Wesen erscheinen."[33]

Unlike most of the writers of Junges Deutschland, however, Müller suffered no persecution for his liberal political opinions. Müller, the ducal librarian and husband of a member of a leading Dessau family, enjoyed the continuous favor of the Duke of Anhalt; not long before his death he even accepted the title of Hofrat to the Dessau court. Many admired his ability to express his political convictions in relatively inoffensive ways in his Trinklieder, *Griechenlieder*, epigrams, and critical essays. Müller apparently realized that it was better to tone down his political commentary than to have his poetry completely censored. His contemporaries' enthusiastic reception of his poetry with a political slant shows that he was reaching sympathetic ears, even though he avoided open expression of his liberal convictions.

CHAPTER EIGHT

The "Literary Legacy"

Für jetzt kommen wir auf ein fünftes und letztes Stück aus der Gruppe der engeren Favoriten—welches nun freilich gar nichts Französisches mehr war, sondern etwas sogar besonders und exemplarisch Deutsches, auch nichts Opernhaftes, sondern ein Lied, eines jener Lieder—Volksgut und Meisterwerk zugleich und eben durch dieses Zugleich seinen besonderen geistig-weltbildlichen Stempel empfangend.... Wozu die Umschweife? Es war Schuberts "Lindenbaum," es war nichts anderes als dies allvertraute "Am Brunnen vor dem Tore."

From Thomas Mann's *Zauberberg*[1]

MÜLLER AND OTHER WRITERS

Heinrich Heine
A study of the early poetry of Heinrich Heine (1797–1856) shows that he was familiar with the poetry of Wilhelm Müller. The first to draw attention to the similarity between Heine's *Lyrisches Intermezzo* and Müller's poetry was an anonymous reviewer of Heine's poems in the *Literarisches Konversationsblatt,* September 23, 1824: "Keine Nachahmung oder Ähnlichkeit, aber eine innere, gleichsam musikalische Verwandtschaft im Anschlagen desselben Tones, in einem ähnlichen Tonfalle, in einer gleich leichten Behandlung der Sprache und im glücklichen Versbaue mit den Liedern Wilhelm Müllers ist mir darin aufgefallen. Doch wer weiss, ob dies nicht mehr ein individuelles dunkles Gefühl als etwas Wirkliches ist?"[2]

In a letter written to Müller dated June 7, 1826, Heinrich Heine acknowledges his obligation to the Dessau poet for his understanding of the rhythms and language of the German folk-song tradition. He confesses to Müller that the *Waldhornistenlieder* had strongly influenced his *Lyrisches Intermezzo.* Heine claims that he prefers Müller's poetry to that of Ludwig Uhland and Friedrich Rückert; after Goethe, Müller is his favorite lyric poet. The following excerpts from Heine's letter to Müller are quoted from the *Blätter für literarische Unterhaltung,* August 15, 1845, where it was first published by F. Max Müller—nineteen years after it was written:

Ich bin gross genug, Ihnen offen zu bekennen, dass mein kleines Intermezzo-Metrum nicht blos zufällige Ähnlichkeit mit Ihrem gewöhnlichen

Metrum hat, sondern dass es wahrscheinlich seinen geheimsten Tonfall Ihren Liedern verdankt, indem es die lieben Müller'schen Lieder waren, die ich zu eben der Zeit kennen lernte, als ich das Intermezzo schrieb. . . . Ich glaube erst in Ihren Liedern den reinen Klang und die wahre Einfachheit, wonach ich immer strebte, gefunden zu haben. Wie rein, wie klar sind Ihre Lieder und sämmtlich [*sic*] sind es Volkslieder. In meinen Gedichten hingegen ist nur die Form einigermassen volkstümlich, der Inhalt gehört der conventionnellen [*sic*] Gesellschaft. Ja, ich bin gross genug, es sogar bestimmt zu wiederholen, und Sie werden es mal öffentlich ausgesprochen finden, dass mir durch die Lektüre Ihrer 77 Gedichte zuerst klar geworden, wie man aus den alten, vorhandenen Volksliedformen neue Formen bilden kann, die ebenfalls volksthümlich sind, ohne dass man nöthig hat, die alten Sprachholperigkeiten und Unbeholfenheiten nachzuahmen. Im zweiten Theile Ihrer Gedichte fand ich die Form noch reiner, noch durchsichtig klarer—doch, was spreche ich viel von Formwesen, es drängt mich mehr, Ihnen zu sagen, dass ich keinen Liederdichter ausser Goethe so sehr liebe wie Sie. Uhlands Ton ist nicht eigenthümlich genug und gehört eigentlich den alten Gedichten. . . . Unendlich reicher und origineller ist Rückert, aber ich habe an ihm zu tadeln Alles was ich an mir selbst tadle: wir sind uns im Irrthum verwandt, und er wird mir oft so unleidlich, wie ich es mir selbst werde. Nur Sie, Wilhelm Müller, bleiben mir also rein geniessbar übrig, mit Ihrer ewigen Frische und jugendlichen Ursprünglichkeit.[3]

This was probably not the first time that Heine had written to Müller. In the 1890s F. Max Müller still possessed a copy of Heine's *Tragödien nebst einem lyrischen Intermezzo* from 1823 with the following personal inscription: "Als ein Zeichen seiner Achtung und mit dem besonderen Wunsche, dass der Waldhornist das lyrische Intermezzo seiner Aufmerksamkeit würdige, überreicht dieses Buch der Verfasser."[4]

Heine wrote flattering letters to many people who he thought might be of assistance to him in his struggle to gain recognition as a writer. Nevertheless, Heine's admiration for Müller appears to have been genuine; the Dessau poet is mentioned four times in Heine's writings. Two of the references appeared after Müller's death in 1827. The quoting of the "Vineta" in *Die Nordsee III* and the singing of Müller's songs by the carousing students on the Brocken in *Die Harzreise* have been mentioned earlier. In *Reisebilder III: Reise von München nach Genua* (Chap. 26), Heine shows in 1829 that he is very familiar with the series of articles Müller wrote during 1820 and 1821 on the numerous travel books dealing with Italy. Heine laments Müller's premature death exclaiming, "Ah, he was a German poet!"

Was überhaupt italienische Reisebeschreibungen betrifft, so hat W. Müller vor geraumer Zeit im "Hermes" eine Übersicht derselben gegeben. Ihre Zahl ist Legion. Unter den ältern deutschen Schriftstellern in diesem Fache sind, durch Geist oder Eigentümlichkeit, am ausgezeichnetsten: Moritz, Archenholz, Bartels, der brave Seume, Arndt, Meyer, Benkowitz und Rehfus. Die neueren kenne ich weniger, und nur wenige davon haben

mir Vergnügen und Belehrung gewährt. Unter diesen nenne ich des
allzufrüh verstorbenen W. Müllers "Rom, Römer und Römerinnen"—ach,
er war ein deutscher Dichter!— . . .⁵

Several years later in *Die romantische Schule; drittes Buch,* Heine praises
Müller's poems in the folk-song style and compares him favorably to
Ludwig Uhland:

> Wilhelm Müller, den uns der Tod in seiner heitersten Jugendfülle entris-
> sen, muss hier ebenfalls erwähnt werden. In der Nachbildung des
> deutschen Volkslieds klingt er ganz zusammen mit Herrn Uhland; mich will
> es sogar bedünken, als sei er in solchem Gebiete manchmal glücklicher und
> überträfe ihn an Natürlichkeit. Er erkannte tiefer den Geist der alten
> Liedesformen und brauchte sie daher nicht äusserlich nachzuahmen; wir
> finden daher bei ihm ein freieres Handhaben der Übergänge und ein
> verständiges Vermeiden aller veralteten Wendungen und Ausdrücke.⁶

Following three earlier studies which mention Müller's influence on
Heine,⁷ a 1902 article by an American, John S. Nollen, treats in detail
the influence that Müller had upon the early poetry of Heine:

> The argument for the influence of Müller upon Heine in the passages to
> be quoted rests upon the following facts: that there is no corresponding
> similarity with all the mass of other lyric poetry studied; that the parallel
> passages, almost without exception, appear in Müller's poetry earlier than
> in Heine's; that the coincident passages in Heine's verse belong almost
> exclusively to the years 1821–1824, or are later echoes from these years,
> the very ones for which Heine testifies to Müller's influence upon him.⁸

During this time (beginning in 1821) Heine was in Berlin as a mem-
ber of the intellectual circle around Rahel Varnhagen von Ense, whose
literary salon Müller had frequented during his years of study in Berlin
(1815–1817). Although he was in Dessau while Heine was in Berlin,
Müller maintained contact with Karl August Varnhagen von Ense, who
wrote him in 1824, requesting anecdotal material about Prince Leopold
of Anhalt-Dessau for a biographical sketch to be included in *Biogra-
phische Denkmale.* When the volume appeared in 1825, Varnhagen von
Ense credited Müller as a source of information: "Handschriftliche
Mittheilungen von Herrn Hofrath und Bibliothekar Wilhelm Müller in
Dessau."⁹ Ernst Elster notes that Heine studied Varnhagen's book in
1826 and took the motto for *Die Nordsee* from the book.

Although Müller and Heine moved in the same circles in Berlin,
there is no record that they ever met face to face. Whether or not they
had actually met is not important—they read each other's poetry.
Müller wrote a review of seventeen of Heine's poems (later incorpo-
rated into his *Lyrisches Intermezzo*) for the *Aurora, 1823;* "Siebzehn
Lieder von H. Heine, der unlängst eine Gedichtsammlung zu Berlin
herausgegeben hat, verdienen Aufmerksamkeit. Es herrscht in ihnen

ein freier, eigenthümlicher Klang, und unter einigen unbedeutenden und verfehlten zeichnen sich mehrere durch Originalität der Empfindung aus, z. B. das 8., 13., 14., 15. und andere mehr."[10] Heine had also read Müller's works. In 1826 he writes Friedrich Merkel from Lüneburg that he is forwarding along with his letter a copy of a work by Müller.[11]

The Nollen article lists seventy-two separate passages from Heine's early poetry, especially from *Lyrisches Intermezzo, Heimkehr, Neuer Frühling,* and *Harzreise,* which parallel lines by Müller. For example:

> "Und es fragen mich die Freunde,
> Was ich doch so traurig bin."[12]

> "Ich weiss nicht, was soll es bedeuten,
> Dass ich so traurig bin." (*Die Heimkehr*)

> "Wir sassen so traulich beisammen
> Im kühlen Erlendach."[13]

> "Mein Liebchen, wir sassen beisammen,
> Traulich im leichten Kahn." (*Lyrisches Intermezzo*)

In addition, a prose passage in Müller's *Rom, Römer und Römerinnen* may have been the inspiration for Heine's thrice-repeated phrase, "Auf die Berge will ich steigen," in the rhymed prologue to *Die Harzreise.* Müller had written "Und so will ich Dich denn heute in freier, grüner Natur für das trockene Feld schadlos halten, das Du in ihnen mit mir durchwandert hast. Auf die Berge wollen wir steigen und uns umschauen in der blühenden Gegend: wir wollen in die Hütten des Landmannes treten, nach seinen Geschäften ihn befragen und von seinen Früchten kosten."[14] A stanza from Heine's poem reads as follows:

> Auf die Berge will ich steigen,
> Wo die frommen Hütten stehen,
> Wo die Brust sich frei erschliesset,
> Und die freien Lüfte wehen.[15]

Elster credits Müller's influence on *Lyrisches Intermezzo* not only in the rhythm and form, but also in the number of poems. Elster mentions Müller's *Siebenundsiebzig Gedichte aus den hinterlassenen Papieren eines reisenden Waldhornisten* as a possible explanation for Heine's almost superstitious use of numbers divisible by eleven. *Lyrisches Intermezzo* contained sixty-six poems when it was first published. Heine balanced the deletions and insertions so that the *Intermezzo* still had sixty-six poems in its second publication in *Das Buch der Lieder.* In 1824 Heine published poems from *Die Heimkehr* under the title "Dreiunddreissig Gedichte von H. Heine." *Die Heimkehr* itself contained eighty-eight poems. Twenty-two poems make up the two cycles of the *Nordseebilder*. In *Neuer Frühling* the total is forty-four.[16]

Two recent studies credit Müller as having been a "teacher" of Heinrich Heine. The first study, published in 1970 by Nigel Reeves in the Oxford German Studies, maintains that Müller showed him (Heine) "how to create the all-important spirit of simplicity that had already fascinated him in the folk-song."[17] In his study of the Biedermeier period, Friedrich Sengle refers in several places to techniques of Müller which influenced the development of Heine, especially in terms of the folk-song style and the use of the song cycle.

Ludwig Uhland, Justinus Kerner, Gustav Schwab, Alexander Baron von Simolin, and Ferdinand Freiligrath

Several poems were written in honor of Wilhelm Müller during his lifetime. After his sudden and untimely death, many articles and memorials appeared.[18] To date no collection of these various works has been published.

During Müller's trip to Stuttgart and the surrounding area in August 1827, he visited a poet whom he much admired—Ludwig Uhland (1787–1862). The older poet wrote the following lines at the time of Müller's departure:

> Wohl blühet jedem Jahre
> Sein Frühling, süss und licht,
> Auch jener grosse, klare—
> Getrost! er fehlt dir nicht;
> Er ist dir noch beschieden
> Am Ziele deiner Bahn,
> Du ahnest ihn hienieden,
> Und droben bricht er an.[19]

A few days later, on September 15, 1827, Müller and his wife visited Justinus Kerner (1786–1862) in Weinsberg. Kerner wrote these lines in his guests' travel diary before they departed:

> Nicht wie Geister, nein! wie Sterne
> Kamt ihr freundlich in der Nacht,
> Ja, so ernst und mild wie Sterne,
> Hat uns euer Bild gelacht.
> Oft wenn schweigt der Welt Getümmel
> Wird's so treten in den Himmel
> Den die Lieb uns angefacht.[20]

When Kerner received the news of Müller's death about three weeks later, he remembered the coincidence with the ominous black cross on the wet Greek flag and composed the following sonnet:

Du kamst zu mir, ein Stern in stiller Nacht,
Warst mit der Sonne Wiederkehr verschwunden,
Von Liedern nicht und nicht von Hellas Wunden
Ward da gesprochen oder still gedacht.
Nein! von des Erdentraumes kurzen Stunden,
Vom Tag, wo unser Innerstes erwacht,
Vom Wiedersehn in bess'rer Welten Pracht,
Hat sich hier Geist mit Geist nur eng verbunden.
Der Morgen kam und in des Nebels Schleier
Sah ich dein bleiches Bild nur ferne schweben,
Die Leichenfahn' vom alten Turme wehen,
Die Glocken läuteten zur Sonntagsfeier,
Und mir im Herzen fühlt' ich's mächtig beben:
Fahr wohl! fahr wohl! Dich werd' ich wiedersehen![21]

Gustav Schwab (1792–1850) published the following memorial poem
in *Morgenblatt für gebildete Stände* on October 18, 1827:

Des Himmels Schützlinge, die Sänger
Der Erd' und ihrer Lieblichkeit,
Hiess das Geschick sonst gütig länger
Verweilen in der flücht'gen Zeit.
Es gab dem graugelockten Greisen
Die junge Leyer in den Arm,
Und liess sie Wein und Liebe preisen
Von langer Spätlingssonne warm.
Doch Dich, der an der Jugend Borne
Die unerschöpften Lieder sang,
Und lächelte, wenn nicht im Zorne
Die Leyer, Freiheit fordernd, klang:
Ach, warum riss vom Quell der Musen,
Und aus der treuen Liebe Wacht,
Und von des Herzensfreundes Busen
Dich früh die schwarze Mitternacht?
Wir fragen nicht: Du warst der Bote
Von eines Volkes Aufersteh'n,
Gesandt noch vor dem Morgenrothe,
Und bei der kühlen Lüfte Weh'n.
Da hat Dein Sang sich aufgeschwungen,
Noch eh' der Tag im Osten graut;
Jetzt ist die Sonne durchgedrungen:
Wohl Dir, Du hast sie noch geschaut.
Der Hauch in Deinen Liedern lebte,
Der einst Hellenenbrust geschwellt,
Vor dem verklärten Auge schwebte

Des Jugendvolkes Götterwelt.
Und Deine Sendung war vollendet;
Da trat aus der Gestalten Chor
Der sanfte Jüngling, abgewendet
Mit der gesenkten Fackel vor.
Still griffest Du zum Wanderstabe,
Du zogst noch durch Dein Erdenland.
Und grüsstest auf dem Weg zum Grabe
Noch manches Herz, das Dich verstand.
Und schied'st, und liessest Deine Lieben;
Dein reicher Morgen war gelebt;
Uns aber ist Dein Lied geblieben,
Das durch die Brust lebendig lebt.[22]

The four sonnets of Alexander Baron von Simolin (1800–1871) about his friend Müller have not been reprinted since their original publication in Brockhaus's *Urania, 1828.* Each of Simolin's sonnets— "Der Waldhornist," "Der Grieche," "Der Winzer," and "Eros"—emphasizes a different theme from Müller's poetry. Since the sonnets are of more biographical than literary interest, only the first sonnet, "Der Waldhornist," is reproduced here.

Nicht in den Saal voll heller Winterkerzen
Geh' ich zu lauschen auf des Waldhorns Klänge,
Wo Berg an Berg sich reiht in stolzer Menge
Und frisch die Quellen in den Thälern scherzen.

Zum neuen Thron des knospengrünen Märzen,
In Waldesweite und an Stromeslänge,
Da führ' mich hin, dass muntere Gesänge
Des Wunderhornes scheuchen meine Schmerzen.

Denn horch, dort bläst ein Wandrer durch die Auen
Aus tiefem Busen Jubelton' und Klagen
Auf seinem Waldhorn unsern Hirten vor.

Wir eilen hin, zu hören ihn, zu schauen,
Und müssen seine Zauberlieder tragen
Im Herzen fort, sind sie verrauscht dem Ohr.[23]

Ferdinand Freiligrath (1810–1876), who was acquainted with F. Max Müller, wrote "Wilhelm Müller; Eine Geisterstimme" in Stuttgart on December 1, 1872, on the occasion of a flood on the Baltic coast. Freiligrath's poem shows a more than casual knowledge of the cycle

"Muscheln von der Insel Rügen," in which Müller's "Vineta" is included. Only five of the eleven stanzas of Freiligrath's work are reprinted here.

Was schreckt von meinen Pfühlen
Mich Schlafenden empor?
Was braust wie tausend Mühlen
Und Bäche mir zum Ohr?
O weh, das sind nicht Bäche,
O weh, das ist kein Wehr—
Das ist die Küstenfläche,
Und über ihr das Meer!

Das ist, wo Möwen fliegen,
Die Sturmflut aus Nordost;
Das ist der Strand von Rügen,
Von Wellen übertost;
Das ist, ertränkt, ertrunken,
Des Pommern Uferstrich—
Aufs neue jäh versunken,
Ruft mein Vineta mich.

O ferne, ferne Tage!
Einst sucht' ich Muscheln hier,
Sang froh zum Ruderschlage
Meerfrische Lieder mir!
Pries Mönkguts ros'ge Bräute—
Dazu dann, dumpf und matt,
Scholl nachts mir das Geläute
Der alten Wunderstadt. . . .

Ich weiss, in diesen Tagen
Fehlt's nicht an Liederschall;
Ihr helft mit Singen und Sagen
Wohl auch in solchem Fall.
Da singt denn von den meinen
Manch Lied auch, ernst bewegt,
Wie Schubert euch die kleinen
Herrlich ans Herz gelegt!

So sei's! Auf dass sein Sänger
Sich Rügen treu erweist!
Auf dass am Deichesprenger,
Am Belt, es immer heisst:
Auch er war rasch zur Stelle,

Auch er zu dieser Frist—
Der wackre Müllergeselle,
Der reisende Waldhornist![24]

Henry Wadsworth Longfellow
The subject of Longfellow (1807–1882) as a "transmitter of German culture" has been treated by James Taft Hatfield.[25] Longfellow's acquaintance with Müller's poetry is first recorded by the American writer in his sketchbook of his travels in France, Spain, and Italy, *Outre-Mer: A Pilgrimage Beyond the Sea,* which appeared anonymously in installments in 1833. In December of 1827 Longfellow was inspired by Müller's "Est Est!"[26] to make a midnight visit to the tomb of Bishop John Defoucris in the cathedral at Montefiascone near the Italian lake of Bolsena. Longfellow writes in *Outre-Mer: A Pilgrimage Beyond the Sea:*

> I passed a night at Montefiascone, renowned for a delicate Muscat wine, which bears the name Est, and made a midnight pilgrimage to the tomb of the Bishop John Defoucris, who died a martyr to his love of this wine of Montefiascone.
>
> > "Propter nimium Est, Est, Est,
> > Dominus meus mortuus est."
>
> A marble slab in the pavement, worn by the footsteps of pilgrims like myself, covers the dominie's ashes. There is a rude figure carved upon it, at whose feet I traced out the cabalistic words, "Est, Est, Est." The remainder of the inscription was illegible by the flickering light of the sexton's lantern.[27]

In Chapter 8 of *Hyperion: Book Two* (1837), Longfellow published a brief discussion of Müller's poetry, giving his own translations of the last stanza of "Abendreihn" and the complete "Wohin" from *Die schöne Müllerin:*

> "I am persuaded," said Flemming, "that, in order fully to understand and feel the popular poetry of Germany, one must be familiar with the German landscape. Many sweet little poems are the outbreaks of momentary feelings;—words to which the song of birds, the rustling of leaves, and the gurgle of cool waters form the appropriate music. Or perhaps I should say they are words which man has composed to the music of nature. Can you not, even now, hear this brooklet telling you how it is on its way to the mill, where at daybreak the miller's daughter opens her window, and comes down to bathe her face in its stream, and her bosom is so full and white, that it kindles the glow of love in the cool waters?"
>
> "A most delightful ballad, truly," said the Baron. "But, like many others of our little songs, it requires a poet to feel and understand it. Sing them in the valley and woodland shadows, and under the leafy roofs of garden walks, and at night, and alone, as they were written. Sing them not in the loud world,—for the loud world laughs such things to scorn. It is Müller who says, in that little song where the maiden bids the moon good evening:—

'This song was made to be sung at night,
And he who reads it in broad daylight
Will never read the mystery right;
And yet it is childlike easy!'

"He has written a great many pretty songs, in which the momentary, indefinite longings and impulses of the soul of man find an expression. He calls them the Songs of a Wandering Horn-player. There is one among them much to our present purpose. He expresses in it the feeling of unrest and desire of motion, which the sight and sound of running waters often produce in us. It is entitled, 'Whither?' and is worth repeating to you." [Longfellow's translation of Müller's "Wohin" follows.]

"There you have the poetic reverie," said Flemming, "and the dull prose commentary and explanation in matter of fact. The song is pretty; and was probably suggested by some such scene as this which we are now beholding. Doubtless, all your old national traditions sprang up in the popular mind as this song in the poet's."[28]

In *Voices in the Night* (1839) Longfellow included his translation of Müller's "Schiff und Vogel" under the title "The Bird and the Ship." Longfellow omitted the sixth stanza, however, for its suggestion of "impropriety."

Sie tanzen und springen den ganzen Tag,
Und klimpern und spielen und trinken,
Und wer nicht mehr tanzen und trinken mag,
Seiner Nachbarin muss er winken.[29]

Longfellow also knew Müller's *Bibliothek deutscher Dichter des siebzehnten Jahrhunderts*. The American's *Poets and Poetry of Europe* (1845) includes "Annie of Tharau," his translation of Simon Dach's "Anke von Tharau," which he had found in Müller's *Bibliothek deutscher Dichter*. "The Bird and the Ship" and "Whither" were also republished in this collection.

Longfellow's collection *The Belfry of Bruges* (1845) contains twelve aphorisms translated from the Logau volume of Müller's *Bibliothek deutscher Dichter*. One of these translations, "Retribution," is the source of an often-quoted proverb:

Though the mills of God grind slowly,
    yet they grind exceeding small;
Though with patience he stands waiting,
    with exactness grinds he all.[30]

Another example of Longfellow's debt to Müller is found in *The Golden Legend* (1851), in which Prince Henry tells the story of the Fastrada legend to his bride Elsie. Longfellow's source was Müller's "Die Sage vom Frankenberger See bei Aachen."[31]

German Writers Influenced by the Griechen-Müller
Müller's *Griechenlieder* were well known and often imitated.[32] Anastasius
Grün (Anton Alexander Graf von Auersperg, 1806–1876) produced
several poems in which Wilhelm Müller's influence may be traced, for
example, "Des Klephten Gaben," "Drei Farben," and "Das Land der
Freiheit." A poem in Grün's anonymously published collection,
Spaziergänge eines Wiener Poeten (1831), was dedicated to Alexander
Ypsilanti and was written in the same meter as Müller's well-known
poem about the Greek hero. *Spaziergänge eines Wiener Poeten*, which was
published by Hoffmann and Campe in Hamburg, is one of the first
collections of the Junges Deutschland movement.

Joseph Christian von Zedlitz (1790–1862) wrote *Die Totenkränze* and,
in 1849, published *Das Soldatenbüchlein*, both of which show Müller's
influence in content and form. In later poems Zedlitz adopted the
meter of *Die Griechenlieder*. Ernst Grosse (born 1801), who published
Gedichte zum Besten der Griechen (1823) in collaboration with Heinrich
Stieglitz (1801–1849), wrote obvious imitations of Müller's *Griechen-
lieder*, such as "Der Greis auf Samos," "Der Hydriotenknabe," "Lieder
athenischer Jungfrauen," and "Die 500 der heiligen Schar." (Cf.
Müller's "Der Greis auf Hydra," "Der kleine Hydriot," "Die Jungfrau
von Athen," and "Die heilige Schar.")

The author of *Peter Schlemihls wundersame Geschichte* also borrowed
from Müller. Adelbert von Chamisso (1781–1838), who wrote several
poems glorifying the Greek cause, adopted the metrical pattern of
Müller's *Griechenlieder* in his poem "Sophia Kondulimo und ihre
Kinder." Two Chamisso poems, "Georgis" and "Die verratene Liebe,"
were based on neo-Greek folk songs taken from Müller's translation of
Fauriel's collection. The latter poem (which begins "Da nachts wir uns
küssten, o Mädchen, / Hat keiner uns zugeschaut") provided the text
for Robert Schumann's setting of 1840 (Opus 40). Müller's literal trans-
lation of the neo-Greek poem reads "O Mädchen, als wir uns geküsst, da
war es Nacht. Wer sah' uns?—"[33] His freely translated version of the
Greek appeared in "Reime aus den Inseln des Archipelagus" under the
title "Wer hat's verrathen?" ("Als wir uns küssten, war es Nacht. Wer hat
es denn gesehn?"). This poem may have been the source for an incident
described in Eduard Mörike's (1804–1875) *Das Stuttgarter Hutzelmännlein*
(1853).[34]

Müller's success in arousing interest in the Greek cause with his *Grie-
chenlieder* inspired poets during the Polish revolt of 1830–1831.[35] The
Polenlieder of Count August von Platen-Hallermünde (1796–1835)
were written as a cycle of more than a dozen poems (which, however,
were censored at the time of their writing and did not appear until
1839). Nikolaus Lenau (1802–1850) and Julius Mosen (1803–1867)
also wrote songs espousing the cause of the Poles. A new wave of
enthusiasm for the Polish cause swept Europe during the 1840s; Georg

Herwegh (1817–1875) wrote "An den König von Preussen," and Moritz Hartmann (1821–1872), a member of the 1848 Frankfurt Parliament, produced the cycle "Krakau."

Müller's patriotic lyrics are also reflected in the poem "Rheinlied" ("Sie sollen ihn nicht haben") which brought renown to the otherwise unknown poet Nikolaus Becker (1809–1845).

Thomas Mann

Schubert's setting of Müller's "Am Brunnen vor dem Tore" ("Der Lindenbaum") is the fifth song in the song cycle *Die Winterreise*. Despite its artistic origin, "Der Lindenbaum" has become a folk song, sung by many who have no knowledge of its origin. Thomas Mann (1875–1955) used the familiar art/folk song in an ironic way as a symbolic musical device with which to close his monumental novel, *The Magic Mountain*.

One of Mann's most striking uses of music in the novel is to be found in the fourth from the last section, "Fullness of Harmony" ("Fülle des Wohllauts"), in which he describes the five favorite record selections of his "simple hero," Hans Castorp. The fifth—and most beloved—selection of Castorp is "Am Brunnen vor dem Tore," to which Mann had alluded earlier in the chapter without naming the song:

> There was a long list of *lieder*, sung to piano accompaniment by famous prima donnas; some of these were the lofty and conscious creation of individual artists, others simple folk-songs, still others fell between the two categories, in that they were products of an intellectual art, and at the same time sprang from all that was profoundest and most reverent in the feeling and genius of a people—artificial folk-songs, one might call them, if the word artificial need not be taken to cast a slur on the genuineness of their inspiration. One of these Hans Castorp had known from childhood; but from now on began to attach to it a quite special love and clothe it with many associations, as shall be seen hereafter.[36]

The importance that Mann placed upon the art/folk song is apparent from the great detail in which he describes it and in the significance that it has for his "simple hero." (Only a small section of the chapter is quoted here; the reader is directed to the entire chapter and conclusion of the novel.)

> And now we come back to the fifth and last piece in his group of high favourites; this time not French, but something especially and exemplarily German; not opera either, but a *lied*, one of those which are folk-song and masterpiece together, and from the combination receive their peculiar stamp as spiritual epitomes. Why should we beat about the bush? It was Schubert's "Linden-tree," it was none other than the old, old favourite, *"Am Brunnen vor dem Tore."* . . .
>
> But wherein lay Hans Castorp's conscientious and stocktaking misgiving, as to the ultimate propriety of his love for the enchanting *lied* and the

world whose image it was? What was the world behind the song, which the motions of his conscience made to seem a world of forbidden love?

It was death.

What utter and explicit madness! That glorious song! An indisputable masterpiece, sprung from the profoundest and holiest depths of racial feeling; a precious possession, the archetype of the genuine; embodied loveliness. What vile detraction! . . .

One need have no more genius, only much more talent, than the author of the *"Lindenbaum,"* to be such an artist of soul-enchantment as should give to the song a giant volume by which it should subjugate the world. Kingdoms might be founded upon it, earthly, all-too-earthly kingdoms, solid, "progressive," not at all nostalgic—in which the song degenerated to a piece of gramophone music played by electricity. But its faithful son might still be he who consumed his life in self-conquest, and died, on his lips the new word of love which as yet he knew not how to speak. Ah, it was worth dying for, the enchanted *lied!* But he who died for it, died indeed no longer for it; was a hero only because he died for the new, the new word of love and the future that whispered in his heart.

These, then, were Hans Castorp's favourite records.[37]

The reason for Mann's lengthy discourse on "Am Brunnen vor dem Tore," the "enchanted Lied worth dying for," becomes clear at the very end of the novel: it is a foreshadowing of Castorp's idealistic plunge into almost certain death on the battlefield of the "Great War." Our hero is singing words from the familiar song from the pessimistic *Die Winterreise* as the reader glimpses him among the dying soldiers on the muddy battlefield:

There is our friend, there is Hans Castorp! . . . He is running, his feet heavy with mould, the bayonet swinging in his hand. Look! He treads on the hand of a fallen comrade; with his hobnailed boot he treads the hand deep into the slimy, branch-strewn ground. But it is he. What, singing? As one sings, unaware, staring stark ahead, yes, thus he spends his hurrying breath, to sing half soundlessly:

"And loving words I've carven
Upon its branches fair—"

He stumbles, No, he has flung himself down, a hell-hound is coming howling, a huge explosive shell, a disgusting sugar-loaf from the infernal regions. He lies with his face in the cool mire, legs sprawled out, feet twisted, heels turned down. . . .

Shame of our shadow-safety! Away! No more!—But our friend? Was he hit? He thought so, for the moment. A great clod of earth struck him on the shin, it hurt, but he smiles at it. Up he gets, and staggers on, limping on his earth-bound feet, all unconsciously singing:

"Its waving branches whi—ispered
A mess—age in my ear—"

and thus, in the tumult, in the rain, in the dusk, vanishes out of our sight. Farewell, honest Hans Castorp, farewell, Life's delicate child! . . . [38]

The reader's final glimpse of the young soldier leaves the song unfinished. The final words, "Komm her zu mir, Geselle, Hier findst du deine Ruh'," are left unsung. However, they are familiar to most readers, thereby providing yet another hint as to the probable—but not certain—fate of "Life's delicate child" (as the intellectual Italian, Herr Settembrini, was wont to call him).

Incidentally, Castorp refers throughout the novel to Herr Settembrini as the "hand-organ man" ("der Drehorgelmann"). Is this characterization of Herr Settembrini, who greets Hans Castorp at the beginning of his sojourn on the mountain and who bids him a sad farewell at the end of the novel, meant to conjure up an image of the "Leiermann," whose song brings *Die Winterreise* to a close on such a haunting note?

In his *Doktor Faustus*, which was published more than twenty years after *Der Zauberberg*, Thomas Mann borrows directly from Theodor Storm's *Ein stiller Musikant* and his own *Der Zauberberg* by connecting death and music with the works of Franz Schubert.[39] Although his composer protagonist Adrian Leverkühn had many favorite works, a melancholy song in *Die Winterreise*, "Der Wegweiser," receives special attention in *Dr. Faustus*, and its emotional effect on Leverkühn is described:

> But Schubert's always twilit genius, death-touched, he liked above all to seek where he lifts to the loftiest expression a certain only half-defined but inescapable destiny of solitude, as in the grandly self-tormenting "Ich komme vom Gebirge her" from the Smith of Lübeck and that "Was vermeid' ich denn die Wege, wo die andern Wandrer gehn?" from the *Winterreise*, with the perfectly heart-breaking stanza beginning:
>
> > "Hab' ja doch nichts begangen
> > Dass ich Menschen sollte scheu'n."
>
> These words, and the following:
>
> > "Welch ein törichtes Verlangen
> > Treibt mich in die Wüstenei'n?"
>
> I have heard him speak to himself, indicating the musical phrasing, and to my unforgettable amazement I saw the tears spring to his eyes. . . .[40]

Mann's ironic treatment of Castorp's fatalistic fascination with the art/folk song "Der Lindenbaum" and of Leverkühn's emotional attachment to "Der Wegweiser" relies heavily on the reader's familiarity with Schubert's *Die Winterreise* and its literary and musical connotations. Through Schubert's masterpiece, Müller's lyrics have become part of the German cultural heritage.

Alexander Solzhenitsyn
Since its composition on the composer's deathbed in Vienna 150 years ago, Schubert's *Die Winterreise* has enjoyed international recognition,

even in the Soviet Union. Nobel Prize winner Solzhenitsyn obviously felt that the song cycle was familiar enough to the Russian public to use it as a dramatic device at the emotional crisis in his drama *Candle in the Wind* (*Sveča na vetru*), which was written in 1960 and which appeared in London in the *Student* in 1968, having been neither published nor performed in the Soviet Union. The Russian play also appeared in Frankfurt am Main in 1969 (in *Grani*, no. 71) and in 1970—*Sobranie Sochineniy v shesti tomakh* (*Collected Works in Six Volumes*).

It is in Solzhenitsyn's rejection of hedonism as a moral option that the writer uses the opening song from *Die Winterreise*, "Gute Nacht" ("Fremd bin ich eingezogen"), in the death scene, where the seventy-year-old professor of music bids farewell to his daughter Alda, a child of a former marriage. The dying professor and his much younger wife represent the hedonistic view of life which Solzhenitsyn rejects. The melancholy text that Solzhenitsyn uses is the Russian version by S. Zayaitsky, which follows the original text closely, with the exception of the last section, which reads literally: "It has long been time for me / To throw my knapsack from my tired shoulders. / Long time for me to rest, / Somewhere to lie down."[41] The death of Professor Craig while listening a last time to *Die Winterreise* is the emotional high point in the drama. Only a short denouement of the plot involving the conflict between technology and the individual follows.

MAURICE

> . . . Alda dear! Over there, look . . .
> (*pointing to one of the shelves*) Schubert. Get me the *Winterreise*. We'll play it together.

ALDA

> Daddy! Something else! Not the *Winterreise!*

MAURICE

> No, it must be the *Winterreise!* (*pushing her*) Hurry, or I'll never hear it again. A winter journey . . . (*Wiping away her tears, Alda looks around for the library steps, puts them against the bookshelves, and climbs up. Looking out of the window, Maurice talks to himself.*) If Schubert didn't flinch at the age of thirty—what do I have to be frightened of at the age of seventy? And what good is life to someone who does not know how to live? . . . In the middle of a snowstorm . . . a snowstorm . . . Everyone is able to stay inside today, but someone . . .
>
>> I may not choose the season
>> Of my departure hence,
>> I will not stay to reason,
>> But straight the march commence.

ALDA

> (*coming down the library steps*) Here it is, Daddy.

MAURICE

(*absentmindedly*) Good. Play. (*Alda switches on the light by the piano, sits down, and plays the Lied "Gute Nacht." Maurice sings very softly.*)

> A stranger I came hither,
> A stranger hence I go . . .

He is suddenly unable to sing any more and puts his hands to his chest. Alda continues to play, weeping.

BOTH TOGETHER

> Until they say: Begone here,
> Why do I longer wait?
> Let stray dogs bay the moon here
> Before her father's gate.

Alda continues to play while Maurice slowly lies down.

ALDA

(*singing alone*)

> Your sleep shall not be broken,
> Yet o'er your door I'll write,
> This simple farewell token,
> Goodnight, my dear, goodnight.

(*She goes on playing, then looks around in alarm and breaks off.*) Daddy! Daddy!! . . . (*running to him*) Father! Are you alive?! (*shouting*) Father!! (*Shaking all over in anguish, she goes down on her knees and bends over the dying man.*)[42]

Later, Solzhenitsyn ends his drama with a stage direction for a melancholy musical reference to *Die Winterreise;* as the hero Alex stands despondent at a window, the earlier melody from *Die Winterreise* is heard again—this time played by a solo horn. This ironic touch, using that most "romantic" of musical instruments, recalls the emotionalism of the sentimental death scene in the midst of a terrifying futuristic world of a technologically controlled society. Is it perhaps also a subtle allusion to the origin of the lyric itself in Müller's second volume of *Gedichte aus den hinterlassenen Papieren eines reisenden Waldhornisten* ("Poems from the Posthumous Papers of an Itinerant Waldhornist")?

THE POETRY IN TRANSLATION

The First English Translation of a Müller Poem
It has long been thought that Longfellow was the first to introduce Wilhelm Müller's poetry to English-speaking countries with his translations in *Hyperion* in 1839. In 1826, however—thirteen years before the publication of Longfellow's book and a year before Müller's death—a

translation of Müller's "Byron" appeared in Edinburgh in *Janus; or, Edinburgh Literary Almanac.*[43] In 1833 the collection was reissued in Edinburgh as *Literary Rambler; Being a Collection of the Most Popular Entertaining Stories in the English Language*, in which the "Byron" translation was introduced by an editorial note: "The elegant version, which we now venture to insert, has been much handed about in private."[44] The German poem had been brought to England originally by Lord Francis Leveson Gower (b. 1800), the second son of the Duke of Sutherland.

English Translations in British and American Collections

Müller's poems, especially those from *Die schöne Müllerin* and *Die Winterreise*, have appeared in numerous collections of English translations of German poetry. In his reference work, *A Critical Bibliography of German Literature in English Translation*, Bayard Quincy Morgan constructs two tables based on his study of 577 collections of English translations—both British and American.[45] The first table ranks German writers in terms of "frequency"—Morgan's term for "a rough computation of the aggregate amount of selections (counting either a poem or a page as one)." Müller holds *thirteenth* position on the "frequency" list, following Johann Wolfgang von Goethe, Friedrich von Schiller, Heinrich Heine, Ludwig Uhland, Friedrich Rückert, Ferdinand Freiligrath, Emanuel Geibel, Gotthold Ephraim Lessing, Martin Luther, Theodor Körner, Gottfried August Bürger, and Christoph Martin Wieland. Müller precedes, among others, Walther von der Vogelweide, Jean Paul (Johann Paul Friedrich Richter), Johann Gottfried Herder, Adelbert von Chamisso, Paul Gerhardt, Friedrich Gottlieb Klopstock, Novalis (Friedrich von Hardenberg), Joseph von Eichendorff, Ludwig Tieck, Friedrich von Matthisson, Baron Friedrich de la Motte Fouqué, Eduard Mörike, Gustav Schwab, and Johann Christian Friedrich Hölderlin. Müller ranks *fourteenth* (following Martin Luther) among all German writers in "range," B. Q. Morgan's term for "the number of separate volumes in which selections from the poet are printed." Goethe, of course, ranks first on both lists.

In *German Culture in America*, Henry A. Pochmann includes a similar table for American collections alone, which is based on the Morgan bibliography of all published collections—both British and American.[46] According to Pochmann, Müller's poems did not appear in American poetry collections until the period 1840–1849, when two poems were published. During the second half of the nineteenth century, however, Müller's poems were included in many more American collections, probably because of the growing popularity of the Schubert song cycles. In Pochmann's ranking of all German authors who appeared in translation in American collections during 1865–1899, Müller is given the *thirteenth* position (tied with Klopstock and Walther von der Vogelweide) for the number of poems published. Müller follows Goethe,

Uhland, Heine, Rückert, Schiller, Geibel, Nikolaus Lenau, Herder, Chamisso, Luther, and Körner. Müller's poems appeared with greater frequency than those of Tieck, Eichendorff, Gerhardt, Matthias Claudius, August von Platen, de la Motte Fouqué, and Novalis, among others. The chart gives Müller an overall rank of *seventeenth* for the period between 1830 and 1899. During these sixty-nine years, forty-four translations of poems by Wilhelm Müller were included in the American poetry collections examined.

Among the more important British and American collections which included Müller poems are those of William Cullen Bryant, Alfred Baskerville, and Karl Buchheim. Bryant included Müller among the twelve German poets in the large poetry collections he edited: *A Library of Poetry and Song* (1871) and *A New Library of Poetry and Song* (1876). These two collections appeared in several editions, one as recently as 1970. The Baskerville collection, which was published in both Germany and the United States, appeared in fourteen editions between 1853 and 1886. In the introduction to one of the several editions of his collection, Karl Buchheim writes: "I cannot help recommending at the same time to all English readers of German, who are lovers of poetry, the poems of Wilhelm Müller, which deserve to be better known in this country." Warner's *A Library of the World's Best Literature* contains twelve poems from *Die schöne Müllerin*, as well as the "Vineta." The poetry is introduced by a three-page biography and a brief discussion of Müller's works: "He died just as his genius was maturing . . . And so, although no poet voice had a more vigorous ring when it sang in the cause of freedom, it is probable that Müller will be chiefly remembered as the singer of winter journeys and wanderers' joys, of mill-stream melodies and the lays of love."[47]

English Translations in British and American Journals
Eight poems by Müller appeared in five British journals between 1842 and 1851.[48] The British magazines were the *Dublin University Magazine*, which was very friendly toward German authors; *Ainsworth's Magazine*; *The Patrician*; *(Coburn's) New Monthly Magazine and Humorist*; and *The Westminster and Foreign Quarterly Review*, which was founded by Jeremy Bentham and edited by Sir John Bowring and John Stuart Mill.

During 1842–1852 eight periodical publications printed works by Müller in New York, Boston, New Orleans, and Washington, D.C.[49] These American publications were the transcendentalist journal *The Dial: A Magazine for Literature, Philosophy, and Religion; Southern Quarterly Review; The United States Magazine and Democratic Review; The Literary World: A Journal of Science, Literature, and Art; The Knickerbocker: New York Monthly Magazine; Littell's Living Age; New York Evening Post;* and *To-Day: A Boston Literary Journal.*

Müller's poems were sometimes quoted in reviews of newly published collections of poetry. The poem most often translated into English is Müller's "Vineta," which appeared seven times in England and the United States between 1842 and 1852. "Alexander Ypsilanti" appeared twice in 1850 and 1851. "Schiff und Vogel," "Der Glockenguss zu Breslau," "Achelous und das Meer," "Die Braut," and "Die Jungfrau von Athen" each appeared once. The article in the *Dial* was a lengthy review written by Margaret Fuller about Müller's translation of Fauriel's collection of neo-Greek folk poetry.

Translations into Languages Other Than English
There are several documented instances of the translation of Müller's poetry into languages other than English. "Der kleine Hydriot" was translated into Serbian by J. Jovanović-Zmaj. Three Müller poems from the "Muscheln von der Insel Rügen"—"Einkleidung," "Bräutigamswahl," and "Die Braut"—were translated into Polish by J. Grajnert. In 1891 Albert Weiss, not realizing that these were translations of German poems, retranslated them into German from the Polish in his *Polnische Dichtung in deutschem Gewande* (1891).⁵⁰ Eduard Hobein translated the cycle *Die schöne Müllerin* and four songs from the "Wanderlieder eines rheinischen Handwerksburschen" into Low German— *De smuke Möllersdochter (In'n Winter to lesen)* in *Bömings un Blomen ut frömden Gor'n*. A friend of Heine, Hippolyte Carnot (1801–1888), translated Müller's *Griechenlieder* into French in 1828 under the title *Chants helléniens*. As recently as the 1950s Jean Jacques Brand translated *Die schöne Müllerin* and *Die Winterreise* into French.⁵¹

Recognition of Wilhelm Müller in the United States
American contributions to the field of Müller research have been many. The 1906 critical edition of the poetry was the work of James Taft Hatfield of Northwestern University. Professor Hatfield also collaborated with Philip Schuyler Allen of the University of Chicago in publishing Müller's Berlin diary, along with a large number of his letters. An additional eight articles about Müller were published by Hatfield independently. In his published dissertation on the German folk-song influence in Müller's poetry, Allen was the first to analyze this relationship. He also wrote five articles about Müller's poetry. Two early investigators into the relationship between Heine's early poetry and that of Müller, John Snodgrass and John Nollen, were Americans. Theses dealing with Müller were written by Richard P. Koepke, Joseph C. Blair, and Alan P. Cottrell. Cottrell has since published a study in book form. Articles about Müller were published by Frank Spiecker, Wolfgang Stechow, and Anna E. Miller. A six-page biography of Müller in English appeared in the Boston Journal *Germania* in 1894.⁵²

Many of Müller's poems entered into the common song treasury of the German people and were carried with them wherever they wandered and settled. A tribute was paid to Wilhelm Müller in 1883, when his son F. Max was invited to attend the ceremonies commemorating the two hundredth anniversary of the establishment of the first German colony on American soil. The invitation to F. Max Müller was accompanied by the following statement: "We think we can count upon your presence with us at least in spirit, for your immortal father, as he lives in his songs, has been companion to us Germans everywhere in America, and will add his sanction to our festival."[53]

Conclusion

Many have labeled Wilhelm Müller a Romanticist, and it can scarcely be denied that much of his life and many of his works indeed exhibit Romantic traits. In Berlin he was influenced by Fouqué, Uhland, Brentano, Tieck, and others, with whom he shared an intense interest in the German past and whose styles and ideas he adopted as his own. Much of his poetry testifies to a Romantic interest in the folk song. Schubert's masterpieces *Die schöne Müllerin* and *Die Winterreise* have Romantic themes and guarantee Müller a small but secure niche in cultural history. The Romantic love of wandering was reflected in his many trips, and he died shortly after satisfying a lifelong dream of making a Rhine journey to "the source of the treasure of the Nibelungen."[1]

It is always dangerous, however, to attempt to place any writer into a single literary movement, style, or philosophy. Most writers reflect more than one of the various literary, social, and political trends current at the time of their activity, and Wilhelm Müller was no exception. While the so-called Romantic traits are perhaps most obvious in Müller's work, he was, nonetheless, also the author of some "Classical" writing and was vitally concerned with the politics of modern Greece and with Greek literature, both classical and modern.

Müller led a conservative, Biedermeier life as a teacher and librarian in provincial Dessau. He was a loving husband and father who enjoyed being with his family. In his definitive work on the Biedermeier period, Friedrich Sengle mentions Müller repeatedly and shows how Müller's forms, themes, symbols, and interests all reflect the times between the Restoration and Revolution, 1815 and 1848.[2]

At the same time, Müller's liberal convictions and stirring, patriotic *Griechenlieder* have earned him the label of "forerunner of the writers of Junges Deutschland." In one of his epigrams Müller explains that his "small gifts" are written for the "small" times in which he lives. He hopes, however, that his perceptive readers will see a whole in the many things he produces:

> Die liebe kleine Zeit will Kleines haben,
> Drum bring' ich ihr so viele kleine Gaben.
> Aus vielen Tagen wird ja doch ein Jahr—
> Sei ganz und sieh ein Ganzes in der Schaar.[3]

Wilhelm Müller is not *just* the poet of the Schubert song cycles. A versatile and prolific poet, translator, literary critic, editor, scholar, and prose writer, his creative work brought him recognition in intellectual circles far away from provincial Dessau, and his simple lyrics were adopted by the general populace as folk songs. His lyrics have become a Leitmotiv with significance for twentieth-century writers Thomas Mann and Alexander Solzhenitsyn. While the survival of Müller's poetry is due to a quirk of fate—Schubert's choice of his lyrics for two immortal song cycles—it should not be forgotten that Müller's achievements during his short life span are remarkable. In addition, his standing among his contemporaries, their admiration for him, and his influence on them should stimulate not only literary historians but any scholar interested in the intellectual and cultural life of early nineteenth-century Germany.

Appendix A

A CHRONOLOGY OF THE LIFE AND WORKS OF WILHELM MÜLLER
(1794–1827)

This chronology is the first such ever compiled and is based on a survey of all available primary and secondary sources.

1794	
October 7	Birth in Dessau of Johann Ludwig Wilhelm Müller, the son of master tailor Christian Leopold Müller (June 1, 1752–June 23, 1820) and Marie Leopoldine Cellarius (March 15, 1751–May 7, 1808), who married on February 10, 1780
1797	Only surviving child in the family at the age of three
1800	
October 12	Adelheid von Basedow Müller born (died April 4, 1883)
1808	Death of Wilhelm's mother; confirmation; first attempts at poetry
1808–1809	Father remarried to Marie Gödel Seelmann (February 13, 1769–March 9, 1853). Wilhelmine, Müller's half sister born of this marriage, eventually married Pastor Francke of Raguhn
1812	Wilhelm passed the *Abitur* examination
July 3	Matriculation at the University of Berlin (founded in 1810)
1813	
February 10	King of Prussia called for volunteers for the War of Liberation
February 16	Müller enlisted in the Prussian army with permission of the Duke of Anhalt
February 24	Withdrawal from the University of Berlin
May 2	Fought in the Battle of Lützen or Gross-Görschen (French victory with heavy losses)
May 20–21	Fought in the Battle of Bautzen, east of Dresden (Napoleon's victory, but with great French losses)
May 26	Fought at Haynau (Chojnow today)
August 30	Fought in Battle of Kulm (Victory over the French General Vandamme)
October 16–19	"Battle of the Nations" (*Völkerschlacht*) at Leipzig (Lieutenant Müller in the depot at Prague)

1814	Müller's military service in Brussels; first love affair; sonnets
November 18	Left Brussels; visited Dessau en route to Berlin

1815	
January	Return after the war to philology studies at the University of Berlin
January 4	Berlinische Gesellschaft für deutsche Sprache founded
June 12	Müller's first visit to the Deutsche Gesellschaft
July 26	Became member of the Deutsche Gesellschaft
August 4	Met Baron de la Motte Fouqué
September	Wrote the foreword to the *Blumenlese aus den Minnesingern*
October 11	Read the introduction to his *Blumenlese* at the Deutsche Gesellschaft
October 21	Müller's twenty-first birthday; first entry in his Berlin diary, a record of his friendship with Luise Hensel
October	Read E. T. A. Hoffmann's *Kreisleriana*; Goethe's *Dichtung und Wahrheit*; Gottfried von Strassburg's *Tristan und Isolde*; Schleiermacher's writings; the poetry of the medieval troubadour Geoffrey Rudel
December	Read *Der arme Heinrich*; Ludwig Uhland's poetry; Adolf Müllner's *Die Schuld*

1816	MAJOR PUBLICATIONS:
	Blumenlese aus den Minnesingern: Erste Sammlung. Berlin: Maurer, 1816. (Müller's modern German translations of Middle High German poetry)
	Bundesblüthen. Berlin: Maurer, 1816. (Reprinted in "The Earliest Poems of Wilhelm Müller," by James Taft Hatfield, 1898. Other contributors: Müller's friends from the War of Liberation, Wilhelm Hensel, Count Friedrich von Kalckreuth, Count Georg von Blankensee, and Wilhelm von Studnitz)
January	Publication of *Bundesblüthen*; difficulties with the censor; read Novalis's writings with Luise Hensel; read several of his poems in the Deutsche Gesellschaft
February 28	Met Clemens Brentano
February 28–29	Visited Baron de la Motte Fouqué with Wilhelm Hensel
March 1	Date of the second introduction to the *Blumenlese*
May	Frequent visits to the home of the wealthy and influential Friedrich August von Stägemann
June	Presented theories on the *Nibelungenlied* in the Deutsche Gesellschaft
August 2	Announcement of Müller's translation of Christopher Marlowe's *Doctor Faustus*
October	Four-week visit in Dessau
November 10	Kissed Luise Hensel on the cheek
End of November	Origin of *Die schöne Müllerin* poetry cycle as a social game in the Stägemann home
December 4	Read "Der Glockenguss zu Breslau" to Luise Hensel
Christmas	At Hensels' and Stägemanns'; Clemens Brentano also present

1817	MAJOR PUBLICATIONS: *Frauentaschenbuch für das Jahr 1817.* (Ballad) *Der Gesellschafter oder Blätter für Geist und Herz, 1817.* (Prose "Flower Interpretations"—Blumendeutungen; "Der Glockenguss zu Breslau"; "Oper und Schauspiel, nebst einigen Bemerkungen über das Theater im Allgemeinen und das Berliner Theater im Besonderen"; literary debate with Adolf Müllner; translations from Old Scottish, Old Spanish, Thomas Gray, etc.) *Wiener Zeitschrift für Kunst, Literatur und Mode, 1817.* (Poems) *Zeitung für die elegante Welt, 1817.* ("Der Birkenhain bei Endermay")
February 20	Lectured at the Deutsche Gesellschaft on the topic "Die Abschriften der altdeutschen Werke aus der Dresdner Bücherei"
August 19	Granted permission from the Duke of Anhalt-Dessau to accompany Baron von Sack on a journey to Italy and Greece with a commission from the historical-philological section of the Berlin Akademie der Wissenschaften
August 20	Departure for Vienna with Baron von Sack
September–October	Acquaintance in Vienna with leaders of the Philikí Etairía (Hetaireia), the group supporting Greek independence from Turkey
November 6	Left Vienna with Baron von Sack and the artist Julius Schnorr von Carolsfeld
November 17	Arrived in Trieste
November 19	Date of Arnim's foreword to the translation of Marlowe's *Faustus*
November 20	Departure for Florence via Ferrara and Bologna
Mid-December	Stay in Florence
1818	MAJOR PUBLICATIONS: *Frauentaschenbuch für das Jahr 1818.* (Three poems) *Gaben der Milde.* Berlin, 1818. (Three poems) *Der Gesellschafter, 1818.* (Blumendeutungen, poems) *Janus.* Vienna, 1818. (Two poems) *Doktor Faustus: Tragödie von Christoph Marlowe.* Introduction by Ludwig Achim von Arnim. Berlin: Maurer, 1818. (Müller, translator) *Die Sängerfahrt.* Berlin, 1818. (Four poems, including "Die Sage vom Frankenberger See") *Wünschelruthe.* Göttingen, 1818. ("Wanderlieder")
January 4	Arrival in Rome with Baron von Sack
Easter	Decision to leave Baron von Sack's expedition
Easter to May	Visited Naples, Pompeii, and Paestum
May 29	Return to Rome
July	Vacation in countryside outside of Rome (Albano)
August	Saved Friedrich Rückert from drowning
August 14	Return to Rome
August 30	Left Rome for Germany via Orvieto, Perugia, Florence, Fiesole, Verona, Tyrol, Munich, Dresden

December 3	Visit in Dresden at the Karl Försters'; read "Die Monate" to Förster, Count Otto Heinrich von Loeben, Baron Ernst Otto von der Malsburg, and Karl August Böttiger, the director of the Museums of Antiquity in Dresden
Early December	Arrival in Dessau
December 28	Application for a teaching position in Dessau
1819	MAJOR PUBLICATIONS: *Frauentaschenbuch für das Jahr 1819.* (Three poems) *Der Gesellschafter, 1819.* ("Goethes Osterie in Rom"; "Briefe aus Albano"; Sonnets ["Die zwölf Monate"]; "Bruchstücke aus meinem römischen Tagebuch"; "Drei Könige")
January	Return to Berlin; continuation of negotiations with Dessau officials about his job application by letter from Berlin
Spring	Wrote *Rom, Römer und Römerinnen;* taught part-time; wrote for the *Gesellschafter*
Summer	Organized ducal library; Berlin trip where he met with Helmina von Chézy
September 1	Back in Dessau; sent announcements to friends asking for items for his new literary journal, *Askania: Zeitschrift für Leben, Literatur und Kunst*
October	Changes in the organization of the Hauptschule
Winter	Worked on *Askania*
December	Began author-publisher relationship with Friedrich Arnold Brockhaus, who asked if Müller would write a "Gesamtrezension der deutschen Reisebeschreibungen über Italien"
December 20	Accepted the offer of Brockhaus to review the German travel writings about Italy
1820	MAJOR PUBLICATIONS: *Askania: Zeitschrift für Leben, Literatur und Kunst.* Edited by Wilhelm Müller. Vol. 1, no. 1–6, January–June, 1820. (Seven poems) *Konversationsblatt, 1820.* Vienna, 1820. (Two poems) *Frauentaschenbuch für das Jahr 1820.* (Two poems) *Gesänge der jüngeren Liedertafel in Berlin, 1820.* No. 122. ("Der Arche Noäh") *Der Gesellschafter, 1820.* ("Der Ackerbau der Römer") *Hermes, 1820.* (Three reviews: "*Hans Sachs,* hrsg. von J. G. Büsching"; "*Hans Sachs* von F. Furchau"; "*Reisebeschreibungen über Italien*") *Literarisches Wochenblatt, 1820.* (Six reviews: "*Paul Flemings erlesene Gedichte* von Gustav Schwab"; "*Die neuesten Romane von dem Verfasser des Waverley*"; "*Heinrichs Dichten und Trachten,* hrsg. von Karl Ludwig Blum"; "*Calderóns Schauspiele,* übersetzt von O. von der Malsburg"; "*Askania*"; "*Fürst Wladimir und seine Tafelrunde*") *Rom, Römer und Römerinnen: Eine Sammlung vertrauter Briefe aus Rom und Albano mit einigen späteren Zusätzen und Belegen.* 2 vols. Berlin: Duncker und Humblot, 1820.

Siebenundsiebzig Gedichte aus den hinterlassenen Papieren eines reisenden Waldhornisten. Dessau: C. G. Ackermann, 1821. (Published in October, 1820, but dated 1821; contains I. "Die schöne Müllerin"; II. "Johannes und Esther"; III. "Reiselieder"; IV. "Die Monate"; V. "Ländliche Lieder"; VI. "Musterkarte")

January–June	Published six issues of *Askania* in Dessau
January 17	Official appointment as librarian of ducal library
Easter	Freed from teaching obligations in grade school
June	Failure of *Askania*
May–June	Worked on reviews of German writings about Italy
June 23	Death of Müller's father
June–July	Journalistic work for Brockhaus
August	Four weeks in Dresden; met Tieck; read *Die schöne Müllerin* aloud
September	Journalistic work for Brockhaus
October	Trip to Berlin
October 28	Dedicated a copy of the *Siebenundsiebzig Gedichte aus den hinterlassenen Papieren eines reisenden Waldhornisten* to Adelheid von Basedow
October 29	Sent copy of *77 Gedichte* to Brockhaus
November	Volume I of *77 Gedichte* appeared (dated 1821); engagement to Adelheid von Basedow
November 30	Copy of *77 Gedichte* sent to Goethe
December	Continued work for Brockhaus; submitted first section of reviews of Italian writings

1821

MAJOR PUBLICATIONS:

Allgemeine Enzyklopädie der Wissenschaften und Künste in alphabetischer Folge von genannten Schriftstellern bearbeitet. Edited by Johann Ersch and Johann Gruber. 1821. (Vol. 7, B—Barzellen; "Bernardino Baldi"; "John Banks")

Frauentaschenbuch für das Jahr 1821. (Poems: "Ungeduld" or "Ich schnitt' es gern in alle Rinden ein"; "Des Postillions Morgenlied")

Der Gesellschafter, 1821. (Three *Griechenlieder*)

Hermes, 1821. ("Reisebeschreibungen über Italien"; "Über deutsche Litteratur")

Literarisches Konversationsblatt, 1821. [Reviews: "*Der Abt* von dem Verfasser des Waverley"; "Streifereien durch die Almanachslitteratur von 1821"; "Litterarische Stadtgespräche aus London" (in five issues); "Byrons *Marino Falieri, Doge von Venedig*"; "*Vaux de Vire* de Basselin"; "Taschenbücher für 1822. (W. v. Schütz, Gustav Schwab, Friedrich Rückert, Helmina von Chézy, Count Otto von Loeben, Ludwig Tieck)"; "*Travels of Cosmos III, Grand Duce of Tuscany*"; "*Lyrische Blätter* vom Grafen Platen." Probably by Müller: two more "Litterarische Stadtgespräche aus London"; "Litterarische Notizen aus Schweden"]

Lieder der Griechen. 2 vols. Dessau: Christian Georg Ackermann, 1821.

Siebenundsiebzig Gedichte aus den hinterlassenen Papieren eines reisenden Waldhornisten. (See listing for 1820)
Urania, 1821. ("Erinnerungen aus Florenz"; "Bacchus in Toscana")
Zeitung für die elegante Welt, 1821. ("Erinnerungen aus Toskana")

March 6	Alexander Ypsilanti began the Greek Revolution by proclaiming a revolt in Moldavia and appealing to the Russian Czar for aid
March 25	Official day of celebration of Greek independence
April 10	Sent poem on Byron to Brockhaus
May 21	Marriage to Adelheid von Basedow (1800–1883)
June 3	Wrote to Brockhaus about the reviews of English books
June 13	Last of reviews on literature about Italy submitted
June 26	Greek hero Ypsilanti defeated by Turks at Dragashan and imprisoned by Austrians
Early August	Trip to Leipzig with Adelheid
September–October	Wrote for Brockhaus
October 18	Sent *Griechenlieder* to Brockhaus
November	Heavy correspondence with Brockhaus; trouble with censor over *Griechenlieder;* much criticism of contemporary politics in his letters to Brockhaus
December 9	Visit from Wilhelm Hensel, who sketched a picture of Müller and Adelheid; consideration of a move to Dresden
December	Letters to Fouqué; new edition of *Griechenlieder* (others sold out in six weeks); trouble with censor; *Griechenlieder* sold out
New Year's	Visit in Leipzig
1822	MAJOR PUBLICATIONS:

Allgemeine Enzyklopädie der Wissenschaften und Künste in alphabetischer Folge von genannten Schriftstellern bearbeitet. Edited by Johann Ersch and Johann Gruber. 1822. (Vol. 8, Bas—Bendorf; "Basilicata"; "Basselin"; "Belluno"; Vol. 9, Bene—Bibeh; five articles)
Bibliothek deutscher Dichter des 17. Jahrhunderts. Edited by Wilhelm Müller. Leipzig: Brockhaus, 1822. (Vol. 1— Martin Opitz; Vol. 2—Andreas Gryphius; Vol. 3— Paul Fleming)
Hermes, 1822. [Two reviews: "Ariosts *Rasender Roland* und dessen Übersetzungen von Gries und Streckfuss" and "Über die deutschen Übersetzungen des Homers (F. A. Wolf, K. L. Kannegiesser, Konrad Schwenck)"]
Literarisches Konversationsblatt, 1822. [Reviews: "Calderón, übersetzt von O. von der Malsburg"; "Taschenbücher für 1822 (E. T. A. Hoffmann)"; "*Östliche Rosen* von Rückert"; "Drei neue Tragödien von Byron (*Cain: A Mystery; Sardanapal; The Two Foscari*)"; "*Der Seeräuber* vom Verfasser des Waverley"; "*Gedichte* von O. von der Malsburg"; "Ein Besuch bei John Clare in dem Dorfe Helpstone in Northamptonshire"; "Fünf litterarische Stadtgespräche aus London"; "*Timbuctoo*

(nach Cochelets Reisebeschreibung)"; "*Die Legende von den heiligen drei Königen von Johann von Hildesheim* von Gustav Schwab"; "Aus Casanovas *Memoiren*, 2. Bd.";
"Deutsche Taschenbücher für 1823 (Raupach, Heine, Platen, Rückert, E. T. A. Hoffmann)"; "*Halidon Hill, a Dramatic Sketch* by W. Scott"; Probably: "Brief aus Novarino, von G. F. aus Dessau, Adjutanten des Generals Normann, an einen Freund in Dessau"; "Griechenlied—Der Bund mit Gott"]
Lieder der Griechen. Zweites Heft, 1822. Dessau: Ackermann, 1822.
Der Obernigker Bote. Breslau, 1822. ("Scenen aus . . . Peter Squenz" and "Dem elterlichen Brautpaare")
Der Sammler. Vienna, 1822. (Scottish poem; "Rabenfrühstück")
Urania, 1822. ("Wanderlieder"; "Kritik Lord Byron als Dichter"; "Assonanzen"; "Ländliche Lieder")

January	Back in Dessau
January 16	Sent *Winterreise* to Brockhaus
January–February	Much correspondence with Brockhaus
March 30	Date of dedication to *Bibliothek deutscher Dichter des 17. Jahrhunderts,* Vol. 1
April 20	Daughter Auguste born (died 1868)
April 22	Sent Vol. 1 of *Bibliothek deutscher Dichter* to Brockhaus
July 6	Vol. 2 of *Bibliothek deutscher Dichter* dedicated at Dessau
July 27–August 12	Trip to Dresden and Leipzig; visited Ludwig Tieck; saw Carl Maria von Weber; stayed with Baron Kalckreuth
September 8	Dedicated Vol. 3, *Bibliothek deutscher Dichter*
Fall	Visit from Baron Alexander von Simolin from Kurland
September 26	Finished Vol. 3, *Bibliothek deutscher Dichter*
October 7–15	Trip to Magdeburg
October 20	Complained of "weak eyes"
November–December	Work for Brockhaus
November 26	Dedication to Vol. 4, *Bibliothek deutscher Dichter*

1823   MAJOR PUBLICATIONS:

Allgemeine Enzyklopädie der Wissenschaften und Künste in alphabetischer Folge von genannten Schriftstellern bearbeitet. Edited by Johann Ersch and Johann Gruber. 1823. [Vol. 11, Bleiberg—Bonzen; "Trajano Boccalini"; "Bojardo"; "Bologna"; "Bologna (Stadt)"; "Bolognesischer Dialekt"; "Bolognesische Malerschule"; "Bolognesischer Schuh"; "Francesco Bolognetti"; "Bolscherezk, auch Bolscherezkoi Ostrog"; "Guidobaldo Bonarelli della Rovere"; "Prospero Bonarelli della Rovere"; "Pietro Bonarelli della Rovere"]
Aurora für 1823. Mannheim, 1823. ("Tafellieder"; "Geselligkeit des Weins"; "Die freie Elbe"; "Romanzen")
Bibliothek deutscher Dichter des 17. Jahrhunderts. Edited by Wilhelm Müller. Leipzig: Brockhaus, 1823. (Vol. 4—Georg Rudolf Weckherlin; Vol. 5—Simon Dach, Robert Roberthin, Heinrich Albert)
Deutsche Blätter für Poesie, Litteratur, Kunst und Theater.

Breslau, 1823. ["Devisen zu Bonbons" (Fourteen poems); "Tafellieder" (Nineteen); "Strafgedichte ('Die neuen Kreuzritter'; 'Gegen die Pharisäer')"; *Die Winterreise* (End; ten songs); "Leo, Admiral von Cypern: Trauerspiel in vier Aufzügen" (only Act 1)]

Hermes, 1823. ("Gries' und Streckfuss' Übersetzungen von Tassos *Befreitem Jerusalem*"; "Über die Gedichte des Thomas Moores")

Literarisches Konversationsblatt, 1823. ["Zwei Taschenbücher, 1823, *Cornelia* and *Penelope* (Ludwig Tieck)"; "Fünf litterarische Bemerkungen"; "Eine Stimme für Griechenlands Freiheit aus Frankreich"; "*Werner,* A Tragedy of Lord Byron"; "Thomas Moore's *Love of the Angels*"; "*Graf Gordo,* Trauerspiel von Ernst Grosse"; "*Der Schultheiss von Zalamea* von Calderón de la Barca"; "*Shakespeares Schauspiele,* erl. von Franz Horn"; "Adamantios Korai an seine Landsleute"; "Neun deutsche Taschenbücher, 1823 (Gustav Schwab, Ludwig Tieck, Ludwig Robert, Helmina von Chézy, Karl Förster, Count Otto von Loeben, Friedrich Rückert)"; "*Ritterzeit und Ritterwesen,* Vorlesungen von Johann Gustav Büsching"; "Shakespeares *Troilus und Kressida,* übers. von Beauregard Pandin"; "Mark Bozzari. Probe aus einer neuen Sammlung von Griechenliedern von Wilhelm Müller"]

Morgenblatt für gebildete Stände, 1823. ("Die Maiottenwitwe"; "Belustigungen aus der deutschen Litteraturgeschichte des siebzehnten Jahrhunderts. Simon Dach und der grosse Kurfürst von Brandenburg"; "Belustigungen . . . der Trompeter Gabriel Voigtländer")

"Herr Peter Squenz: Oder die Komödie zu Rumpelskirch, Posse in zwei Abtheilungen, nach Gryphius und Shakespeare frei bearbeitet." *Jahrbuch deutscher Nachspiele.* Vol. 2, 1823.

Neue Lieder der Griechen. Leipzig: Brockhaus, 1823.

Neue Lieder der Griechen. Zweites Heft. Leipzig: Brockhaus, 1823.

Taschenbuch zum geselligen Vergnügen aus dem Jahre 1823. ("Der ewige Jude"; "Amor in der Vigne"; "Weinlied")

Urania, 1823. ("Wanderlieder"; "*Die Winterreise, in 12 Liedern*"; "Ländliche Lieder")

January	Turks failed to take Missolunghi at Gulf of Corinth; Müller's lengthy quarrel with school principal Stadelmann about his obligations at school; work on *Griechenlieder*
January 22–23	Trip to Leipzig with the Liedertafel
February–March	Extensive correspondence with Brockhaus
Easter	Request for relief from school duties
June	In Dresden with Carl Maria von Weber; honored by Dresden Liedertafel
July	Two-week vacation in Berlin at the Hensels'; met Fanny Mendelssohn; heard *Die schöne Müllerin* performed (probably Ludwig Berger's setting)
August 20	Death of Friedrich Arnold Brockhaus

August 30
August–November

December 6

1824

Dedication to Vol. 5 of the *Bibliothek deutscher Dichter*
Letters to Heinrich Brockhaus, F. A. Brockhaus's son
and successor
Friedrich Max born (godfather, Carl Maria von Weber)
(died 1900)

MAJOR PUBLICATIONS:
*Allgemeine Enzyklopädie der Wissenschaften und Künste in
alphabetischer Folge von genannten Schriftstellern bearbei-
tet.* Edited by Johann Ersch and Johann Gruber.
1824. (Vol. 12, Boochanpoor—Brezow; ten articles
including "Sebastian Brandt"; Vol. 13, Briänsk—Bu-
kuresd; twenty-one articles including "John Brown";
"George Villiers Buckingham"; and various English
and Italian personalities)
Allgemeine Literatur-Zeitung, 1824. ("Bernhard Thiersch,
Über das Zeitalter und Vaterland des Homer"; "Bernhard
Thiersch, *Urgestalt der Odyssee*")
Bibliothek deutscher Dichter des 17. Jahrhunderts. Edited by
Wilhelm Müller. Leipzig: Brockhaus, 1824. (Vol. 6—
Friedrich von Logau, Hans Assmann von Abschatz)
Konversationslexikon. 6th rev. ed. Leipzig: Brockhaus,
1824–1826. ("Atterbom"; "Byron"; "Campbell";
"Clare"; "Coleridge"; "Cornwall"; "Crabbe"; "Italie-
nische Reisen"; "Literaturgeschichte"; "Th. Moore";
"Rückert"; "G. Schwab"; "Schwedische Literatur";
"Starke"; "Thiersch"; "L. Uhland"; "Walther v. d.
Vogelweide"; "Weckherlin")
Literarisches Konversationsblatt, 1824. ["Deutsche Ta-
schenbücher für 1824"; "Litterarische Notizen aus
England"; *"Les Hermites en prison* par E. Jouy et A. Jay"
(in two issues); "Bemerkungen über die Novellen des
Verfassers von Waverley—W. Scott"; *"Rossinis Leben
und Werke* (nach Stendhal)" (in two issues); "Berli-
nische wissenschaftliche und Kunstnachrichten";
"Lord Byrons *Don Juan*"; *"The Adventures of Hayii Baba
of Ispahan*"; *"St. Ronans Brunnen,* Walter Scotts neue-
ster Roman" (in two issues); *"Leberecht Hirsemenzels,
eines deutschen Schulmeisters, Briefe aus und über Italien,*
hrsg. von Ernst Raupach"; *"Griechenlieder* (von Wai-
blinger, H. Stieglitz, E. Grosse, Chr. Bork)"; *"Beiträge
zur Poesie* . . . von Eckermann"; *"Casimir Delavigne und
Alphonse de Lamartine I, II (L'Ecole des Vieillards-La Mort
de Socrate)*"; "Rossini und seine Mütze in London";
"The Deformed Transformed by Byron"; "Litteratur-
briefe aus London" (in ten issues); "Litteraturbriefe
aus Paris" (in eleven issues); *"The Life and Times of
Salvator Rosa* by Lady Morgan"; "Über Palimpseste";
"Byron (Gedicht)—English translation in *Literary
Rambler,* 1823"; *"Walladmor* (von W. Alexis)"; "Klop-
stocks Säkularfeier in Quedlinburg" (two issues);
"Englische Zeitungen"; "Leichenrede auf Lord By-
ron, gehalten von Spiridion Trikupi, gedruckt auf Be-
fehl der griechischen Regierung"; *"The Second Sight*

(aus der *Literary Gazette*)"; "Missolunghi, nach Pouqueville, usw"; "P. J. de Béranger"; "Casimir Delavigne: *Trois messéniennes nouvelles*"; "Byroniana"; "*Neugriechische Volkslieder* von Wilhelm Müller" (Six poems); "Briefe an eine Dame über die Almanachs-Literatur des Jahres 1825 (Schwab, Raupach, Rückert, Maler Müller, Robert, von der Malsburg)" (several issues); "*Königsmark, der lange Finne* (Roman von James Paulding"); *Der Vexierte* (von Ch. F. Meurer)"; "Griechenland in den Jahren 1823 und 1824"; "Russische Poesie"; "Washington Irving"; "Litterarische Notizen aus England" (numerous uninitialed articles); "Litteraturund Kunstnotizen aus dem Österreichischen"]

Morgenblatt, 1824. ["Belustigungen aus der deutschen Literaturgeschichte des siebzehnten Jahrhunderts. Deutsche Kernsprüche von Hans Assmann Freyherrn von Abschatz"; "Alexander und Diogenes" (Trinklied); "Amorettenspiele" (Four poems); "Zukunft" (Trinklied)]

Gedichte aus den hinterlassenen Papieren eines reisenden Waldhornisten. Zweites Bändchen. Dessau: Ackermann, 1824. ("Tafellieder für Liedertafeln"; "Die Winterreise"; "Ländliche Lieder"; "Wanderlieder"; "Devisen zu Bonbons")

Homerische Vorschule: Eine Einleitung in das Studium der Ilias und Odyssee. Leipzig: Brockhaus, 1824. (Second edition in 1836)

Neueste Lieder der Griechen. Leipzig: Leopold Voss, 1824. (Seven held back by the censor; two in Schall and von Holtei's *Deutsche Blätter;* translated into French in 1828)

Taschenbuch zum geselligen Vergnügen aus dem Jahre 1824. (Four poems)

Urania, 1824. ("Italienische Ständchen in Ritornellen"; "Epigramme aus Rom 1818")

Zeitung für die elegante Welt, 1824. ["Markos Bozzaris: Eine biographische Skizze" (in four issues)]

1824	Franz Schubert's *Die schöne Müllerin* published; Müller given title of Hofrat in Dessau court
January–February	Correspondence with Heinrich Brockhaus about unpublished *Griechenlieder* and *Homerische Vorschule*
March 16	Contract for *Homerische Vorschule* signed
April 15	Dedication to Vol. 6 of *Bibliothek deutscher Dichter*
April	Heard Weber conduct *The Seasons* in Dresden; visited Weber at his villa Osterwitz
May 24	Dedication of *Homerische Vorschule* written
May 29–June 13	Vacation at Villa Grassi of Baron Kalckreuth outside Dresden
June	Stopped off in Leipzig on way to Dresden; saw Count Loeben and Otto von der Malsburg; took mineral baths for poor health; celebrated Tieck's birthday with him; wrote "Frühlingskranz aus dem Plauenschen Grunde," published in 1826
June 16	Back in Dessau

June 20   Byron's death in Greece

July 2   Celebration of one hundredth anniversary of Klopstock's birth in Quedlinburg (Adelheid sang a solo, and Wilhelm published a report in the *Literarisches Konversationsblatt*)

July   Worked on Fauriel translation and critique of Goethe's *Kunst und Alterthum, 1823*

August 8   F. A. Wolf died

October 20   Complained to Brockhaus that he couldn't work as much in winter due to poor eyesight

October   Worked on *Der Dreizehnte*

November   Worked on Byron biography, *Der Dreizehnte*, and "Frühlingslieder"; Vol. 2 of *Gedichte aus den hinterlassenen Papieren eines reisenden Waldhornisten* appeared

1825   MAJOR PUBLICATIONS:

Allgemeine Enzyklopädie der Wissenschaften und Künste in alphabetischer Folge von genannten Schriftstellern bearbeitet. Edited by Johann Ersch and Johann Gruber. 1825. [Vol. 14, Part 1, Bulacan—Byrom [*sic*]; twelve articles including "John Bull"; "Michelangelo Buonarroti"; "Robert Burns"; "Samuel Butler"); Vol. 14, Part 2, C—Calza (Eighteen articles)]

Allgemeine Literatur-Zeitung. Halle, 1825. ("*Chants populaires de la Grèce Moderne*, Recueillis et publiés . . . C. Fauriel"; "*Die Hölle des Dante Alighieri*, übersetzt und erläutert von K. Streckfuss"; "Besprechung von 8 Schriften über Byron (1822/25)"; "*Ariosts fünf Gesänge*, übersetzt von K. Streckfuss")

Bibliothek deutscher Dichter des 17. Jahrhunderts. Edited by Wilhelm Müller. Leipzig: Brockhaus, 1825. (Vol. 7— Julius Wilhelm Zincgref, Andreas Tscherning, Ernst Christoph Homburg, Paul Gerhardt)

Der Gesellschafter, 1825. ["Literarhistorische Cúriositäten" ("Der Schädel des Mönches"; "Lord Byrons Menagerie"; "Lord Byrons Selbstporträt"); "Mein erstes Sonnett. Zum Geburtstage eines Freundes, 1814"; "Bukovallas"; "Anekdota Bacchia"; "Alte und neue Weisheit (Tafellied)"; "Der Ausflug eines jungen Elfen"; "Vevros und sein Rappe"; "Der sterbende Matrose")]

Fauriel, Claude, comp. *Neugriechische Volkslieder.* Translated by Wilhelm Müller. 2 vols. Leipzig: Leopold Voss, 1825. ("I. Geschichtliche Lieder; II. Romantische und Häusliche Lieder nebst Anhang. Mit dem neugriechischen Texte.")

Literarisches Konversationsblatt, 1825. ["Litteraturbriefe aus London" (several); "Byroniana" (several); "Briefe an eine Dame über die Almanachslitteratur des Jahres 1825" (several authors, including Rückert, Platen, Schmidt von Lübeck); "Litteraturbriefe aus Paris"; "Unnötige Rechtfertigung des Rezensenten der Taschenbücher für 1825"; "George Waddington über

Griechenland und die Griechen in den Jahren 1823
und 1824"; "Der Bund der Hetairia (nach Wadding-
ton)"; "Französische, englische und deutsche Überset-
zungen neugriechischer Volkslieder. Von Wilhelm
Müller." (Compares French of Nep. L. Lemercier,
English of R. Brinsley Sheridan, and his own
German—which he prefers); "*Chansons Nouvelles* de
Béranger"; "Zwei neue Gedichte des Alphonse de
Lamartine ("Chant du Sacre" and "Le dernier Chant
du Pèlerinage de Childe Harold")"; "Deutsche Über-
setzungen neugriechischer Volkslieder von Wilhelm
Müller"; "*Goethes Philosophie*, hrsg. von Fr. K. Julius
Schütz"; "Taschenbücher auf 1826 (Ludwig Tieck,
Gustav Schwab, Ernst Raupach)"]

Morgenblatt, 1825. ["3 Tafellieder"; "Der Charon der
Neu-Griechen"; "Frühlingslied"; "Bürgers 'Leonore'
und ein neugriechisches Volkslied"; "Bilder aus dem
neugriechischen Volksleben—Die Kinderwelt, Braut-
wahl, Verlobung, Hochzeit"; "Belustigungen aus der
deutschen Literaturgeschichte des siebzehnten Jahr-
hunderts. Lobhudeley in Anagrammen." (On name
of Joh. Rist; plus two Rist poems)]

Lieder der Griechen, Erstes Heft. 2nd enl. ed. Dessau:
Ackermann, 1825.

Taschenbuch zum geselligen Vergnügen aus dem Jahre 1825.
Edited by A. Wendt. ["Lieder vom Meere" (Seven
poems); "Die Umkehr"; "Est, Est (Romanze)"]

Zeitung für die elegante Welt, 1825. ["Deutsche Blätter-
und Blumensprache"; "Das Königreich Yvetot"
(Three issues)]

January–February	Worked on Byron biography in Dessau
January 25	Published critique of Goethe's *Über Kunst und Alterthum, 1823*
February 25	Turks began siege of Missolunghi
February 27	Wrote dedication to Vol. 7 of *Bibliothek deutscher Dichter*
March 1	Finished Byron biography
March—April	Four weeks in Berlin; met Fanny Mendelssohn
April 14	Back at Dessau working on Fauriel translations
July 28	Departed for vacation on Rügen with poet Adolf Fried-rich Furchau (Inspired "Muscheln von der Insel Rügen")
August 7	Traveled to Putbus, later Stralsund and Rostock
August 15	Visit in Berlin; ate at Mendelssohns'; Felix Mendels-sohn present
August 20–22	Return to Dessau
August 30	Left on brief trip to Magdeburg
September–October	Work in Dessau for Brockhaus
November 7	Dedication to Vol. 8 of *Bibliothek deutscher Dichter*
November 9	Working on *Der Dreizehnte*
December 7	Submitted *Der Dreizehnte* to Brockhaus
December 11	"Muscheln von der Insel Rügen" submitted
End of year	Began work on Ersch und Gruber *Enzyklopädie* again
After Christmas	Trip to Dresden via Leipzig; return week after New Year's

1826

MAJOR PUBLICATIONS:

Allgemeine Enzyklopädie der Wissenschaften und Künste in alphabetischer Folge von genannten Schriftstellern bearbeitet. Edited by Johann Ersch and Johann Gruber. 1826. [Vol. 15, Camaldulenser—Cazouls les Beziers; 124 articles including many Italian terms, "Caravaggio"; "Capri"; "Carew"; "Henry Carey"; "Baldassare Castiglione"]

Allgemeine Literatur-Zeitung. Halle, 1826. [Reviews of three novels: *"Walladmor.* Frei nach . . . W. Scott. Von W. . . . .s,* 2. verb. Aufl. Hrsg. . . . von W. Alexis"; *"Königsmark, der lange Finne . . .* Vom . . . W. Irving. Aus dem Engl. vom Übersetzer der *Jungfrau vom See";* "*Der Vexirte . . . Roman";* "*Volkslieder der Serben metrisch übersetzt . . .* Talvj"; *"Das neue Leben . . . des Dante Alighieri.* Übersetzt und hrsg. von F. v. Oeynhausen"]

Bibliothek deutscher Dichter des 17. Jahrhunderts. Wilhelm Müller, ed. (Vol. 8—Johann Rist, Daniel Georg Morhof; Vol. 9—Georg Philipp Harsdörffer, Johann Klaj, Siegmund von Birken, Andreas (Scholtz) Scultetus, Justus Georg Schottel, Adam Olearius, Johannes Scheffler—Angelus Silesius)

Blätter für literarische Unterhaltung, 1826. ["Missolunghi"; "Literarische Abendunterhaltungen auf dem Lande" (several); "Schenkendorf"; "Homerica" (in several issues); "Lamartine in zwei deutschen Übersetzungen"]

Frauentaschenbuch für das Jahr 1826. ["Romanzen und Lieder" (Six poems); "Feldblumenstrauss" (Four poems); "Kleine Liebesreime aus den Inseln des Archipelagus"]

Der Gesellschafter, 1826. ["Zwei Trinklieder"; "Erotische Tändeleien" (Nine poems)]

Griechisches Feuer auf dem Altare edler Frauen. . . . M. G. Saphir, ed. No. 1. Berlin: 1826. (Seven *Griechenlieder)*

Literarisches Konversationsblatt, 1826. ["Die Taschenbücher für 1826 (Rückert)"; "Einige Worte über Fr. A. Wolf"; *"Shakespeare,* erl. von Franz Horn"; "*Malsburgs Calderón,* 6 Bd."; "Homerica"]

Mitternachtsblatt, 1826. (Four poems)

Morgenblatt, 1826. ["Erotische Tändeleien" (Thirty poems); "Hundert deutsche Reimsprüche"]

"Missolunghi." Dessau: Juni, 1826.

"Missolunghi: Ein Gedicht zum Besten der Griechen." Dresden: Walther, 1826. (Republished 1837)

Siebenundsiebzig Gedichte aus den hinterlassenen Papieren eines reisenden Waldhornisten. Vol. 1. 2nd ed. Dessau: Ackermann, 1826.

Neuer Nekrolog der Deutschen. Zweiter Jahrgang, 1824. Ilmenau, 1826. ("Ernst Friedrich Georg Otto Freiherr von der Malsburg")

Taschenbuch zum geselligen Vergnügen aus dem Jahre 1826. F. Philippi, ed. (Four Frühlingslieder)

Urania aus dem Jahre 1826. "Frühlingskranz aus dem Plauenschen Grunde, 1824" (Nine poems)
Zeitgenossen. New series. Vol. 5, no. 17, 1826. ("Byron")
Zeitung für die elegante Welt, 1826. ["Solomon von Golau redivivus, oder: Deutscher Sinnsprüche Erstes Hundert"; "Lieder aus Franzensbad bei Eger" (Thirteen poems); "Zwei neugriechische Volkslieder" ("Auf den Tod des Markos Bozzaris"; "Auf den Tod des Georgis"); "Reise von Wunsiedel nach Bayreuth"]

December 31– January 1	New Year's Eve celebrated in the home of Ludwig Tieck
January 9	Return from Dresden via Leipzig
January 22	Worked on Ersch and Gruber *Enzyklopädie*
March	Caught whooping cough from his children
April	Sent first 100 epigrams to Brockhaus
April 23	Fall of Missolunghi
May	Epigrams appeared in *Zeitung für die elegante Welt*
Summer	Moved into new house in library building
June 5–18	Recuperation at Luisium, ducal country house
June 7	Wrote to Heinrich Heine
June 12	Wrote dedication to Vol. 9, *Bibliothek deutscher Dichter*
June	Last Griechenlied, "Missolunghi," published
July–August	"Cure" at Franzensbad in Bohemia (Czechoslovakia)
July 15	Sent copy of "Missolunghi" to Dresden Griechenverein
August 17	Return trip via Bayreuth, Wunsiedel, Nuremberg, Bamberg, Coburg, Rudolstadt, Jena, Weimar
August 23	Arrival in Weimar
August 24	Saw Goethe
August 26	Attended tea party at Goethe's home
August 28	Attended Goethe's birthday party
August 31	Arrival in Dessau
September	Work on *Debora* (finished by October 1)
October 17	Letter to Tieck with dedication of new edition of 77 *Gedichte*
October 23	Sent Cotta 100 epigrams
November 20	Simolin staying with Müllers until the New Year
December	Dramaturge for Dessau amateur court theater

1827

MAJOR PUBLICATIONS:

Allgemeine Enzyklopädie der Wissenschaften und Künste in alphabetischer Folge von genannten Schriftstellern bearbeitet. Edited by Johann Ersch and Johann Gruber. 1827. (Vol. 16, Cea—Chiny; seventy-three articles, including "Chaucer"; Vol. 17, Chiococca—Claytonia; forty-three articles, including "Cicerone" and "Charles Churchill"). Section II, Vol. 1, H—Hamburgh, 1827. Edited by Georg Hassel and Wilhelm Müller. (Eighty-seven articles on English and Italian topics; etymology; artists; ornithology; "Albrecht von Halberstadt"; "Franz Hals")
Allgemeine Literatur-Zeitung. Halle, 1827. [Review of *"Das Fegefeuer (Das Paradies)* des Dante Alighieri, übersetzt von K. L. Kannegiesser. 2. sehr veränderte Aufl."]

Bibliothek deutscher Dichter des 17. Jahrhunderts. Edited by Wilhelm Müller. Leipzig: Brockhaus, 1827. (Vol. 10, Johann Christian Günther) (Vol. 11–14 edited and published by Karl Förster in 1828, 1831, 1837, 1838)

Blätter für literarische Unterhaltung, 1827. ["Litterarische Abendunterhaltungen auf dem Lande" (Three articles); "*Handbuch für Reisende in Italien* von Neigebaur"; "Die Frithjofsage"; "*Dante Alighieris lyrische Gedichte,* italienisch und deutsch von Kannegiesser"; "*Homerica. Irrfahrten des Odysseus . . .* von Hedw. Hülle (1826)"; "Cas. Delavigne, *Sept messéniennes nouvelles*"]

Deutscher Regentenalmanach, 1827. ("Leopold Friedrich, Herzog von Anhalt-Dessau")

Frauentaschenbuch für das Jahr 1827. ["Die schöne Kellnerin (von Bacharach) und ihre Gäste" (Nine poems)]

Der Gesellschafter, 1827. ("Hänschen und sein Herr: Gesellschaftslied zu Goethes Geburtstag, 1827")

Hermes, 1827. ["Über die neueste lyrische Poesie der Deutschen (Ludwig Uhland und Justinus Kerner)"]

Jahrbücher für wissenschaftliche Kritik, 1827. (Reviews: "*Die elegischen Dichter der Hellenen . . .* übers. und erläutert von W. E. Weber"; "*Lieder von Schmidt von Lübeck.* 2. verm. Aufl."; "*Gedichte* von Justinus Kerner")

Konversationslexikon. 7th ed. Leipzig: Brockhaus, 1827. (Sixty-five articles on early and contemporary writers, including a long article on "Deutsche Poesie"; "Johannes Agricola"; "Heinrich Christian Boije"; "Simon Dach"; "Sebastian Francke"; "Gottfried von Strassburg"; "Brüder Grimm"; "Georg Philipp Harsdörffer"; "Johann Klaj"; "Heinrich von Kleist"; "Konrad von Würzburg"; "Jakob Michael Reinhold Lenz"; "Hrabanus Maurus"; "Max von Schenkendorf"; "Christian Wernicke"; "Julius Wilhelm Zincgref")

Lyrische Reisen und epigrammatische Spaziergänge. Leipzig: Voss, 1827. [Dedication to Simolin; "Lieder aus dem Meerbusen von Salerno" (*Taschenbuch zum geselligen Vergnügen aus dem Jahre 1825*); "Ständchen in Ritornellen aus Albano" (*Urania, 1824*); "Reime aus den Inseln des Archipelagus" (*Frauentaschenbuch aus dem Jahre 1826*); "Frühlingskranz aus dem Plauenschen Grunde" (*Urania, 1826*); "Muscheln von der Insel Rügen" (*Urania, 1827*); "Deutscher Sinnsprüche Erstes Hundert"; "Lieder aus Franzensbad" (*Zeitung für die elegante Welt, 1826*); "Reise von Wunsiedel," two neo-Greek folk songs, "Die schöne Kellnerin und ihre Gäste" (*Frauentaschenbuch aus dem Jahre 1827*); "Berenice" (*Morgenblatt, 1826*); "Epigrammatische Spaziergänge" (*Zeitung für die elegante Welt, 1827*)]

Morgenblatt, 1827. ["Kleine Liebeslieder aus den Inseln

des Archipelagus" (Thirteen poems); "Vater-
ländisches" (Five poems, including "Morgengruss aus
Luisium")]
Neuer Nekrolog der Deutschen. Vol. 3, 1825. Ilmenau,
1827. ("Otto Heinrich Graf von Loeben")
Taschenbuch zum geselligen Vergnügen, 1827. Leipzig:
Voss, 1827. ["Des Trinkers Jahreszeiten" (Four
poems)]
Urania aus dem Jahre 1827. [*Der Dreizehnte;* "Muscheln
von der Insel Rügen" (Fifteen poems, including
"Vineta")]
Zeitung für die elegante Welt, 1827. ("Hundert Sprüche
und Sinngedichte")

February–November	Franz Schubert composed *Die Winterreise*
February 14	Submitted all but last chapter of *Debora*
February 19	Finished *Debora*
June	Trip to Zerbst with Liedertafel; two weeks sick in bed
July 1	Dedication to Vol. 10, *Bibliothek deutscher Dichter*
July	Published *Lyrische Reisen und epigrammatische Spazier-gänge*
July 23	Submitted Vol. 10 of *Bibliothek deutscher Dichter*
July 31–September 25	Müller and Adelheid made a Rheinreise
July 31	Leipzig
August 3	Frankfurt (saw Goethehaus; Georg Döring; Müller's friend Simolin)
August 7	Mainz and Rhine River
August 8	Rüdesheim, Bingen, Rochuskapelle and Lorelei
August 13	Cologne
August 16	Bonn (Siebengebirge; visit with August Wilhelm von Schlegel)
August 17	Koblenz
August 18	Bingen
August 19	Wiesbaden
August 20	Frankfurt, Königstein, Falkenstein
August 25–26	Heidelberg
August 27–28	Karlsruhe
August 29–30	Baden-Baden
September 1	Strassbourg
September 3	Karlsruhe
September 5	Stuttgart via Ludwigsburg (saw Gustav Schwab, Wilhelm Hauff, Ludwig Uhland, Friedrich von Matthisson, Friedrich Haug)
September 15	Visit with Justinus Kerner in Weinsberg
September 16	Mergentheim
September 17	Würzburg
September 19	Gotha
September 20	Arrival in Weimar
September 21	Wilhelm and Adelheid visited Goethe
September 23	Left Weimar and arrived in Leipzig
September 24	Visited Brockhaus in Leipzig
September 25	Arrival in Dessau
September 30–October 1	Unexpected death in bed after writing several business letters in the early evening

1828	MAJOR PUBLICATIONS:

Allgemeine Enzyklopädie der Wissenschaften und Künste in alphabetischer Folge von genannten Schriftstellern bearbeitet. Edited by Johann Ersch and Johann Gruber. 1828 [Vol. 2, Hamcken— Harrespur (Forty-five articles including "Georg Friedrich Händel"; "Hansa"; "Hanswurst"); Vol. 3, Harrich—Hebung. Edited by Georg Hassel and A. G. Hoffmann. 1828. (Eleven articles); Vol. 5 (1829), Heinrich—Hequaesi, portrait (a copper etching) of Wilhelm Müller by J. F. Schröter and a mention of him are in the foreword.]
Taschenbuch zum geselligen Vergnügen, 1828. Leipzig: Voss, 1828. (Six poems including "Die vier Jahreszeiten des Trinkers")
Urania aus dem Jahre 1828 (Debora: Novelle)

1829	MAJOR PUBLICATIONS:

Erholungsstunden Zeitschrift. Edited by G. Döring, 1829. (Three poems)
Müller, Wilhelm, and Wolff, Oskar Ludwig Bernhard, eds. *Egeria: Raccolta di poesie Italiane populari.* Leipzig: Ernst Fleischer, 1829.

1830	Gustav Schwab published Müller's *Vermischte Schriften* in five volumes
1831	Karl Förster published Vol. 12 of *Bibliothek deutscher Dichter* (Friedrich Spee von Langenfeld)
1833	Henry Wadsworth Longfellow, *Outre-Mer*
1836	Second edition of *Homerische Vorschule* by Detlev Carl Wilhelm Baumgarten-Crusius
1837	Karl Förster published Vol. 13 of *Bibliothek deutscher Dichter* (Zacharias Lund, David Schirmer, Philipp von Zesen)
	Gedichte—second edition published by Gustav Schwab
1838	Last volume of *Bibliothek deutscher Dichter* published by Karl Förster (Christian Hofmann von Hofmannswaldau, Daniel Caspar von Lohenstein, Christian Wernicke, Friedrich Rudolf Ludwig von Canitz, Christian Weise, Johann von Besser, Heinrich Mühlfort, Benjamin Neukirch, Johann Michael Moscherosch, Nikolaus Peucker)
1839	Henry Wadsworth Longfellow, *Hyperion*
1844	*Griechenlieder* published as collection by Brockhaus with introduction by F. Max Müller
1845	Arthur Müller, *Moderne Reliquien*
1847	Müller's Faust translation appeared in Scheible's *Das Kloster*
1850	Miniatur-Ausgabe of Gustav Schwab
1854	*Moderne Klassiker* edition
1857	Gubitz republished "Oper und Schauspiel," the literary feud between Müller and Adolf Müllner
1858	Brockhaus's fourth edition of *Gedichte*
1864	*Ausgewählte Gedichte* (Brockhaus)
1868	Müller's daughter Auguste died

	F. Max Müller's edition of his father's *Gedichte* appeared with a biography written by the son
1874	*Gedichte,* edited by E. Hermann
1883	Adelheid Müller died on April 4 at the age of 83
1884	*Debora* republished in *Die deutsche Library,* New York. (Also in the *Deutscher Novellenschatz* of Paul Heyse and Hermann Kurz)
	John Snodgrass, "Heine and Wilhelm Müller"
1885	F. Max Müller's biography of his father appeared in the *Allgemeine deutsche Biographie*
1887	Article about Müller's family and childhood by O. Francke
1889	*Gesamtausgabe* (Halle, Bibliothek der Gesamtliteratur)
	Griechenlieder (Halle, Bibliothek der Gesamtliteratur)
1891	Monument erected in Dessau with Grecian marble as part of the celebrations on the one hundredth anniversary of Müller's birth
1894	*Gedichte,* edited by Curt Müller
	Guido Stempel's brief English adaptation of Schwab's biography in *Germania*
1896	Robert Franz Arnold published a chapter on Wilhelm Müller in his lengthy article "Der deutsche Philhellenismus" in *Euphorion*
1898	"Earliest Poems" by James Taft Hatfield
1899	Philip Schuyler Allen, "Wilhelm Müller and the German Volkslied," Ph.D. dissertation, University of Chicago; articles in 1899 (two) and 1901
1900	F. Max Müller died at Oxford on October 28 at the age of 76
1902	John Nollen, article on "Wilhelm Müller and Heine"
1903	"Unpublished Letters" by James Taft Hatfield
	Diary and Letters by Philip Schuyler Allen and James Taft Hatfield
1906	Critical edition of the poetry published by James Taft Hatfield
	Reinhold Steig's article on Wilhelm Müller's translation of Marlowe's *Faustus*
1908	Bruno Hake, "Die schöne Müllerin"
	Aloys Josef Becker, *Wilhelm Müllers Kunstanschauung*
	Karl Goedeke bibliography appeared
	James Taft Hatfield clarified the confusion over the records of Müller's visit with Goethe
1910	Memorial plaque placed in Franzensbad September 8
1911	Two editions of *Faustus* (Berta Badt and Rudolf Frank)
1913	*Faustus* edition by Karl Georg Wendriner
	Gaston Caminade's book *Les Chants des Grecs et le Philhellénisme de Wilhelm Müller*
1914	Hermann Waeschke's article "Wilhelm Müllers Jugendzeit"
1921	Richard Paul Koepke, "Wilhelm Müllers Dichtung und ihre musikalische Komposition," Ph.D. dissertation, Northwestern University

1923	Margaret Richardson's article "Wilhelm Müller's Poetry of the Sea"
1924	Thomas Mann's *Der Zauberberg* published
1926	Philip Schuyler Allen and K. M. Klier, article about Müller and the German folk song
1927	One hundredth anniversary of Müller's death
	Paul Wahl edition of poetry
	Ceremonies and exhibitions at Ducal Library in Dessau
	Heinrich Lohre, *Wilhelm Müller als Kritiker und Erzähler* (mainly Brockhaus correspondence)
	Paul Wahl and Otto Hachtmann, various articles
1928	Alfred Wirth's article "Wilhelm Müller und das Volkslied"
1931	Paul Wahl, *Wilhelm Müllers Rheinreise* (diary, miscellaneous correspondence, and sympathy letters sent to Adelheid after Wilhelm's death)
1933	Frank Spiecker's article "Luise Hensel and Wilhelm Müller"
	Paul Wahl, "Wilhelm Müllers Tod"
1943	Otto Brües's article "Der Griechen-Müller"
1956	*Rom, Römer und Römerinnen.* Edited by Christel Matthias Schröder. Republished in Bremen by Schünemann
1958	Hans Brandenburg, "*Die Winterreise* als Dichtung: Eine Ehrenrettung für Wilhelm Müller"
1960	Joseph Cullen Blair, "Wilhelm Müller's *Doktor Faustus*," M.A. thesis, University of Maryland
	Alexander Solzhenitsyn, *Candle in the Wind* (play)
1963	Alan P. Cottrell, "Wilhelm Müllers lyrische Liederzyklen," Ph.D. dissertation, Ohio State University
1966	Miodrag Ibrovac's book on Claude Fauriel with detailed discussion about Müller's translations of neo-Greek folk songs
	Johannes Irmscher's article on philhellenism in Prussia
	Klaus Günther Just's article "Wilhelm Müller und seine Liederzyklen"
	Hermann Augustin's article on "Der Lindenbaum"
1967	Hans Henning's article on Müller's *Faustus* translation
	Wolfgang Stechow, "Der greise Kopf: Eine Analyse"
1968	Johannes Irmscher's article "Der Dessauer Dichter Wilhelm Müller und der deutsche Philhellenismus"
1970	Alan P. Cottrell, *Wilhelm Müller's Lyrical Song Cycles*
	David B. Greene's "Schubert's '*Winterreise*': A Study in the Aesthetics of Mixed Media"
	Cecilia C. Baumann, "The Life and Works of Wilhelm Müller," Ph.D. dissertation, Northwestern University
	Nigel Reeves, article on Heine and Müller
	Müller's translation of Marlowe's *Faustus* republished in *Faust—Theater der Jahrhunderte*, edited by Margret Dietrich
1971	*Wilhelm-Müller-Kunstpreis* established in Dessau
	Ulla Machlitt's article "Wilhelm Müller—Liederdichter der späten deutschen Romantik"

	Joachim Schulze's article "O Bächlein meiner Liebe. Zu einem unheimlichen Motiv bei Eichendorff und Wilhelm Müller"
1973	H. Lowen Marshall, "Symbolism in Schubert's *Winterreise*"
1975	The essay "Wilhelm Müller und die Romantik," by Rolf Vollmann, in Arnold Feil's book on *Die schöne Müllerin* and *Die Winterreise*
1977	One hundred and fiftieth anniversary of Müller's death
	Commemorations in Dessau; publication of special Müller issue of *Zwischen Wörlitz und Mosigkau,* which includes a listing of the holdings of the Stadtbibliothek Dessau prepared by Irmgard Lange
	Günther Hartung's article "Wilhelm Müller und das deutsche Volkslied" appeared in the *Weimarer Beiträge*
1978	One hundred and fiftieth anniversary of Schubert's death
	Edition of *Rom, Römer und Römerinnen* published in the German Democratic Republic, edited by Wulf Kirsten

APPENDIX B

THE DEDICATION OF THE WILHELM MÜLLER MONUMENT IN DESSAU IN 1891

Dessau, den 1. October 1891

Aus Anhalt.

Die Einweihung des Wilhelm Müller Denkmals bewegte bereits Tags zuvor alle Bewohner Dessaus. Es wurden die Tribünen vor dem verhüllten Denkmal in der Cavalierstraße erbaut und allenthalben sah man bereits am 29. September die Häuser mit Fahnen geschmückt, da nachmittags die hohen Herzoglichen Herrschaften erwartet wurden. Höchstdieselben trafen auch nach 5 Uhr ein und fuhren unter dem Jubel der Bevölkerung nach dem Schlosse. Von den Angehörigen des verewigten Dichters war bereits Professor Max Müller aus Oxford mit seiner Familie in Dessau angekommen und hatte im Kaiserhof Absteigequartier genommen. Professor Max Müller, unser geehrter Landsmann, ist wohl der erste Anhaltiner, dem für seine Verdienste der hohe Orden pour le mérite verliehen wurde; auch ist der berühmte Gelehrte zum Mitglied der französischen Akademie ernannt worden.

Nach 6 Uhr endigte das Festmahl und die Festgäste begaben sich nach dem Herzoglichen Hoftheater, wo man Goethes "Iphigenie auf Tauris" gab. Als die Hohen Herrschaften das Theater betraten, erhob sich Herr Oberbürgermeister Dr. Funk und ließ das prinzliche Ehepaar hochleben. Sodann intonierte das Orchester Glucks Ouverture zu "Iphigenie in Aulis" (mit Richard Wagners Schluß); vorher sprach Frl. Gläser einen schwungvollen, von Herrn Geheimrath Dr. Hosäus gedichteten Prolog. Dann begann die herrliche Dichtung Goethes, der Stolz des deutschen Literaturschatzes, das Kunstwerk der Verschmelzung edelsten Griechentums mit deutscher Empfindung, eine Aufführung, die eine sehr erfolgreiche war.

Aus: *Hundertvierzig Jahre Theater in Dessau: Zeitspiegel, Geschichte, Anekdote.* (Eine Erinnerungsgabe zur Einweihung des neuen Hauses "Das Dessauer Theater" am Hauptmann-Loeper-Platz 29. Mai 1938.)
Dessau: Dünnhaupt, 1938.
Obige Abschrift entstammt dem Abschnitt: "Das Theater im Spiegel der Zeitung," S. 42/43.

Signatur: 54 021

Notes

Complete publishing information can be found in the Bibliography. The original nineteenth-century spellings have been kept in quotations, except where the sources were unclear or where they show varying spellings, as in *Literarisches Konversationsblatt*. Italics are used wherever quoted sources indicate emphasis.

Preface

1. W. Müller, *Diary and Letters*, ed. note; Wäschke, "Aus Müllers Jugendzeit," p. 58.
2. W. Müller, *Diary and Letters*, ed. note.
3. F. Max Müller, "Wilhelm Müller," p. 683.
4. W. Müller, *Vermischte Schriften*, 1:xix.
5. Nollen, "Heine and Müller," p. 104.

Chapter One

1. W. Müller, *Gedichte* (Hatfield, ed., 1906), p. 4.
2. W. Müller, *Diary and Letters*, p. 97.
3. Ibid., p. 147.
4. Not shoemaker, according to Wäschke, p. 60.
5. Ibid., p. 67.
6. W. Müller, *Rheinreise*, p. 117.
7. W. Müller, *Diary and Letters*, p. 4.
8. Ibid., p. 38.
9. Ibid., p. 31.
10. Spiecker, "Luise Hensel and Wilhelm Müller," p. 266.
11. W. Müller, *Diary and Letters*, p. 52.
12. Ibid., p. 178.
13. Hensel, *Lieder*, p. 23.
14. W. Müller, *Diary and Letters*, pp. 37–38.
15. Ibid., pp. 51, 56.
16. Ibid., p. 8.
17. Ibid., p. 12.
18. Ibid., p. 35.
19. Ibid., p. 84.
20. W. Müller, *Vermischte Schriften*, 1:xxvi.
21. W. Müller, *Diary and Letters*, p. 6.
22. Schnorr von Carolsfeld, *Briefe*, pp. 26, 37.
23. Lohre, *Briefe an F. A. Brockhaus*, p. 364.
24. Schnorr von Carolsfeld, *Briefe*, p. 99.
25. Lohre, *Briefe an F. A. Brockhaus*, p. 293.
26. F. Max Müller, *Auld Lang Syne*, p. 84.
27. Kaden, *Italiens Wunderhorn*, pp. xvi–xvii.
28. Luise Förster, *Karl Förster*, p. 104.
29. Hatfield, "Unpublished Letters," p. 126.
30. Lohre, *Briefe an F. A. Brockhaus*, p. 294.
31. Luise Förster, *Karl Förster*, p. 170.
32. W. Müller, *Diary and Letters*, pp. 163–65.
33. Hatfield, "Unpublished Letters," p. 131.
34. Lohre, *Briefe an F. A. Brockhaus*, p. 294.
35. Ibid., pp. 296–97.

36. May 22, according to Wahl; W. Müller, *Rheinreise*, p. 139.
37. F. Max Müller, *Life and Letters*, 1:1–2.
38. W. Müller, *Diary and Letters*, pp. 109, 155.
39. Lohre, *Briefe an F. A. Brockhaus*, pp. 310, 313.
40. W. Müller, *Diary and Letters*, p. 139.
41. F. Max Müller, *Autobiography*, p. 115; *Auld Lang Syne*, p. 10.
42. Ibid., p. 16.
43. W. Müller, *Diary and Letters*, p. 110.
44. Rudolf Koepke, *Ludwig Tieck*, 2:22.
45. Francke, "Zur Biographie Müller," pp. 33–44.
46. Lohre, *Briefe an F. A. Brockhaus*, p. 74.
47. W. Müller, *Diary and Letters*, p. 111.
48. Ibid., p. 120.
49. Ibid., pp. 139–40.
50. Ibid., pp. 143, 150.
51. Ibid., pp. 147–48.
52. Ibid., pp. 152–53.
53. Ibid., p. 157.
54. Ibid., pp. 163–64, 166.
55. Lohre, *Briefe an F. A. Brockhaus*, p. 340. .
56. W. Müller, *Diary and Letters*, p. 170.
57. Lohre, *Briefe an F. A. Brockhaus*, p. 276.
58. W. Müller, *Rheinreise*, p. 73.
59. Ibid., p. 27.
60. Kerner, *Das Kernerhaus*, pp. 59–60.
61. Unfortunately, the date of this meeting with Goethe has been incorrectly recorded. In his 1885 biography of his father in *Allgemeine deutsche Biographie*, F. Max Müller gives the date of the visit as August 28, 1826, on the return trip from Franzensbad. This is obviously incorrect; Müller's traveling companion during this 1826 trip was Baron Simolin, not Adelheid. The early editions of Burkhardt's *Unterhaltungen mit dem Kanzler Friedrich von Müller* and the fifth volume of Biedermann's *Gespräche* erroneously place the meeting on January 26, 1825 (when Müller was occupied with school duties in Dessau). In 1908 Hatfield reports in the *Goethe Jahrbuch* (pp. 184–90) that a loose page in a manuscript had been reinserted in the wrong place, thus explaining the confusion. Hatfield explains that this filing error had led to the false identification of Müller as the "well-known German poet" who had shown Goethe samples of his "misery-filled" poetry, thereby provoking the old master later to rail to his secretary about the sorry quality of contemporary poetry. Goethe's negative comment, which appears in both Woldemar von Biedermann's *Goethes Gespräche* and Johann Peter Eckermann's *Gespräche mit Goethe in den letzten Jahren seines Lebens*, is in fact criticizing the poetry of Karl Streckfuss (1778–1844), not that of Wilhelm Müller.
62. F. Max Müller, "Wilhelm Müller," p. 688.
63. Goethe, *Werke*, 1:28, 266–67.
64. Ibid., 1:28, 275.
65. Biedermann, *Goethes Gespräche*, 3:449–50.
66. Lohre, *Briefe an F. A. Brockhaus*, p. 278. Although some literary histories have given the date of Müller's death as September 30, 1827, the official record in the Church of St. Johannes in Dessau agrees with the accounts of the relatives that the death occurred during the early hours of October 1, 1827.
67. W. Müller, *Vermischte Schriften*, 1:lx–lxi.
68. Hatfield, "Zu *Müller als Kritiker*," p. 565.
69. Schulze, "Müllers letzte Lebensjahre."
70. Wahl, "Müllers Tod," pp. 46–50, 62. Wahl's article is discussed here in detail because it is not well known and is available in the United States only at Harvard University. Recent Müller scholars seem to be unaware of the Wahl article. For example, Johannes Irmscher of the Humboldt University in East Berlin still writes in 1968 of Müller's "easy death" ("sanfter Tod") in his otherwise well-documented article about Müller as a philhellene (p. 73); Cottrell writes in his 1970 book of a heart attack which killed Müller "suddenly and painlessly" (p. 7).

71. Friedrich von Matthisson's unpublished autograph book (*Stammbuch*) includes remarks and occasional poetry by Müller and others (including Friedrich von Schiller, Johann Wolfgang von Goethe, Alexander von Humboldt, Johann Gottfried Herder, Christopher Martin Wieland, Gustav Schwab, Johann Kaspar Lavater, Johann Heinrich Pestalozzi, Matthias Claudius, Gottfried August Bürger, Varnhagen von Ense, Elisa von der Recke, and Johann Gottfried Seume). It is located in the Dessau Archives.

72. Wahl's footnote: "*Hof- und Kammerrat* Dr. Franz Olberg (1767–1840)." Wahl, "Müllers Tod," p. 47.

73. Wahl's footnote: "The word *ganzen* was crossed out in the original." Ibid.

74. Wahl's footnote: "Gottlieb Ludwig Schoch (1794–1864)." Ibid.

75. Ibid.

76. Ibid., p. 48.

77. Ibid.

78. "Statut für den 'Wilhelm-Müller-Kunstpreis'."

Chapter Two

1. W. Müller, *Diary and Letters*, p. 5.

2. Becker, *Kunstanschauung Müllers*, p. 87.

3. W. Müller, *Gedichte* (F. Max Müller, ed., 1868), pp. v–vii; Hatfield, "Poetry of Wilhelm Müller," p. 593.

4. Cottrell, "Müllers lyrische Liederzyklen," p. 9.

5. Sengle, *Biedermeierzeit*, 2:517; Hebbel, *Werke*, 12:254.

6. Sengle, *Biedermeierzeit*, 2:518.

7. Cottrell, *Müller's Lyrical Song-Cycles*, pp. 1–2.

8. Nollen, "Heine and Müller," p. 108.

9. Hatfield, "Müllers Dichtungen," p. 2.

10. Sengle, *Biedermeierzeit*, 2:624.

11. Mustard, *Lyric Cycle*, p. 87.

12. Ibid., p. 176.

13. F. Max Müller, *Auld Lang Syne*, p. 49; Gross, "Fouqué und das *Frauentaschenbuch*," p. 54.

14. Wirth, "Müller und das Volkslied," pp. 139–40.

15. W. Müller, *Vermischte Schriften*, 4:105–6.

16. Ibid., p. 105.

17. W. Müller, *Gedichte* (F. Max Müller, ed., 1868), pp. vii–viii.

18. Gumppenberg, *Das teutsche Dichterross*, p. 11.

19. Richardson, "Müller's Poetry of the Sea," p. 323.

20. Heine, *Werke*, 3:102.

21. Richardson, "Müller's Poetry of the Sea," p. 330.

22. W. Müller, *Gedichte* (Hatfield, ed., 1906), p. 327.

23. Allen, "Martin Opitz and Müller," pp. 213–14; "Müller and the German Volkslied," p. 156; Joachim Schulze, "Motiv bei Eichendorff und Müller," pp. 215–23; Schoolfield, *Figure of the Musician*, pp. 54–55.

24. Allen, "Müller and the German Volkslied," p. 89; Hake, *Müller: Sein Leben und Dichten*, p. 44.

25. Spenser, *Poetical Works*, p. 542.

26. W. Müller, *Gedichte* (Hatfield, ed., 1906), p. 10.

27. Gaer, *Legend of the Wandering Jew*, pp. 113–17; Miller, "Wordsworth and Müller," pp. 206–11.

28. Allen, "Müller and the German Volkslied," p. 31.

29. Richardson, "Müller's Poetry of the Sea," pp. 328–29.

30. Moore, *Poetical Works*, p. 292.

31. W. Müller, *Gedichte* (Hatfield, ed., 1906), p. 280.

32. Allen, "Müller and the German Volkslied," p. 157.

33. Allen, "Unpublished Sonnets," pp. 1–9; Wirth, "Studien zu Müller," pp. 125–61.

34. Geiger, *Berlin, 1688–1840*, 2:414.

35. Hatfield, "Unpublished Letters," p. 130.

36. Wirth, "Müller und das Volkslied," p. 138; Allen, "Müller and the German Volkslied," p. 82.

37. Houben, *Der gefesselte Biedermeier,* p. 7; Houben, *Verbotene Literatur,* pp. 520–21.
38. W. Müller, *Diary and Letters,* pp. 94–95.
39. W. Müller, *Gedichte* (Hatfield, ed., 1906), p. vii.
40. W. Müller, *Diary and Letters,* pp. 94–95, 81–82, 84.
41. Hatfield, "Berichtigung," pp. 189–90.
42. Luise Förster, *Karl Förster,* p. 171.
43. Lohre, *Briefe an F. A. Brockhaus,* p. 302.
44. Ibid., p. 186.
45. Nollen, "Heine and Müller," p. 105.
46. Lohre, *Briefe an F. A. Brockhaus,* p. 125.
47. "Siebenundsiebzig Gedichte," *Heidelberger Jahrbücher der Literatur,* p. 986.
48. F. Max Müller, *"Griechenlieder* von Müller," p. 910.
49. For an interpretation of "Im Krug zum grünen Kranze," see Hachtmann, "Müller und wir," pp. 70–77.
50. Mustard, *Lyric Cycle,* p. 78.
51. W. Müller, *Gedichte* (Hatfield, ed., 1906), p. 54.
52. For two interpretations of an important passage in the ballad, consult: Schwarz, "Zu Müllers 'Glockenguss zu Breslau,' " pp. 166–67; Schaaffs, "Zu 'Glockenguss zu Breslau,' " pp. 354–55.
53. [Gustav Schwab], "Müllers Poesie," p. 393.
54. W. Müller, *Rom, Römer und Römerinnen,* 2:187–92.
55. Kempe, *Friedrich Schneider,* p. 156.
56. Lohre, *Briefe an F. A. Brockhaus,* p. 310.
57. Ibid., p. 186.
58. W. Müller, *Gedichte* (Hatfield, ed., 1906), pp. 109–10.
59. Ibid., p. 158.
60. Hatfield, "Political Poems of Müller," pp. 212–21.
61. Heine, *Werke,* 3:62.
62. Wilpert, *Sachwörter der Literatur,* pp. 343–44.
63. W. Müller. *Gedichte* (Hatfield, ed., 1906), pp. 136–37.
64. Ibid., p. 467.
65. Ibid., pp. 179–80.
66. Ibid., p. 242.
67. W. Müller, *Rom, Römer und Römerinnen,* 1:52–57; *Gedichte* (Hatfield, ed., 1906), p. 480.
68. Allen, "Müller and Italian Popular Poetry," pp. 165–66.
69. W. Müller, *Gedichte* (Hatfield, ed., 1906), p. 249.
70. W. Müller and Wolff, *Egeria,* p. 5.
71. W. Müller, *Gedichte* (Hatfield, ed., 1906), p. 258
72. W. Müller, *Vermischte Schriften,* 1:xxxix; Cottrell, *Müller's Lyrical Song-Cycles,* p. 70.
73. Richardson, "Müller's Poetry of the Sea," pp. 327–32; Radermacher, "Die Vineta Sage," pp. 677f.; Minor, [Review, Hatfield's edition of the poetry], p. 94.
74. *Blätter für literarische Unterhaltung,* no. 53 (22 February 1844), p. 211.
75. W. Müller, *Gedichte* (Hatfield, ed., 1906), p. 297.
76. Caminade, *Philhellénisme de Müller,* p. 189.
77. Hachtmann, "Müller und wir," p. 74.
78. Wahl, "Berichte über Müllers Tod," p. 49; Schwab, "Müllers Poesie," p. 394.
79. Hatfield, "Müllers unveröffentlichtes Tagebuch," p. 368.
80. W. Müller, *Gedichte* (Hatfield, ed., 1906), pp. 399–400.
81. Holtei, *Briefe an Ludwig Tieck,* 4:24–30.
82. W. Müller, *Diary and Letters,* p. 5; Deutsch, *Schubert: A Documentary Biography,* pp. 436–37.
83. Lohre, *Briefe an F. A. Brockhaus,* p. 302; W. Müller, *Diary and Letters,* p. 105.
84. Richard Koepke, "Müllers Dichtungen und ihre musikalische Komposition," p. 20.
85. Stechow, " 'Der greise Kopf,' " p. 65.
86. Hachtmann, "Müller und wir," p. 77.
87. For more information on Schubert, see Abraham, *Music of Schubert;* Bell, *Songs of Schubert;* Brown, *Schubert: Critical Biography;* Capell, *Schubert's Songs;* Deutsch, *Schubert: Die*

Dokumente (1914); *Schubert: Die Dokumente* (1964); *Schubert: Documentary Biography; Schubert Reader; Schubert's Letters and Other Writings;* Einstein, *Schubert: Musical Portrait;* Feil, *"Die schöne Müllerin" und "Die Winterreise";* Fischer-Dieskau, *Auf den Spuren der Schubert-Lieder; Schubert: A Biographical Study; Schubert's Songs;* Fröhlich, *Schubert;* Greene, "Schubert's *Winterreise,*" pp. 181–93; Marshall, "Symbolism in Schubert's *Winterreise,*" pp. 607–32.

88. Fischer-Dieskau, *Auf den Spuren der Schubert Lieder,* p. 201.

89. For detailed information on the origin of the song cycle, see Hake, *Müller: Sein Leben und Dichten,* pp. 1–56; Friedländer, "Die Entstehung der Müllerlieder," pp. 301–7; "Die schöne Müllerin," col. 348.

90. Rellstab, *Ludwig Berger,* pp. 110–12.

91. W. Müller, *Diary and Letters,* p. 166.

92. Cottrell, *Müller's Lyrical Song-Cycles,* p. 9.

93. Damian, *Schuberts "Die schöne Müllerin."*

94. W. Müller, *Gedichte* (Hatfield, ed., 1906), p. 3.

95. Just, "Müllers Liederzyklen," pp. 141–42.

96. Feil, *"Die schöne Müllerin" und "Die Winterreise,"* pp. 28–29; Fischer-Dieskau, *Schubert: A Biographical Study,* pp. 267–68.

97. Brown, *Schubert: Critical Biography,* p. 202.

98. Günther Baum, "Das Problem der *Winterreise,*" p. 643.

99. Brandenburg, "*Die Winterreise* als Dichtung," p. 59.

100. Cottrell, *Müller's Lyrical Song-Cycles,* p. 65.

101. Just, "Müllers Liederzyklen," p. 147.

102. Stechow, " 'Der greise Kopf,' " p. 67.

103. Richard Koepke, "Müllers Dichtung und ihre musikalische Komposition," pp. 32–33.

Chapter Three

1. W. Müller, *Vermischte Schriften,* 5:117.

2. W. Müller, *Blumenlese,* p. ii.

3. Ibid., pp. ii–iii.

4. Müller translated the poetry of the following poets for his *Blumenlese:* Kaiser Heinrich, König Konrad, König Wenzel, Herzog Heinrich von Breslau, Markgraf Otto von Brandenburg, Markgraf Heinrich von Meissen, Herzog von Anhalt, Graf Otto von Botenlauben, Markgraf von Hohenburg, Heinrich von Veldeke, Graf Wernher von Honberg, Jakob von Warte, Walther von Klingen, Der von Kürenberg, Kristan von Hamle, Heinrich von Morungen, Reinmar der Alte, Meinloh von Sevelingen, Walther von der Vogelweide, Wolfram von Eschenbach, Albrecht von Johannsdorf, Hartmann von Aue, Ulrich von Liechtenstein, Kristan von Luppin, der Thüringer, der tugendhafte Schreiber, Steinmar von Klingnau, Reinmar von Zweter, Gottfried von Strassburg, and Johannes Hadlaub.

5. W. Müller, *Blumenlese,* pp. 58–59.

6. Grimm, *Kleinere Schriften,* 6:233.

7. Lohre, *Briefe an F. A. Brockhaus,* p. 23; Sokolowsky, *Der altdeutsche Minnesang,* p. 139.

8. Christopher Marlowe wrote *The Tragical History of Doctor Faustus* in 1588 or 1589. Although there were nine editions of the drama between 1604 and 1663, it fell into obscurity during the eighteenth century when no editions were published between 1663 and 1814. It was in 1814 that Sir Charles Wentworth Dilke published it in his *Old English Plays.* After its resurrection by Dilke, Marlowe's *Faustus* has probably gone through more editions than any other English drama not by Shakespeare.

9. Steig, "Müllers Übersetzung von Marlowes *Faust,*" p. 102.

10. Blair, "Müller as Translator of Marlowe's *Dr. Faustus,*" p. 28.

11. W. Müller, *Doktor Faustus: Tragödie von Marlowe,* p. 5.

12. Boas, *Tragical History of Doctor Faustus,* pp. 6, 13.

13. W. Müller, *Marlowes "Faust"* (Badt, ed., 1911), p. 9.

14. Bakeless, *Marlowe: The Man in His Time,* pp. 151–52; Butler, *Fortunes of Faust,* p. 342; Mayer, *Zur deutschen Klassik und Romantik,* p. 13; Heller, *Faust and Faustus,* p. 219.

15. Görne to Baumann, 11 March 1974.

16. Holtei, *Briefe an Ludwig Tieck,* 1:107; Steig, "Müllers Übersetzung von Marlowes *Faust,*" p. 99.

17. Lohre, *Briefe an F. A. Brockhaus*, p. 28; Theens, *Geschichte der Faustgestalt*, p. 88.
18. Max Förster, "Bücherschau," p. 345.
19. W. Müller, *Marlowes "Faust"* (Badt, ed., 1911), p. 20.
20. Blair, "Müller as Translator of Marlowe's *Faustus.*"
21. Ibid., p. 51.
22. Müller, trans. *Doktor Faustus: Tragödie von Marlowe* (Dietrich, ed., 1970), pp. 57–111.
23. Henning, "Marlowes *Faust* in der Übersetzung von Müller," pp. 52–53.

Chapter Four
1. W. Müller, *Gedichte* (Hatfield, ed., 1906), p. 322.
2. Ibid., p. 411.
3. In five journals Müller published both poetry and critical writings: *Gesellschafter, oder Blätter für Geist und Herz* (Berlin); *Literarisches Wochenblatt*, also titled at later dates— *Literarisches Konversationsblatt* and *Blätter für literarische Unterhaltung* (Leipzig); *Morgenblatt für gebildete Stände* (Stuttgart); *Urania* (Leipzig); and *Zeitung für die elegante Welt* (Leipzig). In eight publications Müller contributed only his editorial and critical writings: *Allgemeine Enzyklopädie der Wissenschaften und Künste* (Leipzig); *Allgemeine Literatur-Zeitung* (Halle); Brockhaus's *Konversationslexikon* (Leipzig); *Deutscher Regentenalmanach; Hermes oder Kritisches Jahrbuch der Literatur* (Leipzig); *Jahrbücher für wissenschaftliche Kritik* (Stuttgart); *Neuer Nekrolog der Deutschen* (Ilmenau); and *Zeitgenossen* (Leipzig). Müller's poetry appeared in the following publications: *Aurora* (Mannheim); *Conversationsblatt* (Vienna); *Deutsche Blätter für Poesie, Litteratur, Kunst und Theater* (Breslau); *Erholungsstunden: Zeitschrift für gebildete Leser* (Aarau); *Frauentaschenbuch* (Nuremberg); *Janus* (Vienna); *Mitternachtsblatt für gebildete Stände* (Braunschweig); *Der Obernigker Bote* (Breslau); *Der Sammler* (Vienna); *Taschenbuch zum geselligen Vergnügen* (Leipzig and Vienna); *Wiener Zeitschrift für Kunst, Literatur und Mode* (Vienna); and *Wünschelruthe* (Göttingen).
4. Lohre, ed., *Briefe an F. A. Brockhaus*, pp. 141, 190.
5. Ibid., pp. 174, 234.
6. Häring, *Erinnerungen*, p. 300; Becker, *Die Kunstanschauung Müllers*, pp. 1–2.
7. Guthke, *Literarisches Leben im 18. Jahrhundert*, pp. 237–38.
8. Lohre, *Briefe an F. A. Brockhaus*, pp. 111, 137–38.
9. W. Müller, *Rheinreise*, p. 82.
10. Lohre, *Briefe an F. A. Brockhaus*, pp. 273–74.
11. Ibid., p. 140.
12. Ibid., p. 215.
13. Ibid., pp. 139–40, 292.
14. Ibid., pp. 259, 214.
15. Ibid., p. 326.
16. W. Müller, *Bibliothek deutscher Dichter*, 1:xii.
17. Ibid., 1:ix–x.
18. Hoffmann von Fallersleben, *Mein Leben*, 2:29; *Findlinge*, 1:213–14.
19. W. Müller, *Bibliothek deutscher Dichter*, 11:vii.
20. Brockhaus, *Friedrich Arnold Brockhaus*, 2:372–73.
21. Lohre, *Briefe an F. A. Brockhaus*, pp. 216–17.
22. Hatfield, "Unpublished Letters," p. 141.
23. Lohre, *Briefe an F. A. Brockhaus*, p. 234.
24. "Prolegomena ad Homerum," pp. 307–37.

Chapter Five
1. Fauriel, *Neugriechische Volkslieder*, 1:xii.
2. Ibid., 1:x–xi.
3. Ibid., 1:xii.
4. Ibid., 1:li–lii.
5. [Goethe], "Neugriechisch-epirotische Heldenlieder." For details about Goethe's interest in neo-Greek folk poetry, consult Arnold, "Der deutsche Philhellenismus," pp. 106–17; Dietrich, "Goethe und die neugriechische Volksdichtung," pp. 61–81; Ibrovac, *Claude Fauriel;* Stadtmüller, "Griechische Dichtung," pp. 301–2.
6. Arnold, "Der deutsche Philhellenismus," pp. 109–12; Ibrovac, *Claude Fauriel*, p. 207; F. Max Müller, "Wilhelm Müller," p. 688; *Auld Lang Syne*, pp. 52–53.

7. Lohre, *Briefe an F. A. Brockhaus,* pp. 343–44.
8. Ibrovac, *Claude Fauriel,* p. 203.
9. Caminade, *Philhellénisme de Wilhelm Müller,* pp. 147–56.
10. Ibrovac, *Claude Fauriel,* p. 207.
11. [Fuller], [Review of *Neugriechische Volkslieder* by Fauriel-Müller], p. 179.
12. Ibrovac, *Claude Fauriel,* p. 208.
13. Irmscher, "Müller und der deutsche Philhellenismus," p. 71.
14. W. Müller, *Gedichte* (Hatfield, ed., 1906), p. 346.
15. W. Müller, *Rom, Römer und Römerinnen,* 1:246–48.
16. Ibid., p. 78.
17. "Wilhelm Müllers *Egeria,*" pp. 350–51.
18. Heyse, *Italienische Dichter,* 4:177. See Kaden, *Italiens Wunderhorn,* for a detailed chronological bibliography of Italian and German-Italian folk-song collections and articles on the subject. It also contains an extensive introduction in which German and Italian folk songs are compared in respect to subject matter, language, and poetic forms.

Chapter Six
1. W. Müller, *Rom, Römer und Römerinnen,* 1:73–74.
2. Ibid., p. 21.
3. Noack, *Deutsches Leben in Rom,* p. 265; W. Müller, *Rom, Römer und Römerinnen,* 1:5–6.
4. Ibid., 2:187–88.
5. Ibid., 2:42
6. Ibid., 2: introduction.
7. Lohre, *Briefe an F. A. Brockhaus,* p. 297.
8. Goedeke, *Geschichte der deutschen Dichtung,* 8:256.
9. W. Müller, *Rheinreise,* pp. 139–40.
10. W. Müller, *Rom, Römer und Römerinnen* (Schröder, ed., 1956).
11. Ibid., p. 263.
12. Ibid.
13. Lohre, *Briefe an F. A. Brockhaus,* p. 234.
14. Ibid., p. 271.
15. Ibid., p. 88.
16. W. Müller, "Debora" (in *Deutscher Novellenschatz,* Heyse and Kurz, eds.), 6:3–4.
17. W. Müller, *Vermischte Schriften,* 3:151–52.
18. Cottrell, "Wilhelm Müllers Liederzyklen," pp. 71–73; Lohre, *Briefe an F. A. Brockhaus,* pp. 8–9, 95; Hachtmann, "Wilhelm Müller," pp. 152–53.
19. Wäschke, "Aus Wilhelm Müllers Jugendzeit," p. 64.

Chapter Seven
1. W. Müller, *Gedichte* (Hatfield, ed., 1906), p. 224. There have been several studies on Müller as a philhellene and as the author of the *Griechenlieder.* The first article about these poems was written by his son in 1845. In 1896 Robert Franz Arnold published an extensive study, "Der deutsche Philhellenismus: Kultur- und literarhistorische Untersuchungen," in which he devotes a chapter to "Wilhelm Müller und seine Freunde." In 1913 a French scholar, Gaston Caminade, published a book in French about the *Griechenlieder* and the philhellenism of Müller. A short article by Otto Brües appeared in 1942. Large sections of the 1966 French volumes on Fauriel by Miodrag Ibrovac deal with Müller's philhellenism. In the same year, Johannes Irmscher discussed Müller in "Der Philhellenismus in Preussen als Forschungsanliegen." In 1968 Irmscher published another article, "Der Dessauer Dichter Wilhelm Müller und der deutsche Philhellenismus," which is well documented and well written. The most recent article about this subject was published in 1972 by Hans-Georg Werner.
2. Reinhardt, *Germany: 2000 Years,* 2:509–10.
3. Spencer, *Literary Philhellenism,* p. vii.
4. *Reallexikon der deutscher Literaturgeschichte,* 2:679.
5. W. Müller, *Diary and Letters,* pp. 99–100.
6. Lohre, *Briefe an F. A. Brockhaus,* p. 312.
7. Ibid., p. 304.

8. Arnold, "Der deutsche Philhellenismus," p. 117.
9. W. Müller, *Rheinreise*, p. 81.
10. W. Müller, *Diary and Letters*, p. 102.
11. Lohre, *Briefe an F. A. Brockhaus*, p. 312.
12. W. Müller, *Gedichte*, p. 183.
13. Ibid., pp. 216–17.
14. Lohre, *Briefe an F. A. Brockhaus*, pp. 168–69.
15. Ibid., pp. 307–8.
16. Ibid., pp. 312–13.
17. [Schwab], "Müllers Poesie," p. 390.
18. W. Müller, *Rheinreise*, p. 140.
19. Becker, *Die Kunstanschauung Müllers*, pp. 54–55.
20. Zeydel, Matenko, Fife, eds., *Letters of Ludwig Tieck*, p. 208; Holtei, *Briefe an Ludwig Tieck*, 4:26–27.
21. Hebbel, *Werke*, 12:254.
22. W. Müller, *Gedichte* (Hatfield, ed., 1906), p. 216.
23. W. Müller, *Vermischte Schriften*, 5:156.
24. Bretscher, "History of the Taschenbuch *Urania*," pp. 27–30, 67.
25. Lohre, *Briefe an F. A. Brockhaus*, p. 230.
26. Cedric Hentschel, *The Byronic Teuton*, p. 23.
27. W. Müller, *Vermischte Schriften*, 3:486–87.
28. Johannes Irmscher, "Müller und der deutsche Philhellenismus," p. 48; Kohut, "Wilhelm Müller," p. 237; F. Max Müller, *Auld Lang Syne*, p. 49; *Life and Letters of F. Max Müller*, 2:140, 153, 163, 271.
29. *Dessauer Freiheit*, 28 March 1979.
30. Robertson, *History of German Literature*, pp. 409–10.
31. Lohre, *Briefe an F. A. Brockhaus*, p. 101.
32. Frenzel and Frenzel, *Daten Deutscher Dichtung*, 2:37–62.
33. Ochsenbein, *Die Aufnahme Lord Byrons*, p. 77.

Chapter Eight

1. Mann, *Der Zauberberg*, p. 597.
2. Nollen, "Heine and Wilhelm Müller," p. 105.
3. F. Max Müller, "*Griechenlieder* von Müller," p. 910; Heine, *Briefe* (Daffis, ed., 1906), 1:271–73; *Briefe* (Hirth, ed., 1950), 1:269–70.
4. Nollen, "Heine and Müller," p. 104.
5. Heine, *Werke*, 3:266–67.
6. Ibid., 5:350–51.
7. Müller's influence on the early poetry of Heine has been noted briefly in Goetze, *Heines "Buch der Lieder*," p. 10; Greinz, *Heine und das deutsche Volkslied*, pp. 13, 36, 38, 49, 63, 65, 70, 74, 77, 93; Snodgrass, "Heine and Müller," p. 152.
8. Nollen, "Heine and Müller," p. 109.
9. Hatfield, "Unpublished Letters," p. 138; Heine, *Werke*, 3:90.
10. W. Müller, *Vermischte Schriften*, 5:430.
11. Heine, *Briefe* (Hirth, ed., 1950), 1:283.
12. W. Müller, *Gedichte* (Hatfield, ed., 1906), p. 44.
13. Ibid., p. 12.
14. W. Müller, *Rom, Römer und Römerinnen*, 1:113.
15. Heine, *Werke*, 3:15.
16. Mustard, *Lyric Cycle in German Literature*, p. 101.
17. Reeves, "Heinrich Heine and Wilhelm Müller," p. 54.
18. Goedeke, *Geschichte der deutschen Dichtung*, 8:259, 707.
19. W. Müller, *Vermischte Schriften*, 1:1xiii.
20. W. Müller, *Gedichte* (Hatfield, ed., 1906), p. xxix.
21. Ibid., pp. xxix–xxx.
22. F. Max Müller, "Wilhelm Müller," p. 691.
23. Simolin, "Der Waldhornist," p. 489.
24. Freiligrath, *Werke*, 7:258–60.
25. Hatfield, "Longfellow, Transmitter of German Culture," pp. 41–55, 95–108; *New Light on Longfellow*.

In addition to Longfellow, Hatfield claims that Müller influenced Alfred, Lord Tennyson, and John Greenleaf Whittier.
James Taft Hatfield, "The Poetry of Müller," p. 581. Here Hatfield mentions that he finds parallels between Müller's *Die schöne Müllerin* and Tennyson's "The Window," "The Miller's Daughter," and "Maud."
James Taft Hatfield, "Müllers Dichtungen," p. 2. Here Hatfield comments on parallels in form and spirit between *Die Griechenlieder* and Whittier's *Voices of Freedom*.
Although resemblances between these works of Tennyson and Whittier and Müller's poetry do seem to exist, there does not appear to be any documented proof that the two authors had read Müller's poetry. It is, however, possible that they had read the poetry in one of the many collections in which Müller had been anthologized. (See Morgan's *Critical Bibliography of German Literature in English Translation, 1481–1927*, and Pochmann's *German Culture in America: Philosophical and Literary Influences, 1600–1900*.) Both Tennyson and Whittier showed more than a passing interest in German literature. Tennyson had visited Germany in 1832. Whittier's interest in Germany is discussed in Eastburn, *Whittier's Relation to German Life and Thought*.
26. Cohn, "Zu 'Est, Est,' " pp. 504–6; Richard Meyer, " 'Est, Est' von Müller," pp. 162–65; Sprenger, "Zu Müllers Romanze 'Est, Est,' " pp. 142–43.
27. Longfellow, *Outre-Mer*, pp. 309–10.
28. Longfellow, *Hyperion*, 2:166–69.
29. W. Müller, *Gedichte* (Hatfield, ed., 1906), p. 45.
30. Longfellow, *Complete Poetical Works*, p. 616.
31. Hatfield, *New Light on Longfellow*, pp. 125, 172.
32. Arnold, "Der deutsche Philhellenismus," pp. 136, 147–48, 162–64.
33. Fauriel, *Neugriechische Volkslieder*, 2:89.
34. W. Müller, *Gedichte* (Hatfield, ed., 1906), p. 255; Arnold, "Die Natur verrät heimliche Liebe," p. 295.
35. Ermatinger, *Die deutsche Lyrik seit Herder*, 2:33–36.
36. Mann, *Magic Mountain*, p. 640.
37. Ibid., pp. 650–53.
38. Ibid., pp. 715–16.
39. Schoolfield, *Figure of the Musician*, p. 175.
40. Mann, *Doctor Faustus*, p. 77.
41. Solzhenitsyn, *Candle in the Wind*, p. 125.
42. Ibid., pp. 124–26.
43. Hatfield, *New Light on Longfellow*, pp. 75, 172; "Longfellow, Transmitter of German Culture," p. 102; "Müllers unveröffentlichtes Tagebuch," pp. 362–80. See also Morgan, *German Literature in English Translation*, p. 557.
44. Fiedler, "Zur deutschen Literatur in England," p. 131.
45. Morgan, *German Literature in English Translation*, pp. 577–79.
46. Pochmann, *German Culture in America*, pp. 344–45.
47. Buchheim, *Deutsche Lyrik*, p. xiii; Warner, *World's Best Literature*, 26:10444.
48. Morgan and Hohlfeld, *German Literature in British Magazines;* See Bibliography, Translations, for listing of Müller's poems in British magazines.
49. Goodnight, *German Literature in American Magazines;* Haertel, *German Literature in American Magazines;* See Bibliography, Translations, for a list of Müller's poems in American magazines.
50. Ibrovac, *Claude Fauriel*, p. 208; Bolte, "Zu Müllers 'Muscheln aus Rügen,' " p. 341.
51. Goedeke, *Geschichte der deutschen Dichtung*, 8:265; Heine, *Briefe* (Hirth, ed., 1950), 5:302; W. Müller, *La belle Meunière*, trans. Jean Jacques Brand, Franz Schubert, composer, *Op. 25* (Strasbourg, 1968); *Le Voyage d'hiver*, trans. Jean Jacques Brand, Franz Schubert, composer, *Op. 89* (Strasbourg, 1968); Hugk, "Leserstimmen zu französischen Übertragungen," pp. 339–43, 370–75.
52. Stempel, "Wilhelm Müller: A Sketch," pp. 14–19, 65.
53. Allen, "Müller and the German Volkslied," p. 6.

Conclusion
1. W. Müller, *Rheinreise*, p. 73.
2. Sengle, *Biedermeierzeit*.
3. W. Müller, *Gedichte* (Hatfield, ed., 1906), p. 322.

Bibliography

PRIMARY SOURCES

Allen, Philip Schuyler. "Unpublished Sonnets of Wilhelm Müller." *Journal of English and Germanic Philology* 4, no. 1 (1902): 1–9.

Allgemeine Enzyklopädie der Wissenschaften und Künste in alphabetischer Folge von genannten Schriftstellern bearbeitet. Edited by Johann Ersch and Johann Gruber. Leipzig: Brockhaus, Gleditsch, 1821–1828.

Fauriel, Claude, comp. *Neugriechische Volkslieder.* Translated by Wilhelm Müller. 2 vols. Leipzig: Leopold Voss, 1825.

Hatfield, James Taft. "Another Unpublished Sonnet of Wilhelm Müller." *Journal of English and Germanic Philology* 4, no. 4 (1902):9.

———. "Earliest Poems of Wilhelm Müller." *PMLA* 13, no. 2 (1898):250–85.

———. "Newly-discovered Political Poems of Wilhelm Müller." *Modern Language Review* 1, no. 3 (April 1906): 212–21.

———. "Unpublished Letters of Wilhelm Müller." *American Journal of Philology* 24, no. 2 (April, May, June 1903): 121–48.

Lohre, Heinrich, ed. *Wilhelm Müller als Kritiker und Erzähler: Ein Lebensbild mit Briefen an F. A. Brockhaus und anderen Schriftstücken.* Leipzig: F. A. Brockhaus, 1927.

Müller, Arthur, ed. *Moderne Reliquien.* Berlin: Adolf Gumprecht, 1845, pp. 1–48.

Müller, Wilhelm, ed., vols. 1–10 and Förster, Karl, ed., vols. 11–14. *Bibliothek deutscher Dichter des siebzehnten Jahrhunderts.* 14 vols. Leipzig: F. A. Brockhaus, 1822–1838.

Müller, Wilhelm, trans. *Blumenlese aus den Minnesingern: Erste Sammlung.* Berlin: Maurer, 1816.

———. *Debora.* In *Deutscher Novellenschatz.* Edited by Paul Heyse and Hermann Kurz. 3rd series. 24 vols. Munich: Rudolf Oldenbourg, 1871–1876, 6:1–148.

———. *Diary and Letters of Wilhelm Müller.* Edited by Philip Schuyler Allen and James Taft Hatfield. Chicago: University of Chicago Press, 1903.

———, trans. *Doktor Faustus: Tragödie von Christoph Marlowe (Mit einer Vorrede von Ludwig Achim von Arnim).* Berlin: Maurer, 1818.

———, trans. *Doktor Faustus: Tragödie von Christoph Marlowe.* Edited by Friedrich Notter. In *Das Kloster,* pub. J. Scheible. Stuttgart and Leipzig: J. Scheible, 1847, 5:922–1020.

———, trans. *Doktor Faustus: Tragödie von Christoph Marlowe.* In *Wie der Faust entstand: Urkunde, Sage und Dichtung.* Edited by Rudolf Frank. Berlin: Verlag Neues Leben Wilhelm Borngraeber, 1911, pp. 154–94.

———. *Doktor Faustus: Tragödie von Christoph Marlowe.* Reclams Universal-Bibliothek, no. 1128. Leipzig: Philipp Reclam, 1879.

———, trans. *C. Marlowes "Faust": Verdeutschung von 1818 mit dem Vorwort Achim von Arnims.* Edited by Berta Badt. Munich: E. Rentsch, 1911.

————, trans. *Doktor Faustus: Tragödie von Christoph Marlowe.* In *Die Faustdichtung vor, neben und nach Goethe.* Edited by Karl Georg Wendriner. 4 vols. Berlin: Morawe und Scheffelt, 1913, 1:149–268. Reprinted in Darmstadt: Wissenschaftliche Buchgesellschaft, 1969.

————, trans. *Doktor Faustus: Tragödie von Christoph Marlowe (Mit einer Vorrede von Ludwig Achim von Arnim).* Weltgeist-Bücher, no. 124. Berlin: Weltgeist-Bücher, [1926].

————, trans. *Doktor Faustus: Tragödie von Christoph Marlowe.* In *Gestaltungen des Fausts: Die bedeutendesten Werke der Faustdichtung seit 1587.* Edited by Horst Wolfram Geissler. 3 vols. Munich: Verlag Parcus, 1927, 1:139–210.

————, trans. *Doktor Faustus: Tragödie von Christoph Marlowe.* In *Faust—Theater der Jahrhunderte.* Edited by Margret Dietrich. Munich: Albert Langen—Georg Müller Verlag, 1970, pp. 57–111.

————, and Wolff, Oskar Ludwig Bernhard, eds. *Egeria: Raccolta di poesie Italiane populari.* Leipzig: Ernst Fleischer, 1829.

————. *Gedichte.* Edited by F. Max Müller. Leipzig: F. A. Brockhaus, 1868.

————. *Gedichte.* Edited by E. Hermann. Berlin: Grote, 1874.

————. *Gedichte: Gesamt-Ausgabe.* Bibliothek der Gesamtliteratur, nos. 309–12. Halle: Otto Hendel, [1889].

————. *Gedichte: Gesamt-Ausgabe.* Edited by Curt Müller. Leipzig: Philipp Reclam, [1894].

————. *Gedichte: Vollständige kritische Ausgabe mit Einleitung und Anmerkungen.* Edited by James Taft Hatfield. Deutsche Literaturdenkmale des 18. und 19. Jahrhunderts, no. 187. Berlin: B. Behr, 1906. Reprinted in Deutsche Literaturdenkmale des 18. und 19. Jahrhunderts. Nendeln, Liechtenstein, and New York: Kraus Reprint, 1973.

————. *Gedichte.* Edited by Paul Wahl and Otto Hachtmann. *Die Freunde,* no. 27. Leipzig: Feuer-Verlag, Lothar Joachim, [1927].

————. *Griechenlieder: Neue vollständige Ausgabe.* Leipzig: F. A. Brockhaus, 1844.

————. *Griechenlieder.* Bibliothek der Gesamtliteratur, no. 314. Halle: Otto Hendel, [1889].

————. "Herr Peter Squenz: Oder die Komödie zu Rumpelskirch, Posse in zwei Abtheilungen, nach Gryphius und Shakespeare frei bearbeitet." *Jahrbuch deutscher Nachspiele* 2 (1823):37–98.

————. *Homerische Vorschule: Eine Einleitung in das Studium der Ilias und Odyssee.* Leipzig: F. A. Brockhaus, 1824.

————. *Homerische Vorschule: Eine Einleitung in das Studium der Ilias und Odyssee.* Edited by Detlev Carl Wilhelm Baumgarten-Crusius. 2nd ed. Leipzig: F. A. Brockhaus, 1836.

————. *Lieder der Griechen.* 2 vols. Dessau: Christian Georg Ackermann, 1821–1822.

————. *Lyrische Reisen und epigrammatische Spaziergänge.* Leipzig: Leopold Voss, 1827.

————. *Missolunghi.* Dessau: J. C. Fritsche, 1826.

————. "Oper und Schauspiel: Fehde zwischen Wilhelm Müller und Adolf Müllner." Edited by Friedrich Wilhelm Gubitz. [n.p., 1857].

————. *Rom, Römer und Römerinnen: Eine Sammlung vertrauter Briefe aus Rom und Albano mit einigen späteren Zusätzen und Belegen.* 2 vols. Berlin: Duncker und Humblot, 1820.

————. *Rom, Römer und Römerinnen: Eines deutschen Dichters Italienbuch aus den Tagen der Romantik.* Edited by Christel Matthias Schröder. Bremen: Carl Schünemann Verlag, 1956. Reviewed in Lucya Hentschel. "Rom—Römer—Römerinnen." *Dessauer Kulturspiegel* 3, no. 12 (December 1956):423–24.

————. *Rom, Römer und Römerinnen*. Mit einem Porträt und 32 zeitgenössischen Stichen. Edited by Wulf Kirsten. Berlin, G.D.R.: Rütten und Loening, 1978.

————. *Siebenundsiebzig Gedichte aus den hinterlassenen Papieren eines reisenden Waldhornisten*. Dessau: C. G. Ackermann, 1821 [October 1820]. Vol. 2 published by Ackermann in 1824.

————. *Vermischte Schriften*. Edited by Gustav Schwab. 5 vols. Leipzig: F. A. Brockhaus, 1830.

————. *Wilhelm Müllers Rheinreise von 1827 sowie Gedichte und Briefe*. Edited by Paul Wahl. Dessau: Walther Schwalbe, 1931.

Die Sängerfahrt: Eine Neujahrsgabe für Freunde der Dichtkunst und Mahlerey. Compiled by Friedrich Förster. Berlin: Maurer, 1818.

SECONDARY SOURCES

Abraham, Gerald, ed. *The Music of Schubert*. New York: Norton, 1947.

Allen, Philip Schuyler. "Martin Opitz and Wilhelm Müller." *MLN* 14, no. 7 (November 1899):213–14.

————. "A Volkslied as a Source of Two of Wilhelm Müller's Songs." *MLN* 14, no. 2 (February 1901):37–38.

————. "Wilhelm Müller and Italian Popular Poetry." *MLN* 14, no. 6 (June 1899):165–66.

————. "Wilhelm Müller and the German Volkslied." Ph.D. dissertation, University of Chicago, 1899. Reprinted in *Journal of English and Germanic Philology* 2, no. 3; 3, no. 1; 3, no. 4 (1901).

————, and Klier, K. M. "Wilhelm Müller und das deutsche Volkslied." *Das deutsche Volkslied: Zeitschrift für seine Kenntnis und Pflege* 28 (May 1926):57–61, 73–77.

Armitage-Smith, Julian. "Schubert's *Winterreise, Part I:* The Sources of the Musical Text." *Musical Quarterly* 60, no. 1 (January 1974):20–36.

Arnold, Robert Franz. "Der deutsche Philhellenismus: Kultur- und literarhistorische Untersuchungen" [Chapter 4—"Wilhelm Müller und seine Freunde"]. *Euphorion* 3, supplement 2 (1896):71–181.

————. "Die Natur verrät heimliche Liebe" [Part 2, "Reflexes des Volksliedes in der Kunstdichtung—Mit Beiträgen zu Wilhelm Müller, Chamisso und Mörike"]. *Zeitschrift des Vereins für Volkskunde* 12, nos. 3–4 (1902):155–67, 291–95.

————. [Review of *Wilhelm Müllers Gedichte*, edited by James Taft Hatfield]. *Deutsche Literaturzeitung* 29, no. 44 (31 October 1908):cols. 2788–89.

Atterbom, Per Daniel Amadeus. *Reisebilder aus dem romantischen Deutschland: Jugenderinnerungen eines romantischen Dichters und Kunstgelehrten aus den Jahren 1817 bis 1819*. Edited by Elmar Jansen. Stuttgart: Steingrüben Verlag, 1970. [Original published in 1867.]

Augustin, Hermann. "Ein treues Lied." *Schweizerisches Monatsheft* 46 (1966):85–97.

Bakeless, John. *Christopher Marlowe: The Man in His Time*. New York: William Morrow, 1937.

Baum, Günther. "Das Problem der *Winterreise*." *Neue Zeitschrift für Musik* 111, no. 12 (December 1950):643–44.

Becker, Aloys Josef. *Die Kunstanschauung Wilhelm Müllers: Ein Beitrag zum Verständnis und zur Würdigung seiner künstlerischen Persönlichkeit*. Borna-Leipzig: Robert Noske, 1908.

Bell, A. Craig. *The Songs of Schubert*. London: Alston, 1964.

Biedermann, Woldemar von. *Goethes Gespräche.* Edited by Flodoard von Biedermann. 10 vols. Leipzig: F. W. Biedermann, 1910, 3:449–50; 5:158.

Blair, Joseph Cullen. "Wilhelm Müller as Poet and Translator of Christopher Marlowe's *Dr. Faustus:* A Critical Study." M.A. thesis, University of Maryland, 1960.

Boas, Frederick S. *The Tragical History of Doctor Faustus.* New York: Dial Press, 1932.

Böhm, W. [Review of *Diary and Letters of Wilhelm Müller.* Edited by Philip Schuyler Allen and James Taft Hatfield]. *Deutsche Literaturzeitung* 27, no. 4 (27 January 1906):217.

Bolte, J. "Zu Wilhelm Müllers 'Muscheln aus Rügen.' " *Euphorion* 6 (1899):341.

Brandenburg, Hans. "*Die Winterreise* als Dichtung: Eine Ehrenrettung für Wilhelm Müller." *Aurora* 18 (1958):57–62.

Bretscher, Paul Martin. "The History and Cultural Significance of the Taschenbuch *Urania.*" Ph.D. dissertation, University of Chicago, 1936.

Brockhaus, Heinrich Eduard. *Friedrich Arnold Brockhaus: Sein Leben und Wirken.* 3 vols. Leipzig: F. A. Brockhaus, 1872–1881.

Brown, Maurice. *Schubert: A Critical Biography.* London: Macmillan, 1958.

Brückner, Franz. *Häuserbuch der Stadt Dessau.* Vol. 7. Dessau: Rat der Stadt Dessau, n.d. [ca. 1979], pp. 640–41.

Brües, Otto. "Der Griechen-Müller." *Das innere Reich: Zeitschrift für Dichtung, Kunst und deutsches Leben* 8, no. 11 (February 1942):602–7.

Buchheim, Karl Adolphus. *Deutsche Lyrik.* 10th ed. London: Macmillan, 1904.

Butler, Eliza Marian. *The Fortunes of Faust.* Cambridge: At the University Press, 1952.

Caminade, Gaston. *Les Chants des Grecs et le Philhellénisme de Wilhelm Müller.* Paris: Félix Alcan, 1913.

Capell, Richard. *Schubert's Songs.* 2nd ed. New York: Macmillan, 1957.

Cohn, Egon. "Zu 'Est, Est.' " *Euphorion* 20 (1913):504—6.

Cottrell, Alan P. [Review of "Wilhelm Müllers Liederzyklen *Die schöne Müllerin* und *Die Winterreise*" by Klaus Günther Just]. *English Language Notes,* Supplement ("The Romantic Movement: A Selected and Critical Bibliography") 3, no. 1 (September 1965):116.

———. "Wilhelm Müllers lyrische Liederzyklen." Ph.D. dissertation, Ohio State University, 1963.

———. *Wilhelm Müllers Lyrical Song-Cycles: Interpretations and Texts.* University of North Carolina Studies in the Germanic Languages and Literatures, no. 66. Chapel Hill: University of North Carolina Press, 1970.

Dakin, Douglas. *The Greek Struggle for Independence, 1821–1833.* Berkeley and Los Angeles: University of California Press, 1973.

Damian, Franz Valentin. *Franz Schuberts Liederkreis, "Die schöne Müllerin."* Leipzig: Breitkopf und Härtel, 1928.

Deutsch, Otto Erich. *Franz Schubert's Letters and Other Writings.* Translated by Venetia Savile. New York: Knopf, 1928.

———. *Schubert: A Documentary Biography.* Translated by Eric Blom. London: J. M. Dent, 1946.

———. *Schubert: Die Dokumente seines Lebens und Schaffens.* Munich: Müller, 1914.

———. *Schubert: Die Dokumente seines Lebens und Schaffens.* Cassel: Bärenreiter, 1964.

———. *The Schubert Reader.* Translated by Eric Blom. New York: Norton, 1947.

Dietrich, Karl. "Goethe und die neugriechische Volksdichtung." *Hellas-Jahrbuch: Organ der deutsch-griechischen Gesellschaft* (1929):61–81.

Dilke, Charles Wentworth, ed. *Old English Plays: Being a Selection from the Early Dramatic Writers.* London: Whittingham and Rowland, 1814, pp. 1–92.

Eastburn, Iola Kay. *Whittier's Relation to German Life and Thought. Americana Germania,* no. 20. Philadelphia: University of Pennsylvania Press, 1915.

Eckermann, Johann Peter. *Gespräche mit Goethe in den letzten Jahren seines Lebens.* Edited by H. H. Houben. 21st ed. Leipzig: F. A. Brockhaus, 1925.

Einstein, Alfred. *Schubert: A Musical Portrait.* New York: Oxford University Press, 1951.

Eisenhardt, Günther. "Vertonungen von Gedichten Wilhelm Müllers." *Zwischen Wörlitz und Mosigkau, Schriftenreihe zur Geschichte der Stadt Dessau und Umgebung,* no. 21, "Wilhelm Müller" (1977):7–14.

Erläuterungen zur deutschen Literatur: Romantik. East Berlin: Kollektiv für Literaturgeschichte, 1973, pp. 516–23.

Ermatinger, Emil. *Die deutsche Lyrik seit Herder.* 2nd ed. 3 vols. Leipzig and Berlin: B. G. Teubner, 1925.

Fauriel, Claude. *Chants populaires de la Grèce Moderne.* 2 vols. Paris: Didot, 1824–1825.

Fechner, Gustav Theodor. "Deutsche Lyris [*sic*] und Wilhelm Müller." *Mundts Der Freihafen: Galerie von Unterhaltungsbildern aus den Kreisen der Literatur, Gesellschaft und Wissenschaft* 1 (1838):165–83.

Feil, Arnold. *Franz Schubert, "Die schöne Müllerin" und "Die Winterreise": Mit einem Essay "Wilhelm Müller und die Romantik" von Rolf Vollmann.* Stuttgart: Philipp Reclam jun., 1975.

Fiedler, H. G. "Zur deutschen Literatur in England." *Archiv für das Studium der neueren Sprachen und Literaturen* 121, n.s. 21 (1908):131.

Fischer-Dieskau, Dietrich. *Auf den Spuren der Schubert-Lieder: Werden, Wesen und Wirkung.* Wiesbaden: F. A. Brockhaus, 1971.

————. *The Fischer-Dieskau Book of Lieder: The Original Texts of Over Seven Hundred and Fifty Songs.* Translated by George Bird and Richard Stokes. New York: Knopf, 1977. [First published under the title *Texte deutscher Lieder.*]

————. *Schubert: A Biographical Study of his Songs.* Translated by Kenneth S. Whitton. London: Cassell, 1976.

————. *Schubert's Songs: A Biographical Study.* Translated by Kenneth S. Whitton. New York: Knopf, 1977.

Förster, Luise, ed. *Biographische und literarische Skizzen aus dem Leben und der Zeit Karl Försters.* Dresden: Gottschalck, 1846, pp. 104–5, 163–64, 170–71, 193, 202, 224–26.

Förster, Max. "Bücherschau." *Jahrbuch der deutschen Shakespeare-Gesellschaft* 48 (1912):344–45.

Francke, O. "Zur Biographie des Dichters Wilhelm Müller." *Mitteilungen des Vereins für Anhaltische Geschichte und Altertumskunde, Dessau* 5 (1887):33–44.

Freiligrath, Ferdinand. *Sämtliche Werke.* Edited by Ludwig Schröder. 10 vols. Leipzig: Max Hesse, n.d., 7:258–60.

Frenzel, Herbert A., and Frenzel, Elisabeth. *Daten deutscher Dichtung: Chronologischer Abriss der deutschen Literaturgeschichte.* 2 vols. Munich: Deutscher Taschenbuch Verlag, 1966.

Friedländer, Max. "Die Entstehung der Müllerlieder." *Deutsche Rundschau* 73 (November 1892):301–7.

————. "Die schöne Müllerin." *Deutsche Literaturzeitung,* no. 10 (1892):col. 348.

Fröhlich, Hans J. *Schubert.* Munich: Hanser, 1978.

[Fuller, Margaret]. [Review of *Neugriechische Volkslieder* by Fauriel-Müller]. *Dial: A Magazine for Literature, Philosophy, and Religion* 3, no. 2 (October 1842):153–80.

Gaer, Joseph. *The Legend of the Wandering Jew.* New York: Mentor, New American Library, 1961.

Garland, Henry and Mary. *The Oxford Companion to German Literature.* Oxford: Clarendon Press, 1976.

"Gedichte, welche dem Andenken Wilhelm Müller's gewidmet und kurz nach dem Tode desselben veröffentlicht worden sind." *Mitteilungen des Vereins für Anhaltische Geschichte und Altertumskunde, Dessau* 5 (1887):45–48.

Geiger, Ludwig. *Berlin, 1688–1840: Geschichte des geistigen Lebens der preussischen Hauptstadt.* 2 vols. Berlin: Paetel, 1895.

Georgiades, Thrasybulos G. *Schubert: Musik und Lyrik.* Göttingen, 1967, pp. 387ff.

Goedeke, Karl. *Grundriss zur Geschichte der deutschen Dichtung.* 2nd ed. Dresden: L. Ehlermann, 1884ff.

——, and Tittmann, Julius, eds. *Deutsche Dichter des siebzehnten Jahrhunderts.* 15 vols. Leipzig: F. A. Brockhaus, 1869–1885.

[Goethe, Johann Wolfgang von]. "Neugriechisch-epirotische Heldenlieder." *Über Kunst und Alterthum* 4, no. 1 (1823):54–64, 166–68; no. 2 (1823):49–50, 165–68.

Goethe, Johann Wolfgang von. *Werke.* Weimar: Hermann Böhlaus Nachfolger, 1887–1919.

Goetze, Robert. *H. Heines "Buch der Lieder" und sein Verhältnis zum deutschen Volkslied.* Halle: Ehrhardt Karras, 1895.

Goodnight, Scott Holland. *German Literature in American Magazines Prior to 1846.* University of Wisconsin Philology and Literature Series, vol. 4. Madison: University of Wisconsin, 1907.

Greene, David B. "Schubert's *Winterreise:* A Study in the Aesthetics of Mixed Media." *Journal of Aesthetics and Art Criticism* 29, no. 2 (Winter 1970):181–93.

Greinz, Rudolf. *Heinrich Heine und das deutsche Volkslied: Eine kritische Unterhaltung nach dem Stoffgebiete der Heine'schen Lyrik.* Neuwied and Leipzig: August Schupp, 1894.

Grimm, Jakob. *Kleinere Schriften.* 8 vols. Berlin: Ferdinand Dümmler, 1865–1890, 6:233–40.

Gross, Carl. "*Frauentaschenbuch:* Fouqué und das *Frauentaschenbuch.*" Ph.D. dissertation, University of Münster, 1925.

Gumppenberg, Hanns von. *Das teutsche Dichterross in allen Gangarten vorgeritten.* 6th ed. Munich: George D. W. Callwey Verlag, 1908. Reprinted in Dietze, Walter, ed. *Die respektlose Muse: Literarische Parodien aus fünf Jahrhunderten.* Berlin: Rüttan und Loening, 1968.

Guthke, Karl S. *Literarisches Leben im 18. Jahrhundert in Deutschland und in der Schweiz.* Bern and Munich: Francke, 1975.

Hachtmann, Otto. "Wilhelm Müller." *Mitteldeutsche Lebensbilder* 2 (1927):151–70.

——. "Wilhelm Müller und wir." *Deutsche Rundschau* 213 (October 1927):70–77.

——. "Wilhelm Müllers Novellen." *Anhaltische Rundschau, Sonderbeilage,* no. 229 (30 September 1927).

Häring, Wilhelm [Willibald Alexis, pseud.]. *Erinnerungen.* Edited by Max Ewert. Berlin: Concordia Deutsche Verlags-Anstalt, Hermann Ehbock, 1905, pp. 298–300.

Haertel, Martin Henry. *German Literature in American Magazines, 1846–1880.* University of Wisconsin Philology and Literature Series 4, no. 2. Madison: University of Wisconsin Press, 1908.

Hake, Bruno. *Wilhelm Müller: Sein Leben und Dichten* ["Kapitel IV. Die schöne Müllerin"]. Berlin: Mayer und Müller, 1908.

Hartung, Günter. "Ich kann zu meinen Reisen nicht wählen mit der Zeit. . . . Zum 150. Todestag Wilhelm Müllers." *Dessauer Kalender, 1977*, pp. 66–72.

———. "Wilhelm Müller und das deutsche Volkslied." *Weimarer Beiträge: Zeitschrift für Literaturwissenschaft, Ästhetik und Kulturtheorie* 23, no. 5 (1977):46–85.

Hatfield, James Taft. "Berichtigung des Datums und Inhalts eines Goetheschen Gespräches mit Kanzler Friedrich von Müller." *Goethe-Jahrbuch* 29 (1908):184–90.

———. [Review of *Les Chants des Grecs et le philhellénisme de Wilhelm Müller* by Gaston Caminade]. *MLN* 30, no. 2 (February 1915):54–55.

———. "Erklärung." *Anzeiger für deutsches Altertum und deutsche Litteratur* 30, no. 4 (1906):233–35.

———. *Four Lectures (Original and in Translation) given at German Universities in February 1936*, no. 4—"Longfellow, A Transmitter of German Culture." Evanston, Ill.: Northwestern University Press, 1936, pp. 41–55, 95–108.

———. *New Light on Longfellow with Special Reference to His Relations to Germany.* Boston and New York: Houghton Mifflin, 1933.

———. "The Poetry of Wilhelm Müller." *Methodist Review* 77 (July 1895):581–94.

———. "Wilhelm Müllers Dichtungen." *Der Westen* (Chicago) 44, no. 6, 6 February 1898, p. 2

———. "Wilhelm Müllers unveröffentlichtes Tagebuch und seine ungedruckten Briefe." *Deutsche Rundschau* 110 (March 1902):362–80.

———. "Zu *Wilhelm Müller als Kritiker und Erzähler* von Lohre—eine Buchbesprechung." *MLN* 43, no. 8 (December 1928):564–66.

Hebbel, Friedrich. *Sämtliche Werke.* 2nd ed. rev. 12 vols. Berlin: B. Badt, 1901–1904, 12:254.

Heine, Heinrich. *Briefe.* Edited by Hans Daffis. 2 vols. Berlin: Pan-Verlag, 1906–1907.

———. *Briefe.* Edited by Friedrich Hirth. 6 vols. Mainz: Florian Kupferberg, 1950.

———. *Sämtliche Werke.* Edited by Ernst Elster. 7 vols. Leipzig: Bibliographisches Institut, 1887–1890.

Heller, Otto. *Faust and Faustus: A Study of Goethe's Relation to Marlowe.* Washington University Studies, n.s., Language and Literature, no. 2. St. Louis: Washington University Press, 1931.

Henning, Hans, ed. *Faust-Bibliographie.* Vol. 1. Berlin and Weimar: Aufbau Verlag (Nationale Forschungs- und Gedenkstätten der klassischen deutschen Literatur in Weimar), 1966.

———. "Zum 100. Geburtstag eines seltenen Buches—Marlowes *Faust* in der Übersetzung von Wilhelm Müller (1818)." *Marginalien: Blätter der Pirckheimer-Gesellschaft* (East Berlin) 21 (1967):47–53.

Hensel, Luise. *Lieder von Luise Hensel.* Edited by Joseph Reinkens. Paderborn: F. Schöningh, 1870.

Hentschel, Cedric. *The Byronic Teuton: Aspects of German Pessimism, 1800–1933.* London: Methuen. [1940].

Hentschel, Lucya. "Rom—Römer—Römerinnen." *Dessauer Kulturspiegel* 3, no. 12 (December 1956):423–24.

———. "Wilhelm Müller: Der Dichter der Griechen." *Dessauer Kulturspiegel* 3, no. 12 (December 1956):422.

Hesse, Hermann; Lang, Martin; and Strauss, Emil, eds. *Der Lindenbaum: Deutsche Volkslieder.* Berlin: Fischer, 1910.

Heyse, Paul. *Italienische Dichter seit der Mitte des achtzehnten Jahrhunderts.* 4 vols. Berlin: Wilhelm Hertz, 1889.

Hoffmann von Fallersleben, August Heinrich. *Findlinge: Zur Geschichte deutscher Sprache und Dichtung.* 2 vols. Leipzig: Wilhelm Engelmann, 1860, 1:211–14.

———. *Mein Leben: Aufzeichnungen und Erinnerungen.* 6 vols. Hannover: Carl Rümpler, 1868, 2:29.

———. *Unsere volkstümlichen Lieder.* 3rd ed. Leipzig: Wilhelm Engelmann, 1869.

Hofmann, Hans. *Wilhelm Hauff: Eine nach neuen Quellen bearbeitete Darstellung seines Werdeganges. Mit einer Sammlung seiner Briefe und einer Auswahl aus dem unveröffentlichten Nachlass des Dichters.* Frankfurt am Main: Moritz Diesterweg, 1902, pp. 247–51.

Holtei, Karl von, ed. *Briefe an Ludwig Tieck.* 4 vols. Breslau: Eduard Trewendt, 1864.

Houben, Heinrich Hubert. *Der gefesselte Biedermeier: Literatur, Kultur, Zensur in der guten, alten Zeit.* Leipzig: H. Haessel, 1924.

———. *Verbotene Literatur von der klassischen Zeit bis zur Gegenwart: Ein kritisch-historisches Lexikon über verbotene Bücher, Zeitschriften und Theaterstücke, Schriftsteller und Verleger.* Berlin: Ernst Rowohlt, 1924.

Howarth, David. *The Greek Adventure: Lord Byron and Other Eccentrics in the War of Independence.* New York: Atheneum, 1976.

Hugk, Margarete. "Leserstimmen zu französischen Übertragungen von Lyrik Wilhelm Müllers durch M. Jean Jacques Brand, Lyon-Villeurbanne." *Dessauer Kulturspiegel* 2, nos. 10–11 (October–November 1955):339–43, 370–75.

———. "Wilhelm Müllers Lyrik in französischer Übertragung." *Dessauer Kulturspiegel* 2, nos. 6–7 (June–July 1955):193–96, 229–34.

Ibrovac, Miodrag. *Claude Fauriel et la fortune européenne des poésies populaires grecque et serbe.* Paris: Marcel Didier, 1966.

Irmscher, Johannes. "Der Dessauer Dichter Wilhelm Müller als Sänger der griechischen Freiheit." *Dessauer Kalender, 1969,* p. 11.

———. "Der Dessauer Dichter Wilhelm Müller und der deutsche Philhellenismus." *Hellenika* (Salonika) 21 (1968):48–74. Reprinted in *Dessauer Kalender, 1969,* pp. 11–31, 74.

———. "Der Philhellenismus in Preussen als Forschungsanliegen." *Sitzungsberichte der deutschen Akademie der Wissenschaften zu Berlin,* no. 2 (Berlin, 1966).

———."Wilhelm Müller und das Corpus Inscriptionum Graecarum." *Studia Byzantina, Wissenschaftliche Beiträge, Martin-Luther-Universität Halle-Wittenberg* 23 (1966):49–55.

Just, Klaus Günther. "Wilhelm Müllers Liederzyklen *Die schöne Müllerin* und *Die Winterreise.*" *Zeitschrift für deutsche Philologie* 83 (1964):452–71. Reprinted in Just's *Übergänge: Probleme und Gestalten der Literatur.* Bern: Francke, 1966.

Kaden, Woldemar. *Italiens Wunderhorn: Volkslieder aus allen Provinzen der Halbinsel und Sicilien in deutscher Übertragung.* Stuttgart: Adolf Bonz, n.d.

Kellner, Leon. "Neueste Shakespeareliteratur." *Die Literatur (Das literarische Echo): Halbmonatsschrift für Literaturfreunde* 15 (October 1912–1913):col. 474.

Kempe, Friedrich. *Friedrich Schneider als Mensch und Künstler.* Dessau: Neubürger, 1859.

Kerner, Theobald. *Das Kernerhaus und seine Gäste.* 2nd ed. enl. Stuttgart: Deutsche Verlags-Anstalt, 1897, pp. 59–60.

Koepke, Richard Paul. "Wilhelm Müllers Dichtung und ihre musikalische Komposition." Ph.D. dissertation, Northwestern University, 1924.

Koepke, Rudolf. *Ludwig Tieck: Erinnerungen aus dem Leben des Dichters nach dessen mündlichen und schriftlichen Mittheilungen.* 2 vols. Leipzig: F. A. Brockhaus, 1855.

Kohut, Adolf. "Wilhelm Müller: Eine biographisch-kritische Studie." *Nord und Süd* 71, no. 212 (November 1894): 235–50.

Kopisch, August, comp. and trans. *Agrumi: Volksthümliche Poesien aus allen Mundarten Italiens und seiner Inseln.* Berlin: Crantz, 1838.

Krosigk, Friederike von. "Wilhelm Müller und Franz Schubert." *Anhaltische Rundschau, Sonderbeilage,* no. 229 (30 September 1927).

Kübler-Ross, Elisabeth. *On Death and Dying.* New York: Macmillan, 1969.

Lange, Irmgard. "Der griechische Autor Thomas Nicolaou." *Zwischen Wörlitz und Mosigkau, Schriftenreihe zur Geschichte der Stadt Dessau und Umgebung,* no. 21, "Wilhelm Müller" (1977):22.

———. "Nachweis der in der Stadtbibliothek Dessau vorhandenen Schriften von und über Wilhelm Müller; Zeitungsnotizen und -artikel über Wilhelm Müller." *Zwischen Wörlitz und Mosigkau, Schriftenreihe zur Geschichte der Stadt Dessau und Umgebung,* no. 21, "Wilhelm Müller" (1977):27–30.

———. "Pflege und Erschliessung des Literatur-und Bibliothekserbes der Stadt Dessau." *Der Bibliothekar* 3 (May 1978):257–59.

———. "Wilhelm Müller—Lieder und Gedichte." *Zwischen Wörlitz und Mosigkau, Schriftenreihe zur Geschichte der Stadt Dessau und Umgebung,* no. 21, "Wilhelm Müller" (1977):14–21.

Langer, William L., comp. and ed. *An Encyclopedia of World History.* Boston: Houghton Mifflin, 1948.

Legras, Jules. *Henri Heine, Poète.* Paris: Lévy, 1897.

Longfellow, Henry Wadsworth. *The Complete Poetical Works.* Boston and New York: Houghton Mifflin, n.d.

———. *Hyperion.* 2 vols. New York: Samuel Colman, 1839.

———. *Outre-Mer: A Pilgrimage Beyond the Sea.* Boston and New York: Houghton Mifflin, 1894.

———. *Poets and Poetry of Europe with Introduction and Biographical Notices.* Rev. ed. Boston and New York: Houghton Mifflin, 1888.

Machlitt, Ulla. "Wilhelm Müller—Liederdichter der späten deutschen Romantik." *Zwischen Wörlitz und Mosigkau, Schriftenreihe zur Geschichte der Stadt Dessau und Umgebung.* no. 5, "Dessauer Persönlichkeiten" (1971):19–24.

Mann, Thomas. *Doctor Faustus: The Life of the German Composer Adrian Leverkühn as Told by a Friend.* Translated by H. T. Lowe-Porter. New York: Knopf, 1948.

———. *The Magic Mountain.* Translated by H. T. Lowe-Porter. New York: Knopf, 1953.

———. *Der Zauberberg: Roman.* Special ed. Berlin: G. B. Fischer, 1965.

Marshall, H. Lowen. "Symbolism in Schubert's *Winterreise.*" *Studies in Romanticism* (Boston University) 12 (1973):607–32.

Mayer, Hans. *Zur deutschen Klassik und Romantik.* Pfullingen: Neske, 1963.

Maync, Harry. "Wilhelm Müllers *Faustus.*" *Neue Jahrbücher für das klassische Altertum, Geschichte und deutsche Literatur und für Pädagogik* 33 (1914):721.

Metzmacher, Gerhard. "Landesbücherei Dessau: Wilhelm-Müller-Ausstellung." *Zentralblatt für Bibliothekswesen* 67, nos. 1–2 (1953):48–49.

Meyer, Gustav. *Essays und Studien zur Sprachgeschichte und Volkskunde.* 2 vols. Strassburg: K. J. Trübner, 1885–1893.

Meyer, Richard M. " 'Est, Est' von Wilhelm Müller." *Euphorion* 20 (1913):162–65.

Miller, Anna Elizabeth. "Wordsworth and Wilhelm Müller." *Americana Germanica* 3, no. 2 (1899): 206–11.

Minor, J. [Review of 1906 Hatfield edition of Müller's poetry]. *Zeitschrift für deutsche Philologie* 44 (1912):92–94.

Moore, Thomas. *The Poetical Works.* Boston: Phillips, Sampson, 1857.

Morgan, Bayard Quincy. *A Critical Bibliography of German Literature in English Translation, 1481–1927. Supplement, 1928–1955.* New York and London: Scarecrow, 1965.

————, and Hohlfeld, A. R. *German Literature in British Magazines, 1750–1860.* Madison: University of Wisconsin Press, 1949.

Müller, F. Max. *Auld Lang Syne.* New York: Scribner, 1898.

————. *Chips from a German Workshop.* 3 vols. New York: Scribner, 1871, 3:100–15.

————. "*Griechenlieder* von Wilhelm Müller." *Blätter für literarische Unterhaltung,* nos. 226–27 (14–15 August 1845): 905–8, 909–10.

————. *The Life and Letters of the Right Honorable F. Max Müller.* Edited by Georgiana Adelaide Grenfell Müller. 2 vols. London: Longmans, Green, 1902.

————. *My Autobiography: A Fragment.* New York: Scribner, 1901.

————. "Wilhelm Müller." *Allgemeine deutsche Biographie* 22 (1885):683–94.

Mustard, Helen Meredith. *The Lyric Cycle in German Literature.* Columbia University Germanic Studies, n.s., no. 17. Morningside Heights, New York: King's Crown Press, 1946.

Noack, Friedrich. *Deutsches Leben in Rom, 1700 bis 1900.* Stuttgart: J. G. Cotta, 1907.

Nollen, John. "Heine and Wilhelm Müller." *MLN* 17, nos. 4–5 (April–May 1902): 103–10, 131–38.

Ochsenbein, Wilhelm. *Die Aufnahme Lord Byrons in Deutschland und sein Einfluss auf den jungen Heine.* Bern: Büchler, 1905.

Pochmann, Henry August. *Bibliography of German Culture in America to 1940.* Madison: University of Wisconsin Press, 1953.

————. *German Culture in America: Philosophical and Literary Influences, 1600–1900.* Madison: University of Wisconsin Press, 1957.

Popp, Wolfgang. "Die Dichtung Müllers." Ph.D. Diss., Konstanz, 1968.

"Prolegomena ad Homerum: sive de operum Homericorum priscâ et genuinâ formâ, variisque mutationibus et probabili ratione emendandi. Scripsit Frid. Aug. Wolfius." *American Quarterly Review* 2, no. 4 (December 1827):307–37.

Rachold, Otto. "Zum 100. Todestag Wilhelm Müllers, mitgeteilt von R. Thiem. Wilhelm Müller als Sänger der Griechen." *Serimunt, Cöthen* 2, no. 32 (1927).

Radermacher, L. "Die Vineta Sage." *Zeitschrift für die österreichischen Gymnasien* 60, nos. 8–9 (1909):677f.

[Rahdes]. "Die Werke und wir: Wilhelm Müller und Franz Schubert." *Der Merker: Österreichische Zeitschrift für Musik und Theater* 2, nos. 10–11 (February–March 1911):436–45.

Rammelt, Johannes. "Wilhelm Müller und der Philhellenismus. Zum 100. Todestag des Dichters (1. Oktober 1827)." *Askania, Cöthen,* no. 12 (1927):45–46.

Reallexikon der deutschen Literaturgeschichte. Edited by Paul Merker and Wolfgang Stammler. 4 vols. Berlin: Walter de Gruyter, 1925–1931.

Reeves, Nigel. "The Art of Simplicity: Heinrich Heine and Wilhelm Müller." *Oxford German Studies* 5 (1970):48–66.

Regener, Edgar Alfred. [Review of *Diary and Letters of Wilhelm Müller,* edited by Philip Schuyler Allen and James Taft Hatfield]. *Die Literatur (Das literarische Echo): Halbmonatsschrift für Literaturfreunde* 12 (October 1909–1910): cols. 1713–14.

Reinhardt, Kurt F. *Germany: 2000 Years.* 2 vols. Rev. ed. New York: Frederick Ungar, 1961.

Rellstab, Ludwig. *Ludwig Berger: Ein Denkmal.* Berlin: T. Trautwein, 1846.
Richardson, Margaret E. A. "Wilhelm Müller's Poetry of the Sea." *Modern Language Review* 18 (1923):323–34.
Risse, Joseph. *Franz Schubert und seine Lieder: Studien.* 2 vols. Erfurt: Bartholomäus, 1873.
Robertson, John G. *A History of German Literature.* Edited by Edna Purdie, W. I. Lucas, and M. O'C. Walshe. Rev. enl. ed. New York: British Book Centre, 1966.
Rosenbaum, Alfred. [Review of *Diary and Letters of Wilhelm Müller,* edited by Philip Schuyler Allen and James Taft Hatfield]. *Euphorion* 11 (1904):365–66.
———. "Wilhelm Müllers 'Birkenhain bey Enermay' und anderes." *Euphorion* 15, no. 3 (1908):574–75.
Schaaffs, G. "Zu 'Glockenguss zu Breslau.' " *Euphorion* 29 (1912):354–55.
Schlösser, Rudolf. [Review of Hatfield's "Earliest Poems of Wilhelm Müller"]. *Zeitschrift für deutsche Philologie* 33 (1901–1902):279.
Schnorr von Carolsfeld, Julius. *Briefe aus Italien geschrieben in den Jahren 1817 bis 1827.* Gotha: Fr. Andreas Perthes, 1886.
Schoolfield, George C. *The Figure of the Musician in German Literature.* University of North Carolina Studies in the Germanic Languages and Literatures, no. 19. Chapel Hill: University of North Carolina Press, 1956.
Schrader, Willi. "Wilhelm Müller und das kulturelle Erbe." *Dessauer Kulturspiegel* 1, no. 12 (December 1954):18–20.
Schulze, Joachim. "O Bächlein meiner Liebe. Zu einem unheimlichen Motiv bei Eichendorff und Wilhelm Müller." *Poetica* 4, no. 2 (April 1971):215–23.
Schulze, Robert. "Wilhelm Müller." *Askania, Cöthen,* no. 12 (1927):46–48.
———. "Wilhelm Müllers letzte Lebensjahre und sein Ende." *Anhaltische Rundschau, Sonderbeilage,* no. 229, (30 September 1927).
[Schwab, Gustav]. "Wilhelm Müllers Poesie." *Blätter für literarische Unterhaltung,* no. 98 (28 April 1828): 389–91; no. 99 (19 April 1828):393–94.
Schwarz, Friedrich. "Zu Wilhelm Müllers 'Glockenguss zu Breslau.' " *Euphorion* 18 (1911):166–67.
Sengle, Friedrich. *Biedermeierzeit: Deutsche Literatur im Spannungsfeld zwischen Restauration und Revolution, 1815–1848.* 2 vols. Stuttgart: J. B. Metzler, 1971–1972.
"Siebenundsiebzig Gedichte aus den hinterlassenen Papieren eines reisenden Waldhornisten." *Heidelberger Jahrbücher der Literatur,* no. 62 (1821):985–87.
Simolin, Alexander von. "Der Waldhornist." *Urania* (1828):489.
Snodgrass, John. "Heine and Wilhelm Müller." *Academy,* no. 644 (6 September 1884):152.
Sokolowsky, Rudolf. *Der altdeutsche Minnesang im Zeitalter der deutschen Klassiker und Romantiker.* Dortmund: Ruhfus, 1906.
Solzhenitsyn, Alexander. *Candle in the Wind.* Translated by Keith Armes and Arthur Hudgins. Minneapolis: University of Minnesota Press, 1973.
Spencer, Terence. *Fair Greece! Sad Relic: Literary Philhellenism from Shakespeare to Byron.* London: Weidenfeld and Nicolson, 1954.
Spenser, Edmund. *The Poetical Works.* Edited by J. C. Smith and E. de Selincourt. London: Oxford University Press, 1963.
Spiecker, Frank X. *Luise Hensel als Dichterin: Eine psychologische Studie ihres Werdens auf Grund des handschriftlichen Nachlasses.* Freiburg i/B.: Herder, 1936. Also published in Northwestern University Studies in the Humanities, no. 3. Evanston, Ill.: Northwestern University Press, 1936.

————. "Luise Hensel and Wilhelm Müller." *Germanic Review* 8, no. 4 (October 1933):265–77.

Sprenger, R. "Zu Wilhelm Müllers Romanze 'Est, Est.'" *Zeitschrift für deutsche Philologie* 25 (1893):142–43.

St. Clair, William. *That Greece Might Still Be Free: The Philhellenes in the War of Independence.* London: Oxford University Press, 1972.

Stadtmüller, Georg. "Griechische Dichtung des Mittelalters und der Neuzeit." *Leipziger Vierteljahrsschrift für Südosteuropa* 3 (1939): 298–311.

"Statut für die Verleihung des 'Wilhelm-Müller-Kunstpreises der Stadt Dessau'" and "Träger des 'Wilhelm-Müller-Kunstpreises der Stadt Dessau.'" *Zwischen Wörlitz und Mosigkau, Schriftenreihe zur Geschichte der Stadt Dessau und Umgebung,* no. 21, "Wilhelm Müller" (1977):22–24.

Stechow, Wolfgang. "'Der greise Kopf': Eine Analyse." In *Festschrift für Werner Neuse.* Berlin: *Die Diagonale,* 1967, pp. 65–67.

Steig, Reinhold. "Wilhelm Müllers Übersetzung von Marlowes *Faust.*" *Euphorion* 13 (1906):94–104.

Stempel, Guido. "Wilhelm Müller: A Sketch of His Life and Works." *Germania* (Boston) 6, nos. 1–2 (May 1894):14–19, 65.

Stockley, V[iolet]. *German Literature as Known in England, 1750–1830.* London: George Routledge, 1929.

Swales, Martin. *The German Bildungsroman from Wieland to Hesse.* Princeton Essays in Literature. Princeton: Princeton University Press, 1978.

Taylor, Roland. [Review of *Wilhelm Müller's Lyrical Song-Cycles: Interpretations and Texts* by Alan P. Cottrell]. *Seminar* 7 (1971):247–48.

Theens, Karl. *Doktor Johann Faust: Geschichte der Faustgestalt vom 16. Jahrhundert bis zur Gegenwart.* Meisenheim am Glan: Westkulturverlag Anton Hain, 1948.

Viertel, Annemarie. "Übernahme und Weiterentwicklung des romantischen Erbes durch Heinrich Heine, dargestellt an einem Vergleich zwischen Heines *Lyrischem Intermezzo* und den *77 Gedichten aus den hinterlassenen Papieren eines Waldhornisten* von Wilhelm Müller." *Dessauer Kulturspiegel* 2, nos. 2–4 (February–April 1956): 53–59, 87–92, 129–35.

Voigt, Johannes H. *Max Müller: The Man and His Ideas.* Calcutta: K. L. Mukhopadhyay, 1967.

Wäschke, Hermann. "Aus Wilhelm Müllers Jugendzeit." *Zerbster Jahrbuch* 10 (1914):56–71.

Wahl, Paul. "Die Berichte über Wilhelm Müllers Tod." *Anhaltische Geschichtsblätter,* nos. 8–9 (1933–1934):46–50, 62.

————. "Schätze aus der Dessauer Landesbücherei." *Montagsblatt, Deutsches Heimatblatt Mitteldeutschlands: Wissenschaftliche Beilage der Magdeburger Zeitung* 76 ([1927]):404, 406.

————. "Wilhelm Müller." *Anhaltische Rundschau, Sonderbeilage,* no. 229 (30 September 1927).

————. "Die Wilhelm-Müller-Ausstellung in Dessau." *Askania, Cöthen,* no. 18 (1927):69–70.

————. "Wilhelm-Müller-Ehrungen in Dessau." *Börsenblatt für den deutschen Buchhandel,* no. 42 (19 February 1927):207.

Walzel, Oskar. [Review of *Diary and Letters of Wilhelm Müller.* Edited by Philip Schuyler Allen and James Taft Hatfield]. *Anzeiger für deutsches Altertum und deutsche Litteratur* 30, no. 4 (1906):126–33.

————. [Review of "Der deutsche Philhellenismus" by Robert Franz Arnold]. *Zeitschrift für die österreichischen Gymnasien* 48, no. 11 (1897):994–95.

Wassermann, Felix M. [Review of *Wilhelm Müller's Lyrical Song-Cycles: Interpretations and Texts* by Alan P. Cottrell]. *German Quarterly* 45 (January 1972):170.

Werner, Hans-Georg. *Geschichte des politischen Gedichts in Deutschland von 1815–1840*. 2nd ed. East Berlin, 1972, pp. 125–40.

———. "Wilhelm Müller und der Philhellenismus." *Zwischen Wörlitz und Mosigkau, Schriftenreihe zur Geschichte der Stadt Dessau und Umgebung*, no. 21, "Wilhelm Müller" (1977):3–7.

"Wilhelm Müller als Schüler und Lehrer auf der Dessauer Hauptschule." In *Friedrichs-Gymnasium 1785–1935*. Dessau, 1935.

"Wilhelm Müllers *Egeria*." *Über Kunst und Alterthum* 6, no. 2 (1828):346–51.

"Wilhelm Müllers Todesjahr." *Die Literatur (Das literarische Echo): Monatsschrift für Literaturfreunde* 30, no. 2 (November 1927):94f.

Wilpert, Gero von. *Sachwörterbuch der Literatur*. 4th ed. Stuttgart: Alfred Kröner, 1964.

Wirth, Alfred. " 'Am Brunnen vor dem Tore.' Zur Entstehung von Wilhelm Müllers Gedicht 'Der Lindenbaum.' " *Dessauer Kulturspiegel*, no. 12 (1955):414–15.

———. "Studien zu Wilhelm Müller." *Anhaltische Geschichtsblätter* 4 (1928):125–61.

———. "Wilhelm Müller und das Volkslied." *Mitteldeutsche Blätter für Volkskunde* 3 (1928):136–42.

Wolff, Oskar Ludwig Bernhard, ed. *Enzyklopädie der deutschen Nationalliteratur oder biographisch-kritisches Lexikon der deutschen Dichter und Prosaisten seit den frühesten Zeiten: Nebst Proben aus ihren Werken*. Leipzig: Otto Wigand, 1840, 5:358–61.

Woodhouse, Christopher Montague. *The Philhellenes*. Rutherford, N.J.: Farleigh Dickinson University Press, 1969.

Wütschke, Johannes. "Der Dessauer Dichter Wilhelm Müller." *Dessauer Kulturspiegel* 1, no. 3 (March 1954):17.

———. "Wilhelm Müller. Unser heimatlicher Liederdichter im vormärzlichen Deutschland." *Dessauer Kulturspiegel*, no. 10 (1958):348–51.

Zeydel, Edwin H.; Matenko, Percy; and Fife, Robert Herndon, eds. *Letters of Ludwig Tieck Hitherto Unpublished, 1792–1853*. New York: Modern Language Association of America, 1937.

TRANSLATIONS

Müller, Wilhelm. "Achelous and the Sea." Translated by John T. Adams. *United States Magazine and Democratic Review* 21, no. 110 (August 1847):166.

——— "Alexander Ypsilanti." Translated by C. T. Brooks. *Literary World: A Journal of Science, Literature, and Art* 6, no. 173 (25 May 1850):517.

———. "Alexander Ypsilanti at Munkac." Translated by Jasper Thorson. *(Colburn's) New Monthly Magazine and Humorist* 93 (1851):448.

———. "The Athenian Girl" and "The Mainote's Widow." *Dublin University Magazine: A Literary and Political Journal* 33 (1849):607.

———. "The Bell Founder." Translated by J. T. Hatfield. *Germania* 5, no. 5 (July 1893):135–37.

———. "The Bell Founder of Breslau." Translated by A. Lodge. *The Patrician* 3 (1847):361–63.

———. "The Bird and the Ship." Translated by Henry Wadsworth Longfellow. *Southern Quarterly Review* 1 (1842):502.

———. "The Bride of the Dead." *Dublin University Magazine: A Literary and Political Journal* 23 (1844):171.

———. "On the Death of Lord Byron." Translated by [Lord Francis Leveson Gower]. n.p., 1825.

———. "The Sunken City." Translated by Percy Boyd. *Ainsworth's Magazine* 10 (1846):11.

———. "The Sunken City." Translated by Percy Boyd. *The Westminster and Foreign Quarterly Review* 49 (April–July 1848):261.

———. "The Sunken City." *The Knickerbocker: New York Monthly Magazine* 35 (May 1850):442.

———. "The Sunken City." Translated by James Clarence Mangan. In *A New Library of Poetry and Song.* Edited by William Cullen Bryant. New York: Fords, Howard, and Hulbert, 1877, 2:752.

———. "The Sunken City." Translated by James Clarence Mangan. In *Library of World Poetry being Choice Selections from the Best Poets.* Edited by William Cullen Bryant. 20th ed. New York: J. B. Ford, Avenel Books, 1970, p. 635.

———. "Vineta." *Dublin University Magazine: A Literary and Political Journal* 19 (1842):780.

———. "Vineta." *Littell's Living Age* 33, no. 411 (3 April 1852):149. Reprinted from *New York Evening Post.*

———. "Vineta." *To-Day: A Boston Literary Journal* 2, no. 36 (1852):149.

Warner, Charles Dudley, ed. *A Library of the World's Best Literature.* 30 vols. New York: International Society, 1897, 26:10444. Contains 12 poems from *Die schöne Müllerin* and "Vineta."

Index

142–43, 145–48, 150, 154–56, 162n–64n, 168n, 173, 181
Schwarz, Friedrich, 164n, 181
Scott, Walter, Sir, 39, 43, 83, 142–45, 147, 151
Sengle, Friedrich, 37, 120, 137, 163n, 169n, 181
Seume, Johann Gottfried, 42, 163n
Shakespeare, William, 19–20, 26, 72, 83, 108, 146, 151, 165n, 178
Simolin, Alexander Heinrich, Baron von, xii, 23–28, 53, 122, 145, 152–54, 162n, 168n, 181
Snodgrass, John, 134, 156, 168n, 181
Solzhenitsyn, Alexander, 64, 129–31, 138, 157, 169n, 181
Song cycle, xi, 37–38, 55–57, 62–69, 120, 157, 174, 178, 180
Sonnet, 5, 44–45, 48–49, 140, 142, 171
Spenser, Edmund, 42–43, 163n, 181
Spiecker, Frank X., 6, 134, 157, 161n, 181–82
Sprenger, R., 169n, 182
Stadelmann, Christian Friedrich, 14, 20, 146
Stägemann, Friedrich August von, 7, 62, 140
Stägemann, Hedwig von, 10, 62
Stechow, Wolfgang, 66, 134, 157, 164n–65n, 182
Steig, Reinhold, 73, 156, 165n, 182
Stempel, Guido, 156, 169n, 182
Stieglitz, Heinrich, 126, 147
Storm, Theodor, 36, 54, 129
Streckfuss, Karl, 149, 162n
Studnitz, Wilhelm von, 10, 45, 140

Tennyson, Alfred, Lord, 169n
Tieck, Ludwig, 9–10, 16–17, 19–20, 22–23, 25–26, 41–42, 46–47, 56, 59–60, 63, 72, 74–75, 88, 98, 102, 111, 132–33, 137, 143, 145–46, 148, 150, 152, 164n–65n, 168n, 178, 183
Tiedge, Christoph August, 7

Uhland, Ludwig, 9, 27, 39, 42, 45, 48, 51, 85, 116–18, 120, 132–33, 137, 140, 147, 153–54

Varnhagen von Ense, Karl August, 7, 41, 118, 163n
Varnhagen von Ense, Rahel, 5, 7, 28, 118
Viertel, Annemarie, 182
Vollmann, Rolf, 158, 165n, 175
Voss, Leopold, 92, 148, 153–55, 171–72

Wahl, Paul, xiii, 27, 30–31, 59, 86, 157, 162n–64n, 172–73, 182
Walther von der Vogelweide, 85, 132, 147, 165n
War of Liberation (1813–1814), 1, 3–5, 10, 44–46, 50, 106, 139–40
Wäschke, Hermann, xii–xiv, 156, 161n, 167n, 182
Weber, Carl Maria von, 14, 18–19, 21–22, 49, 60, 88, 145–48
Weckherlin, Georg Rudolf, 85, 87, 145, 147
Wendriner, Karl Georg, 77, 156, 172
Werner, Hans–Georg, 167n, 183
Whittier, John Greenleaf, 169n
Wilpert, Gero von, 164n, 183
Wirth, Alfred, 4, 38, 44, 157, 163n, 183
Wolf, Friedrich August, 3, 8, 11, 14, 21, 78, 88–90, 144, 148–49, 151, 155, 172, 180
Wolf, Hugo, 61
Wolff, O. L. B. (Oskar Ludwig Bernhard), xiii, 54, 95–96, 155, 164n, 172, 183
Wordsworth, William, 43, 52, 163n, 173
Würdig, L., xii, 30
Wütschke, Johannes, 183

Zedlitz, Joseph, 126
Zeune, August, 7, 9
Zincgref, Julius Wilhelm, 85, 87, 126, 149, 153
Zöllner, Karl Friedrich, 35